FEEDING DESIRE

She is beautiful to the eyes, oh my lord, and God gave her
Gave her a breast new and green appearing like two balanced weights . . .
Gave her a waist lined with stripes
Gave her a thigh with stretchmarks reaching from her stomach to her knee
Gave her calves beautiful and soft, you have never seen such creations
Gave her a heel like none a son of Adam ever walked on.

Poem recited by Boukia at Tchin Tabaraden, Niger, 1990

While the Western world adheres to a beauty ideal that says women can never be too thin, the semi-nomadic Moors of the Sahara desert have for centuries cherished a feminine ideal of extreme fatness. Voluptuous immobility is thought to beautify girls' bodies, hasten the onset of puberty, heighten their sexuality, and ripen them for marriage. From the time of the loss of their first milk teeth, girls are directed to eat huge bowls of milk and porridge in one of the world's few examples of active female fattening.

Based on fieldwork in an Arab village in Niger, *Feeding Desire* analyzes the meanings of women's fatness as constituted by desire, kinship, concepts of health, Islam, and the crucial social need to manage sexuality. By demonstrating how a particular beauty ideal can only be understood within wider social structures and cultural logics, the book also implicitly provides a new way of thinking about the ideal of slimness in late Western capitalism. Offering a reminder that an estimated 80% of the world's societies prefer plump women, this gracefully written book is both a fascinating exploration of the nature of bodily ideals and a highly readable ethnography of a Saharan people.

Rebecca Popenoe is Visiting Lecturer in Anthropology at Uppsala University in Sweden. She received her Ph.D. from the University of Chicago and has taught at the University of Virginia and Middlebury College in the US as well as at Stockholm and Linköping universities in Sweden.

FEEDING DESIRE

Fatness, beauty,
and sexuality among
a Saharan people

Rebecca Popenoe

Routledge
Taylor & Francis Group

LONDON AND NEW YORK

First published 2004
by Routledge
2 Park Square, Milton Park, Abingdon, Oxon, OX14 4RN

Simultaneously published in the USA and Canada
by Routledge
270 Madison Ave, New York, NY 10016

Reprinted 2005

Transferred to Digital Printing 2007

Routledge is an imprint of the Taylor & Francis Group, an informa business

© 2004 Rebecca Popenoe

Typeset in Sabon by
Florence Production Ltd, Stoodleigh, Devon
Printed and bound in Great Britain by
TJI Digital, Padstow, Cornwall

British Library Cataloguing in Publication Data
A catalogue record for this book is available from the
British Library

Library of Congress Cataloging in Publication Data
Popenoe, Rebecca, 1962–
Feeding desire: fatness, beauty, and sexuality among a Saharan people/
Rebecca Popenoe.
p. cm.
Includes bibliographical references and index.
1. Muslim women – Azaouak Valley (Mali and Niger)   2. Women,
Arab – Azaouak Valley (Mali and Niger)   3. Overweight women – Azaouak
Valley (Mali and Niger)   4. Sex customs – Azaouak Valley (Mali and Niger)
5. Body image in women – Azaouak Valley (Mali and Niger)   6. Body,
Human–Social aspects – Azaouak Valley (Mali and Niger)
7. Azaouak Valley (Mali and Niger) – Social life and customs.   I. Title.
HQ1170.P65 2003
306.4 – dc 21   2003046664

ISBN 10: 0-415-28095-8 (hbk)
ISBN 10: 0-415-28096-6 (pbk)

ISBN 13: 978-0-415-28095-2 (hbk)
ISBN 13: 978-0-415-28096-9 (pbk)

TO MY PARENTS,
DAVID POPENOE
AND
KATHARINE SASSÉ POPENOE

CONTENTS

CONTENTS

CONTENTS

ILLUSTRATIONS

Plates

Maps

ACKNOWLEDGMENTS

The research on which this work is based was supported financially by generous fellowships from the National Science Foundation, the Social Science Research Council, and the Fulbright Agency of the US Department of Education, to all of which I am deeply grateful. I also thank the Carter G. Woodson Institute for Afro-American and African Studies at the University of Virginia, Middlebury College, and Linköping University in Sweden, each of which provided time, space, and support during work on this project. Thanks also are due the Institut de Recherche en Sciences Humaines in Niamey for allowing me to carry out this research, and for the enjoyable hours spent in their library.

For teaching me to think like an anthropologist I owe a lifetime of gratitude to my teachers first at Bryn Mawr College and then at the University of Chicago, especially Jean Comaroff, John Comaroff, Marshall Sahlins, and Bill Hanks. Jean and John Comaroff especially followed me and supported me along the journey that has become this book, and their power of insight into how social and cultural worlds work continues to awe and inspire me. I would also like to thank my anthropological friends Kenda Mutongi, Adria LaViolette, Meena Khandelwal, Melissa Johnson, Joel Robbins, Sam Bamford, Margo Smith, and Abigail Adams, for veiling in kind encouragement the helpful criticisms of chapters they read. I also thank my anonymous reviewers for making such fine suggestions for its improvement. Please know that any advice I failed to heed in this work I am nonetheless planning to incorporate in future research and writing projects I undertake!

In Niger, Nancy Lowenthal in Niamey and Marcel Jacot in Tahoua and Tchin Tabaraden received me when I surfaced for air, listening sympathetically as the narrative that follows formed in my mind, and entertaining me with their own rich experiences of the wonders of Niger. In France, hospitality that can be rivaled only by that offered in the Azawagh was extended to me by the Marty family and by Aline Tauzin. I thank Peter Raby and Ralph Keyes for their help with getting the Oscar Wilde quotation at the start of the Prologue correct, Claire Ullman for the title as well as for moral support, James L. Webb for advice on the term "Moor," and Kari Örtengren for helping me think through some of the ethical issues involved in writing about a Muslim people after 9/11.

Julene Knox at Routledge masterfully shepherded this manuscript most of the way to publication, proving as she did so what wonderful people book editors can be, contrary to persistent rumors. Most of all I thank her for her faith in my project. I also thank Clare Johnson, Christopher Cudmore, Ruth Whittington, Rosamund Howe, and Margaret Deith for all their cheerful help in the final stages before publication.

Thanks are also due to my many students at Middlebury College, Stockholm University, and Linköping University, who have helped me to see what is interesting in my research and, perhaps just as important, what is not.

Of course the real co-authors of this book are the people of the Azawagh who for unfathomable reasons let me into their lives with such unceasing generosity and warmth. I thank above all my informal research assistant, language tutor, and friend Sidi Mohamed uld Sanad, *chef de poste* of Gazaoua at this writing, and my friend Boukia mint Hamdi, who in her own indomitable personage served as my introduction to her people. I also thank Boukia's daughters, Al-Beytha, Tetou, Denna, and Reqia, for being my substitute daughters while I was too busy getting a Ph.D. to have my own. Others to whom I am forever grateful, and miss often, are: 'Omar, Asseghiyera, and B'eris and their families, formerly of Tchin Tabaraden and now in Niamey; Moussaysa and 'Aichettu at Amassara; Bakka and Aichata in Tassara; Munni, Khadijatou, Natou, and their families in Tassara; Ketti and Daha now in Niamey; Maya, now deceased, and Shweytima in Tchin Tabaraden; Maya mint Oumada and her family in Tassara; and also in Tassara, Minatou and her family; Sakina, Tuma, and Kia; and Nennou and her family. I also thank Minnou and Al-Kahel and their family, for taking such good care of me. (I identify families by the women in them instead of the men, for which, as I discuss in chapter 4, I was always laughed at, but old habits die hard.) And I thank the chief of the Azawagh Arabs, Oumada, and the now deceased *qāḍi* Sidi al-Mokhtar, and Issa Issaka, who was *chef de poste* during my time in Tassara. There are so many others in Tassara, Tchin Tabaraden, Egawan, and out in the bush, who helped me in so many ways to enter and understand the Azawagh Arab world, and I wish I could thank them all by name. When I have changed any names in the work that follows it is not for lack of gratitude, but in case they would rather not be identified, should it come to that, by some thoughtful insight or life struggle they were so trusting and kind as to share with me.

One reason I believe I took to Azawagh Arabs was that they rejoiced in their families, the same people with whom I, at the end of my travels, most like to be. My family has also been an invaluable part of the making of this book. My sister Julie and her husband Dan, "real" scientists both, keep me ever on my guard for social science-y speculation and unfounded generalizations. Any exaggeration that remains, therefore, in the parts of the book I was brave enough to let them read, is my fault alone. And I thank my sister for visiting me all those years ago in Tchin, for "getting" anthropology, and for her uncommon sisterly wisdom, about anthropology as about all things.

To my husband Johan I owe deep gratitude, not least for the many nights on which he traipsed out into the dark, snowy streets of Stockholm, our daughter the night owl in tow, so that I could work for a few hours in peace. His love, support, and encouragement have sustained me through many years of this book's writing.

Lastly, I wish to thank those without whom this book would not be: my parents, Katharine and David Popenoe. Both of them have supported me through every phase of its making, financially, editorially, and most of all emotionally. My father has nursed and shared my fascination with both deserts and social science, delighting with me in the beauty of the Azawagh when he visited me there in 1987, and following the progress of my research with enthusiasm and helpful encouragement ever since. My mother made her visit five years later, surviving *kisra* (a local delicacy) and gunshots in the night to sashay through Tassara in her *ḥawli*, making me legitimate in the villagers' eyes – the loved daughter of a gracious mother – as no one else could have. Thank you both for risking so much to share this world with me. Back at home, my mother has read countless drafts of this manuscript with her unparalleled editorial eye, improving each and every page. Most of all, however, I want to thank my parents for giving me boundless curiosity about the world, and for their equally boundless love and support that has allowed me to follow where that curiosity leads.

Plate 1 Boukia and four of her daughters, El-Beytha, Denna, Reqia, and Maya (Egawan)

PROLOGUE: THERE IS MORE TO BEAUTY THAN MEETS THE EYE

> People say sometimes that beauty is only superficial. That may be so, but at least it is not so superficial as thought is. To me, beauty is the wonder of wonders. It is only shallow people who do not judge by appearances. The true mystery of the world is the visible, not the invisible.
>
> -Oscar Wilde 1994 [1891]

This book seeks to shed light on what beauty ideals mean to society by examining one very different from the taut thinness that has become synonymous with beauty in the contemporary West. In the Sahara desert live about one million Moors for whom the ideal of female beauty has for centuries been to be as fat as possible. Girls are fattened on milk and porridge for several years leading up to puberty to attain the full, abundant, luscious look that is admired by men and women alike, and that is considered sexually desirable. Women work to maintain the folds of fat around their stomach, fleshy behinds, and stretchmarks on every limb by continuing to stuff themselves with particular types of food thought to fatten best. The work that follows explores this ideal among the easternmost group of Moors, here called Azawagh Arabs (a-ZAW-ag), using their ideal of beauty as a window onto their cultural world as well.

Beauty ideals have come under attack in recent years for their associations with the oppression of women and with eating disorders. It has been claimed that they are primarily the result of media pressure or male fantasies, and that as such they can and should be rooted out and abandoned. A differing perspective will be argued here, however: that these ideals persist not primarily because of their imposition by a powerful few or by forces extrinsic to the individuals held in their sway, but because they are deeply embedded in wider cultural values and social structures that we are all party to. While not denying the complex relationship among beauty, the media, and the male imagination, the analysis offered here seeks to

1

shed light on the way in which beauty ideals have deeper and broader well-springs and are an integral and inescapable part of human social life. It follows that, in contrast to the view that beauty ideals are deeply problematic in their very nature, this work finds that investment in their achievement, while potentially burdensome and open to exploitative purposes, is also a kind of cultural work that contributes to the identity, well-being, and honor of both individuals and the social groups to which they belong.

Although certain elements of fashion may be fleeting, random, and superficial, aesthetic ideals are on the whole not random or arbitrary, but are related in complex ways to a society's ideals in other spheres of life. Beauty ideals take their cues from political, social, and economic realities (van Damme 1996). In modern Western societies, for example, where men and women are expected to fulfill similar roles, the ideal female body, in general terms, is mannish – lean and trim – whereas among Azawagh Arabs, where women and men are thought to be very different sorts of creatures, women should look as little like men as possible – round and fleshy. These ideals could be said to express cultural and economic values in another register, and in this way cannot be understood outside of their context. A look at history shows that ideals of beauty tend to change in sync with wider social and economic changes. Look only at dress over the past 200 years in the West, where men's fashion became increasingly somber when new male roles as self-disciplined producers emerged with industrialization, and women's fashion grew increasingly masculine (suits, shoulder pads, pants) as a belief in the equality of the sexes became widespread. My analysis of Azawagh Arab society will show how their beauty ideals also reflect and express social ideals such as "closedness," and are predicated on an economic system in which the fruits of men's active labor are "invested" in passive female bodies. In short, this work attempts to show, in keeping with Oscar Wilde's quip, that the significance of outer appearance is anything but superficial.

Beauty universals and cultural particulars

Neither the contemporary West nor Azawagh Arab society is exceptional in the time and energy they invest in modifying the human body, even though they represent two ends of the spectrum with respect to preferences for body shape and size. All societies have notions of what is beautiful and all societies modify the human body in some way. Archaeological finds from 30,000–50,000 years ago indicate that enhancing the body through adornment of various kinds accompanied the emergence of modern cultural life. Aesthetic ideals and the modification of the human body to achieve them thus appear to be human social universals that have been part of societies throughout history. Even if modern capitalism and the media do their best to profit from the seemingly universal human tendency to want

2

to improve upon nature's givens, modifying and adorning the body to particular ideals appear to be a part of the human condition.

When Sander Gilman (1999: 3), who has written extensively on plastic surgery, states that "[i]n a world in which we are judged by how we appear, the belief that we can change our appearance is liberating," we should not let ourselves think that a world in which people are not judged by appearance exists just over the horizon. "All cultures are beauty cultures," as Nancy Etcoff (1999: 23) puts it in her book, summarizing evidence from anthropology, psychology, and biology which suggests that appearance matters everywhere, and that humans are in some way programmed to respond to beauty, in both its universally shared and its culturally particular manifestations.

Beauty does not lie only in the eye of the beholder. Universal ideals of beauty seem to include symmetry, smooth skin, youthfulness, and, for women, hips that are wider than their waists (Etcoff 1999; Singh 1993). This last ideal holds whether or not the society prefers fatter or thinner women, and the Azawagh Arab example supports this finding – even there it was desirable to have something of an hourglass figure, albeit on a large scale. While societies around the world apparently share these general aesthetic ideals, however, their opinion of which hairstyles, adornment, body size, form of body parts, and many other features are attractive varies widely.

On the issue of what constitutes beauty, researchers have reached the surprising conclusion that what is considered beautiful is often that which is most average. This discovery has its beginnings in the work of the eugenicist Francis Galton (1878) in the 1870s, when he attempted to arrive at the facial features typical of the average criminal. When he superimposed on each other the photographic images of a number of convicted murderers and robbers, he found to his disappointment not the expected sinister facial features of criminality, but a more attractive countenance than any of the criminal mug shots alone presented. In more recent experiments as well, the composite of many faces turns out a face more attractive than that of the individuals that make it up. Humans react positively, in other words, to looks that deviate least from the mean, be it in nose length, lip size, or eye shape (Etcoff 1999: 145).

This begs the question, then, of how it is possible that so many extreme features have come to represent loveliness in diverse societies: bound feet, ringed necks, scarified torsos, corsetted waists, or the elongated flat bodies of contemporary fashion models. Nancy Etcoff (1999: 225) hypothesizes that the extreme thinness of catwalk fashion models, just like the extraordinary size of football players, is a consequence of competition: if being thin is valued, then being a little bit thinner than the next woman will give you an edge. The same could be said for long necks, small feet, or fatness: if looking plump is considered attractive, looking a little plumper than the

3

woman in the next tent will be considered an advantage. A slight leaning toward one favored feature or another readily escalates to an extreme. Thus when thin or very fat bodies become emblems of status, our natural aesthetic instincts to see beauty in what is average are overridden. This argument holds true both for the class-stratified West, where cheap food is fattening and where keeping trim and fit costs money, and for the Arabs in the Azawagh, where being able to consume a lot of food and resist movement has helped elite women distance themselves from lower castes.

Studies in the West, at least, have also found that people seem to respond to beauty in predictable ways. Psychological tests have demonstrated that even small babies react to beauty, staring longer at faces that adults have judged to be more beautiful (Langlois *et al.* 1990). Studies and tests also find that more attractive people have an easier time persuading others of their views, are assumed to be more intelligent, and are more readily let off the hook if accused of a crime (Etcoff 1999: 46–49). Adults judged to be more attractive have an easier time getting not only mates, but also in many cases jobs (Etcoff 1999: 65, 83–85). Fortunately for most of us, beautiful people do not seem to be happier, and indeed their advantages in life are not overwhelming – nothing that a charming personality and a good CV can't overcome (Etcoff 1999: 85–88). That beauty confers advantage does not mean that we should welcome this human instinct – we can choose to try to fight it – but if we want to fight "lookism" we had best start by acknowledging the role appearance seems to play in human life, whether we like it or not.

Fatness and fattening cross-culturally

Although with increasing affluence and Western influence more and more societies across the globe are beginning to adhere to bodily ideals of streamlined, willowy thinness, the vast majority of human societies have had ideals that tend toward plumpness, especially for women. A medical researcher of obesity, Peter J. Brown (1991: 49), estimated on the basis of an analysis of a large set of anthropological data, the Human Relations Area Files, that "the desirability of 'plumpness' or being 'filled out' is found in 81 percent of the societies for which this variable can be coded." Moor society does not seem to have entered into this statistical compilation, since Brown also notes that "[n]o society on record has an ideal of extreme obesity," an observation that is contradicted by both Moor society and some communities of Tuareg. Note that because of its negative connotations the biomedical term "obesity" is misleading in a discussion of positive and admired large bodily ideals in other cultures where fatness is often culturally associated with health, not illness. Indeed the word "fat" is also problematic because of its negative connotations in English, but for lack of a better term I use it in this work.

In addition to a wide literature on fatness as a biomedical condition (see for example Brown 1991; McGarvey *et al.* 1989) and as a stigmatized body form in the West (see for example Bordo 1993; Stearns 1997), a number of studies have tried to ferret out the cultural meanings assigned to bodily "abundance" in societies where it is valued. The medical anthropologist Anne Becker (1995: 5) found that for Fijians, body presentation and size is "not formulated as a project of the self," as in the West, but is profoundly about an individual's embeddedness in a social network. A robust body shows not that one has personally exercised self-discipline, but instead that one is well connected within a community of caring that has kept one well fed. Among Jamaicans, Elaine Sobo (1993: 32) also found that fatness is a positive trait, connoting "happiness, vitality, and bodily health in general." Like Azawagh Arabs, Jamaicans also make a distinction between good, moist fat and bad, dry fat; the goal, especially for women, is a look of plump ripeness. A plump body also indicates "happiness, beauty, and sexual appeal" for working-class women in Egypt (Ghannam 1997: 17). In general, the association around the world between female fatness and happiness, well-being, sexiness, beauty, and social status contrasts starkly with modern Western readings of fatness as indicative of laziness, lack of self-control, ill-health, low status, and unattractiveness.

Even within the United States, however, various subgroups of the population do not share the dominant white value placed on thinness in women. The anthropologist Emily Massara (1989) noted the lack of stigma attached to "obesity" among Philadelphia Puerto Ricans after marriage, since it connoted a successful marriage to a husband who provides adequately for his wife. Fatness has also been shown to possess positive connotations for black American women (Sims 1979; Styles 1980), who associate it with strength, health, and invulnerability (Brown 1991: 47–48); for Mexican-Americans (Ross and Mirowsky 1983); and for Native Americans (Sims 1979; Smithson 1959; Bennett and Zingg 1935). In a study of adolescents in the United States Mimi Nichter (1994) found that in contrast to white American girls who defined an "ideal girl" primarily in terms of a svelte body, African-American girls considered body size generally less important than personality and style factors. These studies all serve to suggest that, even in the face of strict notions of female beauty and health perpetuated by doctors, the media, popular culture, and the dominant white majority, contrasting female bodily ideals have a particular tenacity as markers of identity, honor, and well-being among marginalized and non-dominant ethnic groups within American society.

As the example of married Puerto Rican women above suggests, ideals of body size are not necessarily constant over a woman's life-span. While there are peoples like Fijians and Moors who consider a certain plumpness in females appropriate at all life stages, in many cultures female fatness is particularly cultivated at two moments: just before and just after marriage.

In a number of societies girls are intentionally fattened before marriage, sometimes in quite ritualized ways. According to a missionary account from 1923, the pastoral Banyankole of Uganda began preparing a girl for marriage at age eight by making her drink large quantities of milk every day and restricting her movement, a practice remarkably similar to that of the Moors (Roscoe 1923: 116–117). More common, though, is a briefer period of fattening before marriage. Among the Efik of southern Nigeria, for example, girls spent up to two years in fattening huts to attain a rotundity that, along with clitoridectomy and a special hairstyle, signaled their readiness for marriage (Malcom 1925). Similar practices have been described among other peoples in this region of southern Nigeria, including among the Annang (Brink 1989) and the Igbo (Emecheta 1976).[1] In East Africa the Haya in Tanzania (Weiss 1992: 546) and the Bagesu of Uganda (Roscoe 1915: 173) have had a custom of fattening girls before marriage, and among the Kipsigis of Kenya fatter girls are said to fetch a higher bride-price (Borgerhoff Mulder 1988). In Papua New Guinea there is also at least one society where girls are fattened before marriage (Mosko 1985). Elsewhere women's ability to fatten after marriage signals a successful marriage and a husband who provides well for his family, as among the Puerto Ricans Massara studied and in Greece (Hirschon 1993: 62). Among the Zarma in Niger married women have held contests after the harvest season to see who can become the fattest, valuing especially rolls of fat around the neck (Stoller 1992).

In addition to its associations with female readiness for marriage or the achievement of a successful marriage, fatness has another set of associations around the globe that are ungendered: associations with royalty, power, and elite status. This reading of fatness holds among the Zulu (Gampel 1962), in highland New Guinea (Strathern 1971) and in many parts of Polynesia. Even among the Nigerian Efik who built fattening huts, fatness was something only the elites had the resources to achieve (Malcom 1925).

Just like slenderness in the West, fatness is admired in numerous societies not for any practical function it is seen to achieve, such as fertility, but for its connotations of more abstract aesthetic and social values. For Moors the meanings of female fatness resonate with those found in other societies that value plump female bodies, with primary emphasis on beauty, sexiness, womanliness, and social status. Moors are remarkable, however, in that fattening begins so young, goes on for so long, and is in fact the central preoccupation of women's lives alongside childbearing, child-rearing, and being good Muslims.

A risk posed by generalizing about fattening around the globe is that similar bodily ideals may be seen as the products of a single, universal logic. Yet there is no such universal cultural logic to fattening. The meanings of fatness vary from culture to culture, just as the hourglass figure of

Scarlett O'Hara or a Victorian lady – feminine daintiness – does not have the same set of cultural connotations as the wasp waist of a contemporary supermodel – self-control and fitness. Whether or not there is an underlying biological reason for certain bodily ideals, within any given culture the meanings attached to these ideals are particular to that society and are embedded in its particular political, social, and economic contexts. Even "marriage" and "status" vary in meaning from society to society, so that the more deeply we understand another culture, the less explanatory these seemingly universal terms become.

I return, however, to the one generalization that can fairly be made in connection to bodily fattening around the world and that is crucial to the approach of this book: that all societies socialize the "natural" body in particular ways, whether by fattening, altering body parts (neck elongation or footbinding), piercing, tattooing, cutting hair, genital operations, or merely socializing the body to particular types of clothing (Brain 1979). Put another way, the "natural" body is never enough. To modify and adorn the body so that the person inhabiting that body conforms to his or her particular society, and indeed is made properly human, can be said to be a human universal. This work explores how the universal drive to make the natural body social takes place in one particular cultural setting.

Preview of the book

The Arabs of the Azawagh region considered it impossible to imagine that where I came from women did not want to be fat; indeed, I think they never believed my protests to the contrary. That they were not particularly talkative about fattening themselves suggests how deeply and how successfully the fat female bodily form encapsulates much that is utterly taken for granted by, and utterly dear to, members of this society. When I asked people directly about the aesthetic, they almost invariably answered, "because it is beautiful." To both men and women it seemed a rather nonsensical thing to come asking questions about. The aesthetic, like beauty aesthetics everywhere, seemed so obvious and natural to its adherents that they had little incentive, indeed little cause, to reflect upon it.

To the people among whom I lived, the things it would make sense to inquire about were their history, their Muslim faith, and their place in Allah's world. Consequently, for the first few months of my fieldwork I was frustrated by the chimerical nature of my subject. There it was before me in the flesh, persistently part of women's everyday practice, and yet it seemed to have little presence in discourse. Fattening's centrality to the culture was proclaimed by women's every mouthful, but was relatively absent in the daily conversations of women, men, and children.

Although I did not see it right away, however, I came to realize that the Azawagh Arabs' vision of themselves, and my own particular interest in fattening, were not so unrelated after all. The answers to my questions about fattening lay embedded in those same daily conversations. Both their official version of themselves, as well as their conscious daily concerns, struggles, joys, and aspirations, revolve around a set of understandings of how the world works and what it is to be human that are reflected also in the corporeal story that their female aesthetic tells.

The relative lack of public commentary on the process of fattening itself was due not only to the aesthetic's tacit centrality, I soon learned, but also to the simple fact that fat is sexy, and sex is not something one talks about openly in the Azawagh. By fattening, girls make their bodies desirable to men, but girls and women should not be seen to relish their own sexiness, even though they are well aware of its significance. Thus as girls fatten they also learn to subdue their own behavior, finally beginning to veil when their bodies become fully womanly, and fully sexually desirable, with the first signs of puberty. Although sexuality is the seat of both pleasure and family increase, its potent force is also threatening to family bonds and the social order (cf. Mernissi 1975), and thus it must be kept in check not only behind veils of cloth but also, at least publicly, behind veils of silence. The appeal of female fatness is in this way embedded in a particular Islamic vision of sexuality and desire.

The appeal of fatness is also grounded in a fading nomadic world in which milk is still the most valued of foodstuffs, flowing rich and white from animal udders and invested, so to speak, into the lush, moist fat of women's bodies. In this way the milk that comes from the animals men own and manage is transformed into the stuff of women's status and desirability, and ultimately into the breastmilk that nourishes future generations. Milk and women's bodies encapsulate value, both material and symbolic, for the community as a whole.

Several tropes recur in my analysis: closedness and openness, stillness and mobility, and dryness and wetness. Women's bodies, for example, should be closed, still, and wet on the inside but dry on the outside. These same qualities are significant in different arenas of Azawagh Arab life, such as in understandings of maleness and femaleness and illness and health. By reiterating these themes I do not mean to suggest that all is neat and harmonious across the Azawagh Arab world (cf. Douglas 1982), but merely that a number of qualities that are significant for making sense of the their ideal of beauty do recur in different registers. I also note where conflict occurs, for example around marriage, and how the ideal mediates some of these perduring social tensions, in particular allegiance to one's natal family vs. one's marital family and the control of sexual desire.

My narrative has been shaped by the path I personally traveled in coming to make sense of the Azawagh Arab world, starting in chapter 1 with how I came to their corner of Niger. The following chapter describes what is known about fattening in the past in the Sahara, and then describes the mechanics and discourse of fattening today among Azawagh Arabs as I encountered it.

In Part II, "Self-representations," I devote three chapters to the ways in which Azawagh Arabs talk about themselves: as Muslims (chapter 3); as people defined by their blood relationships to kin (chapter 4); and as herders, traders, and former owners of slaves (chapter 5). In Part III, "Veiled logics," I describe the more implicit cultural logics of the Azawagh Arab world that slowly came to the fore as I partook of their lives: the way they imagine the human body (chapter 6) and the way they use and think about the spaces of the desert and their tents (chapter 7). Finally in Part IV, "Negotiating life's challenges," I examine the way in which Azawagh Arabs negotiate some of what they consider the greatest challenges in their lives, including the maintenance of good health (chapter 8) and the control of desire, sexual and otherwise (chapter 9).

Because the meanings of fattening are both dense and largely unspoken, I will slowly unravel them in each chapter, illustrating as I go the wider contexts in which the value of a laboriously fattened, voluptuous, immobile female body makes utter sense. By this interpretative journey I hope to demonstrate how and why the female body, swathed in heavy folds of cloth and anchoring the family by its weightiness, holds so enduringly the values, reproducibility, and affective center of the Azawagh Arab world.

Part I

ENTERING THE
FIELD

Plate 2 Madi (left) and Sidi Mohamed uld Sanad, my research assistant (Niamey)

1

COMING INTO THE
AZAWAGH

The [Arabs of the Azawagh] are good herders and also excellent traders; their caravans go all the way to Touat [in Algeria]
to bring animals and to exchange mainly ostrich feathers and
skins . . . for *gandouras* [men's robes] and blankets. They
maintain very cordial relations with the French authorities,
but retain nonetheless a pronounced spirit of independence
that pushes them to live apart in the most isolated pastures
of the Azawagh.

-Col. Maurice Abadie 1927: 153

In a mostly empty spot in the center of the map of West Africa lies the
Azawagh region of Niger, a sparsely populated stretch of savanna where
the gently undulating grasslands of the West African Sahel meet the drier,
harsher landscape of the Sahara desert proper. It is roughly the size of
Austria but is home to only about 85,000 people, predominantly from four
ethnic groups. For two years in the mid-1980s and for fifteen months in
the early 1990s I lived in this region, first as a Peace Corps volunteer in a
town of approximately 5000 people, and then in a village of about 700
where I carried out the fieldwork on which this book is based.

The Azawagh

The landscape against which Azawagh Arab women pack their bodies until
overflowing with plentiful, moist fat and veiled folds of allure exhibits
anything but those bountiful traits to the outsider. Desolate, flat semi-desert
under a giant dome of blazing sky, the corner of Niger where most Arabs
live is a land of sparse grass and occasional spindly, thorny acacia trees.[1]
However bleak northwestern Niger appears to one from greener climes, to
Azawagh Arabs the terrain that they consider earth's basic form is rich and
diverse. The dunes that to me were unremarkable, identical swellings rose
as mountains to the men I traveled with, and a tree that I would hardly

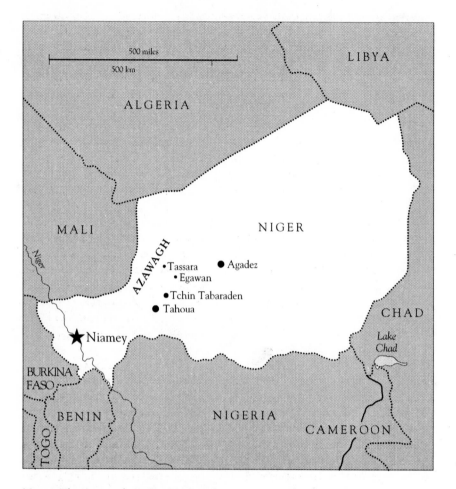

Map 1 The Azawagh region in Niger

notice was a looming landmark. The seemingly meager vegetation provided not only a smorgasbord of grasses for animals, but a well-supplied pharmacy as well. Once when out on a day trip in the desert, an old man and I sat under a tree while he identified no fewer than eleven tiny plants sticking up out of the soil, each no more than an inch high, all more or less indistinguishable to me. He explained carefully which animals ate which, and how each plant benefited or harmed them. Similarly, women could list dozens of local plants that were used to treat human illnesses, explaining in detail how the leaves or bark could be cooked, ground, or combined with other ingredients to soothe all manner of complaints, from constipation to scorpion bites.

Far more ubiquitous than vegetation, sand comes in several varieties: large-grained *lhse'*, deep loose *ramle*, hot *azeyz*. As ubiquitous as the sand is the wind. Though harshest before rainstorms and in the winter season, wind knocks against the landscape incessantly in all seasons. The gusts pick up in the vast desert reaches and trip across the plains, tossing up sand, flapping the tent sides, and constantly blowing this researcher's hair into unbecoming chaos in the absence of the oil and heavy braids that make up the stiff hairstyles of Arab women. From December to March, the winds carry so much sand that the world turns into an anemic yellowish-gray haze for weeks on end. Like sand, the wind comes in many varieties: there is the cool *amerūg*, the hot *irīfi*, and the *zowb'aya* whirlwinds.

While the Azawagh Arabs seem little bothered by the wind in the way I was – the endless, unsettling irritation and the fine grains of sand it deposits in food, ears, and books – they are concerned by the less visible and ultimately more potent ills that it can bring. As a more general term, wind is a metaphor for, even the embodiment of, spirits and forces of evil. To keep such forces at bay, people often quietly recite a prayer as a whirling funnel of dust hurries across the desert. Wind is also the bearer of "heat" and "coldness," forces that reside in bodies and the world and that must always be kept in balance. Like gravity or an electromagnetic field, the wind and the unseen forces it carries silently and invisibly enter all substances, connecting people to the world around them.

This windswept corner of Niger is today home to a patchwork of distinct ethnic groups, comprising a metropolitan desert world of different languages and customs, though all the groups share a faith in Islam. Historically, the dominant ethnic group in the region has been the Tuareg, a better-known Saharan nomadic group whose indigo-turbanned men and silver-bejewelled women have appeared in movies like *The Sheltering Sky* and *Beau Geste*. Like Azawagh Arabs and most other peoples in Niger, the Tuareg used to have a slave caste known as the Bouzou, who are a populous ethnic group in their own right, even as some seem to be assimilating to sub-Saharan black African ethnic groups in the south. Numerous cattle-raising, nomadic Wodaabe Fulani have also long drifted in and out of the zone. The Wodaabe, a group that became Muslim only recently, have been much photographed by outsiders and have been featured in picture books and calendars of Africa, highlighting the way men bedeck themselves in jewelry, paint their faces, and dance before young women to attract lovers. More recently, increasing numbers of Muslim Hausa and Zarma, sub-Saharan black groups that dominate Niger politically and numerically, have arrived in the north as civil servants, government officials, and traders.

The Azawagh has known fighting at several points in its recorded history, beginning with the violent French colonization of the Tuareg at the start of the twentieth century. Since the 1980s when the Azawagh and other

15

Tuareg regions of Niger were hard hit by drought, the Tuareg have waged an on–off guerrilla war for more power and independence within Niger. Azawagh Arabs and Tuareg have raided each other periodically throughout history as the Arabs encroached on Tuareg lands, and simply because raiding generally has been something of a subsistence strategy in this part of the world. Although Arabs and Tuareg were at peace for much of the twentieth century, violence between the groups intensified again in the early 1990s in the context of Tuareg revolts against the government, since the Arabs own vehicles, guns, and other resources that the Tuareg need. This is, at least, the Arab view of matters. There have been so many raids and counter-raids over the years that both sides are no doubt equally guilty of prolonging the fighting, in which many lives have been lost.

The Azawagh Arabs of Niger are concentrated in the north of the region. Their de facto capital is the village of Tassara, my fieldwork site, but a number also live in the county capital, Tchin Tabaraden, where I worked as a Peace Corps volunteer. Both settlements came into being only in the last fifty years and are the products of outside intervention, not indigenous settlement alone. Tchin Tabaraden was established by the French in the middle of the century, and Tassara by the Nigerien government in the 1970s, both essentially as places where the government could station its leaders, schools, and army, in addition to more welcome health clinics and water stations.

Those who live in the northern reaches of the Azawagh make their peace with desiccating heat in the spring, rainstorms of biblical proportions in the brief summer, and chill nights and stinging windstorms in the winter. The sky arches always overhead, huge and distant and endless. There is a desolate beauty to the landscape, and amidst the impermanence of land, air, and people, a kind of stillness and absoluteness that is deeply calming. As bone-thin cows, camels, sheep, and goats scrounge lazily for sustenance on the vast reaches of sand, their owners engage in endless travel to make their trade profitable, retain their autonomy, and remain on land they consider their own and profess to love. Despite the increasing temptations of more urbanized life to the south, the Azawagh Arabs have stuck to this remote region, remaining satisfyingly beyond easy reach of first French and now Nigerien officials, extracting a living from the seemingly most ungenerous of pastoral landscapes, and maintaining a desired nearness to the Arab world to the north.

Who are the "Azawagh Arabs"?

The issue of just who the Azawagh Arabs are and how to label them is a textbook case of a basic ethnographic truth: peoples do not always come in neatly bounded units with a name all agree upon, even if the modern world of nation-states has led us to believe that this should be so.

Descended from Arabs of the Middle East, the people I studied speak a dialect of Arabic, and consider themselves to be simply Arabs. Arabs from the Middle East, however, would not consider them "pure" Arabs and indeed, according to histories written by outsiders, there has been considerable intermarriage with non-Arab peoples over the past five centuries.[2] Their language and culture align them less with the Arabs of northern Africa and more with the Moors of Mauritania, but the Arabs of Niger do not see themselves as such. So who are they and by what name should they be called here?

While the people of northwest Niger whom I studied refer to themselves simply as "Arabs" (*'Arab*), culturally, linguistically, and historically they belong to a group of Arabic speakers across the western parts of the Sahara desert known most commonly in the modern West as Moors. Moor society coalesced between the fifteenth and seventeenth centuries in northwestern regions of the Sahara out of the mingling and intermarriages among local Berbers (the inhabitants of North Africa before the Arabs came), newly arrived Arabs, and sub-Saharan Africans (Webb 1995: 15). Today they number approximately one million and make up the predominant population of Mauritania; they also live in the rural margins of Mali, southern Algeria, and Niger, and are closely related to the predominant ethnic group of Western Sahara. (See Map 2, page 18.)

The "Arabs" of Niger represent the easternmost tip of this group, number between 15,000 and 20,000,[3] and speak a form of Arabic they call Galgaliyya, a variant of the Hassaniyya Arabic spoken in Mauritania. Oral traditions and old Arabic documents relate that about a century ago they moved east into what is now Niger from the area of present-day Mali, and for several centuries before that resided further north in what is now Algeria. Mostly nomadic until the early 1970s, more and more Azawagh Arabs are now settling in small desert communities and, occasionally, in larger towns. Their increasing settlement is due most directly to droughts in the early 1970s and 1980s that forced people into villages to get water and food, where they then stayed, enjoying the nearness to water (from pumps), relatives, and certain material goods.

Across the huge swath of land where Moors, including Azawagh Arabs, reside, they share devotion to Islam, belief in Arabian roots, similar dialects of Arabic, an economy based on herding and trade, a caste-like social structure that leaves much hard labor to former slaves, and many similarities of dress, poetry, ritual practices, and, not least, bodily ideals. In many rural areas of the Moor world the corpulent female aesthetic is still prized, and the fattening of girls continues to take place in parts of Mauritania and Mali (Tauzin 1981, 1987, 1988; Amidié 1985; Brewster 1992; Hildebrand *et al.* 1985) as well as in Niger.

Even if Azawagh Arabs are in some senses essentially the same people as the Moors of Mauritania, the term "Moor" is not particularly

Map 2 The approximate location of Moors in Africa

appropriate to the Nigerien context. First and foremost, the Arabs of Niger do not consider themselves one with the inhabitants of Mauritania. Second, the term "Moor" is of European derivation (from Latin, referring to the people of North Africa) and is not used in the local language anywhere in the "Moor" world, as far as I know. Third, the term also has a long history of European usage to refer to Berber and Arab peoples of other times and places, for example the Moor invasion of Spain and Othello the Moor, where it means Berber North Africans. The term is therefore a confusing one to use for the "Arabs" in Niger.

Since not only they themselves but all the other ethnic groups around them also called the Nigerien Moors simply "Arabs," this term is the one most sensitive to local habits. The simple "Arab," however, is too general and misleading in the wider context I write within. Therefore I felt compelled to find a more satisfactory ethnic label that would work both for those I write about and for myself and Western readers. When I asked the people themselves how I should refer to them, I learned a great deal about their self-image from their answers: they suggested that I call them "Yemeni Arabs" or "Saudi Arabs," harking back to their putative roots in Yemen and Saudi Arabia as companions of the Prophet Muhammad. Rejecting the potential complications of these admittedly intriguing suggestions, I have finally chosen the neologism "Azawagh Arabs," after the region of Niger where they live, to refer to the people whom this book concerns, a name to which people I spoke to about it acceded.

There is one additional aspect of Moor and Azawagh Arab society that complicates the process of group naming, and that is that they are caste societies. Among Azawagh Arabs there are three main castes: (1) the "white" or "free" Arabs; (2) the former slave caste, called *haratin*; and (3) the small artisan caste, also called blacksmiths in Western languages. The hierarchy of these castes is imagined in terms of skin color, with the former slave caste termed "black" and the artisans considered of intermediate skin color, though in reality there are very dark-skinned "white" Arabs as well as very light-skinned "black" Arabs. What more accurately distinguishes the castes is descent, status, and a lack of intermarriage across caste lines.

Even though slavery has been officially outlawed by the Nigerien government since 1960 and even though all "white" Arabs now pay the freed slaves to work for them, remnants of master–slave relationships still exist. *Haratin* still fetched water and did small tasks for their former masters at their bidding, and, in return, the former masters gave gifts to their former slaves on holidays and helped them in times of need. The segregation was also perpetuated geographically; the *haratin* all lived on the north side of the town where I did fieldwork, and the "white" Arabs lived in the center and at the southern end. Even as one could see the former master–slave relationship slowly evolving into something more akin to ranked ethnic distinctions, the racialized inequalities of the situation were often uncomfortable for a Westerner.

The complexity of the caste situation will be explored further in chapter 5. For now, I will note that the existence of slavery has been crucial to the persistence of fattening, which is only possible for girls who do not have to do household work. Indeed, when I asked "white" Arab women who were not fattening why they had stopped, a not infrequent answer was, "Our slaves have left; how can we fatten?" The *haratin* had not themselves taken up the practice of fattening their daughters, but they nonetheless appreciated and strove for the same aesthetic.

Peace Corps prelude: Tchin Tabaraden

My initial contact with Niger, and with Azawagh Arabs, came in 1985. That year I joined the Peace Corps as a health volunteer and was sent to Tchin Tabaraden, a town of about 5000 people. A sprawling, dusty place at the end of a long gravel road, Tchin Tabaraden consists of a grid of sandy lanes lined by adobe walls, behind each of which stretches a yard of more sand with a mud house or tent. Of the many ethnic groups in the town, the Azawagh Arabs were the least visible, not because of their small number but because the men dress in the same flowing robes and turbans that the Tuareg wear and are generally fluent speakers of the Tuareg language, Tamajeq, while Arab women, whose dress is distinctive, rarely leave their compounds. In the two years I lived and worked there, I learned to speak Hausa (the most widely spoken language in Niger) and some Tamajeq, before finding myself drawn to the Azawagh Arab world.

The first time I saw a group of Arab women was during my first week in Tchin Tabaraden. From the steps of the health clinic where I worked I gazed upon a group of five or six women as they came waddling slowly toward us en masse across the sand, swaying under the flowing, filmy, all-covering, sari-like *hawli*s they wore, the end pulled up over their high hairdos, framing their chubby faces. Only many months later would I begin to learn to see perfected feminine comportment in what I at first could only see as unattractive lumbering. If Evans-Pritchard could confess to symptoms of "Nuer-osis" when embarking on his now legendary work on the Nuer (1969: 13), I will also risk the confession that I found my first sight of these women somewhat off-putting. Their unwieldy bodies, hair piled on top of their heads with a few braids hanging down, rounded full faces, and their slow swaying approach went against most conceptions I previously entertained of appealing womanly conduct and appearance. Furthermore, none spoke any Hausa except for one woman brought along as spokesperson, and none appeared particularly eager to defer or adapt to the rituals and culture expected at the government clinic. They all heaved to a squatting position outside the door while the one Hausa speaker proudly and heavily mounted the steps and went about getting the nurses' attention. I learned later that by virtue of their light skin and supposedly prestigious Islamic descent, the Arabs considered themselves superior to the dark-skinned Hausa, and indeed to most other peoples, including Europeans, a sentiment that did not always endear them to the non-Arab government officials with whom they had regularly to contend. (It might be added that the Hausa also considered themselves superior to the "bush" Arabs who were not "real" Arabs anyway!)

I do not remember how the clinic scene played itself out. I know that several months later an Arab woman came into the clinic alone but for three young daughters, displaying little knowledge of Hausa but an open-ness to the Hausa nurses and good humor unusual for Arab women in this setting. She came so that her three girls could be weighed and, when found underweight, could start receiving weekly rations of aid food that was still being given out in the wake of the 1984 drought. Her name was Boukia, and I took to her immediately. I made several follow-up visits to her tent, and within a few months, despite language barriers, we had become what for lack of a more nuanced term I will call friends. She and her lively girls were my introduction to the Azawagh Arab world. Poorer than most Arabs, they struggled to get by. None of her daughters fattened seriously even after their rapid recovery from the drought-inflicted weight loss. Boukia herself, however, bore the stretchmarks on her upper arms that testified to her girl-hood fattening, and her daughters did go through periods when they tried to get plumper.

Surrounded daily by a multi-ethnic gaggle of women at the health clinic, I had quickly realized, from banter, body practices, and commentary on my own inadequate physical state, that a plump body was a highly desir-able feature of adult womanhood among all the ethnic groups in the area: the Hausa, Tuareg, Wodaabe, Bouzou, and Arabs. It was the last of these groups, however, who clearly excelled at achieving great bulk. As I got to know individual Azawagh Arab women, I noticed that they often ate by stuffing their mouths full of couscous and swallowing it down with large quantities of water, without chewing. Their hefty beauty and allure was accentuated by several layers of cloth surrounding the lower half of their bodies under their filmy *ḥawli*s, as well as by their slow, swinging walk on the relatively rare occasions when they emerged from their compounds into the town's dusty public spaces.

It was not until I had been in Tchin Tabaraden for almost a year, however, that I realized that the process of getting fat begins in a routinized and enforced way early in a girl's childhood. One hot Saharan afternoon I strolled into an Arab compound to see a girl of nine or ten sitting with a large bowl of porridge before her, and beside her an older woman force-fully pulling one of the girl's fingers backwards toward her arm and urging her in no uncertain terms to eat on. The girl cried and protested, but slowly continued raising an oversized ladle of the milky gruel to her lips, swal-lowing huge mouthfuls at a time. Some other people lay around in the compound, but no one took much notice. No one explained to me what was going on, but the scene was for me an epiphany of sorts about why Arab women looked the way they did and how they got that way. More questions were raised than answered by what I had witnessed, however. As I encountered the practice of fattening in different contexts and spent more time with Boukia and other Arab families, I became increasingly curious to understand this foreign bodily ideal more deeply.

Fieldwork: Tassara

I visited Tchin Tabaraden twice after my Peace Corps years before returning to the Azawagh for a long period of research – once briefly in 1989, and again for two months the following winter to begin learning Galgaliyya Arabic. I returned for fieldwork proper in the summer of 1991, and stayed until the fall of 1992. Because of the large size and predominantly non-Arab population of Tchin Tabaraden, I chose to do my fieldwork in the smaller, de facto capital of the Azawagh Arabs 120 kilometers to the north, a village of about 700 people called Tassara (see Plate 8, page 152).

With increased settlement of former nomads, the establishment of a government presence, and the drilling of a deep water hole, Tassara became a magnet for Arabs suffering from the drought, and the increasing population put pressure on the fragile ecosystem of the Sahel, as the southern edge of the Sahara desert is called. The installation of a deep artesian well around the time of the 1973–4 drought lured a number of *ḥaraṭīn* settlers, and in the coming decade "white" Arabs began building houses there as well. By the early 1990s both the religious leader (*qāḍi*) and the chief (*ṣulṭān*) resided most of the time in Tassara.

In the early 1990s about a third of the town were "white" Azawagh Arabs, a third their former slaves the *ḥaraṭīn*, and a third outsiders from other Nigerien ethnic groups (mostly Hausa and Zarma), including a few tradespeople, several teachers, two nurses, and a handful of guards, soldiers, and policemen. Governments everywhere are notoriously suspicious of nomads because they are hard to control, and Tassara had been carefully conceived and equipped by the national government to monitor and discipline nomadic peoples resistant to being wards of a state to which they have until recently felt little connection. There are two government elementary schools, one French and one Franco-Arabic, and a small market around the town center, though there is no weekly market with livestock as in some larger towns in the region.

When I first went up to Tassara, with a Swiss development worker, Marcel Jacot, who was the only other Westerner (*neṣrāni*)[4] working in the Azawagh, I found that the women had already heard about me, and had even been expecting my arrival a month earlier. Apparently, when my application for research permission was accepted in Niamey, word had been sent notifying those in Tassara of my impending arrival. Although my original plan had been to go not to Tassara but to a tent village where my friend Boukia from Peace Corps days now lived, this news was not relayed, and the women (little realizing what a pest I would turn out to be) urged me to come live with them. Deciding I would need the presence of houses for my sanity and that it would generally make sense to be at the cultural and political center of the world I had come to study, I chose to settle there.

Although I knew almost no one when I arrived in Tassara, many of the women and men were relatives of people I knew in Tchin Tabaraden. I had heard about several of them before and even met a few when they visited their families in Tchin Tabaraden. I was not an entirely unknown quantity to them either. Only a few Westerners (*anaṣāra*) had lived in the Azawagh over the last few decades, so those who had spent time there became known, and this included me from my two years in the Peace Corps. Many knew of my friendship with Boukia, knew that my father had once visited me in Tchin Tabaraden, and no doubt knew many other things of which I am not aware.

On my second visit to Tassara, when I went to move in, I drove north alone. It was August 1991. After the day's drive north from the capital Niamey to Tchin Tabaraden, I waited several days there until another vehicle was driving the 120 kilometers to Tassara so that I could follow it on the sandy, often vanishing tire tracks that passed for a road. When the time finally came to leave, I fell in behind the Arab-owned pick-up truck, its bed filled with young Arab men and sacks of grain, as we headed out through the camel market at the north end of town, the dust from their wheels puffing up in a cloud before me. Within half an hour, however, they seemed to forget to keep my little blue Suzuki in their rearview mirrors, and the distance between us grew and grew until I was alone on the bumpy, occasionally disappearing tracks, too unschooled in desert driving to take the pot-holed, tricky "road" at their speed. For a while I enjoyed the feeling of freedom and space as the endless sea of desert spread out all around me, passing a few lone herders, some tents in the distance, and a few abandoned wells. After almost two hours, though, as numerous tire tracks crisscrossed each other and seemed to go off in every possible direction, I began to get nervous. Finally I spotted a person in the distance, a Wodaabe cow herder sauntering along with his herds. I headed over to him, and slowed to a stop.

Using Hausa, I called out a greeting. As he responded and walked over, I saw, to my great surprise, that he was Sodinge, a Wodaabe man I had known from my Peace Corps days. He greeted me warmly and did not seem the least bit surprised that a lone Western woman he knew should appear over the horizon in an electric blue Suzuki, in what I still considered very much the middle of nowhere. After going through the usual litany of greeting questions and answers – how is your family, how are you, how is your work, how is your family again, etc. – he assured me that I was on the right track and should only continue north. To me, that I ran into Sodinge there, on my first venture alone to Tassara, seemed like a supernatural sign, but with time I came to see that one never really was alone in the desert – over the next dune or round the next grove of trees was always some welcome form of civilization or some old acquaintance.

23

Heading off again, the hot wind and anxiety starting to sap my energies, I finally passed the encampment of Amassara that lies a few kilometers to the south of Tassara. With great relief I began summoning my forces for my arrival in the place where I was planning to ensconce myself, essentially uninvited, for the next year and a half. I rounded a large area of thorny bushes and came in sight of the town. On a barely sloping plain of gray-white sand, Tassara looks like a handful of play adobe houses rolled like dice across it, landing in a scattering of vague order. The empty holes of windows in the mud blocks stare out like dark eyes, as if the village had long been deserted by its inhabitants. Only on the slight rise to the west of the town where the military have a small camp are trees visible: fragile, light green, willowy *neem* trees, transplanted from far away in place of the scraggy acacias that otherwise dot the landscape. A line of cows, some goats, and a few *ḥaraṭin* women on donkeys were making their way slowly across the gray expanse that is Tassara's wide doorstep, on their way to the watering troughs on the southeast edge. The sky arched over it all, dwarfing any significance such an unlikely settlement might have.

I rolled into the town and pulled up at the walled enclosure where the town head lived, remembered from my first brief visit with the Swiss Marcel Jacot, and stopped the car in front of the high mud wall. Soon a gaggle of children were crowding around my car, peering through the windows at my crammed-in belongings, and staring at my pale skin and windswept hair. The noise of my car engine also provoked the curiosity of some adults, so I did not need to push open the swinging corrugated tin door to the yard to announce my presence. Several adult men welcomed me cautiously but graciously, and invited me to come in and sit down with the women under the tent. They were, as might be expected, as uncertain about what to do next as I was. Someone was told to bring me water, and tentative conversation took place. It was inappropriate for the men to sit with me and the other women, but I could not really talk much to the women since my Arabic was not yet very good, and only the men spoke Hausa.

What happened then? I ate – porridge and sauce, and a bowl of fresh milk that I only later realized the value of – and then I slept, on a camp cot someone had that they probably thought was what we Westerners sleep on. I remember the wind flapping at the tent sides and my blanket all night, and a general feeling of dizziness at the strangeness of what I was getting myself into. The next morning, still overwhelmed by the prospect of the adventure before me, I discovered old tea crates in the corner of the yard that were appointed with tiny mats and cushions – girls' dollhouses, it turned out. Inside them lay small, round dolls whose strange fat shapes seemed to encapsulate all I had come to study. Amidst my confusions, anxieties, and sun-drenched weariness, I felt an immense curiosity to understand this world to which I would soon form a deep attachment.

The kind, government-appointed Hausa mayor, Issa Issaka, had arranged with some of the local Arab leadership that I should rent a conveniently empty two-room adobe house, with cement plastering that made it one of the most elegant in Tassara. Later the same day I parked my Suzuki jeep in the sandy yard – a bit of walled-off desert really – and began settling in. The first days passed in a blur, but within six weeks I felt fully ensconced, though I still had problems with the language. My standard Arabic studied in the United States was of limited help, only one woman in town spoke the Hausa I knew, and my Tamajeq – which more Arab women knew – began fading as I crammed more Galgaliyya Arabic into my head. I would occasionally corner young men who knew Hausa and some French into helping me with linguistic questions, but they were generally too mobile for any permanent tutoring arrangement. Eventually I arranged with an Azawagh Arab friend in Tchin Tabaraden from Peace Corps days, Sidi Mohamed, known simply as Sidi, to sit with me regularly whenever I went to Tchin or he to Tassara. Over the year he helped me tremendously to learn the frustratingly difficult language, and gave me numerous insights into his culture as well.

I spent the mornings visiting with women in their tents, came home and wrote field notes during the afternoon when most people napped, and then ventured out again in the late afternoon as the heat of the day began to wane. As the months wore on I occasionally took out my notebook and wrote things down when I spoke to women, but more often I engaged in the daily chatter as much as I could and later at home noted down from memory what had transpired. I performed some more formal, structured interviews, to ask about genealogies, traditional plant medicines, the nature of hot and cold, stories of the past, or to write down songs. On several occasions I interviewed both the *sulṭān*, or traditional chief, and the *qāḍi*, or religious judge/leader, about history and Islam. Although I taped these interviews with men, women were worried that if I taped their voices I could carry them somewhere and play them back to unknown men, something deemed almost equivalent to exposing their very bodies to strangers; hence I tape-recorded very few conversations with women.

I also spent a considerable amount of time with *haratīn*, the former slave population who made up at least half of the Galgaliyya-speaking population of Tassara. Generally more open than their former "Arab" masters, they both accepted me readily and shared with me many of the insights that inform this work. I was, however, considered a "white," and as such was not privy to expressions of sentiment toward the *haratīn*'s former masters. On one or two occasions I caught some bitterness being expressed or a slight being made, but when I asked for clarification I was told it was nothing.

It was more difficult to converse freely with men than with women in this highly sex-segregated society, but my anomalous outsider status allowed me considerable latitude to go where Arab women would not. I went into the market, a place where the only other representatives of the female sex were non-Arab girls, and bantered with the men in their shops while buying things I needed. Many young men befriended me and would come to chat in the evenings; they were interested to talk to someone from the wider world about politics, culture, and foreign affairs, and, once they grew comfortable (which usually did not take very long), sex. Middle-aged married men were the most difficult group for me to talk with, perhaps because of their fear of suspicious wives, though a number of older men treated me as their daughter and taught me much. With my jeep I possessed transportation services that were much in demand, and I found men would often open up to me in a different way in the privacy of the car.

But I tried never to travel alone with one man. As the Arab proverb goes, where one man and one woman are alone together, there will always be a third present – the devil. It is generally not thought plausible, by either women or men, that a woman and a man could be alone together anywhere and not have sex. Such is the nature of attraction and desire, maleness and femaleness, as I will discuss in the following chapters. Even when I once traveled with a stooped, gray-haired, spindly elder, his equally elderly wife teased me about what might happen between us.

Outside my house I always wore the toga-like *ḥawli* of Azawagh Arab women – a stretch of wide cloth several meters long, wrapped around the body and knotted over the shoulders – and before older, married men I kept the end of it appropriately over my head in a sort of veil. Before the religious leaders I made sure that my hair was completely covered, as was appropriate. I did not veil my face as Azawagh Arab women do, but I fell within the lines of what is viewed as appropriate covering. With collar bones protruding and not a stretchmark to be found on my upper arms, I believe many women considered me a poor specimen of my sex, and were therefore less bothered than they might otherwise have been by my carrying on casual conversations with their husbands, sons, brothers, and perhaps paramours. Indeed, when women asked me if we Western women menstruated, I was always reminded that I was not entirely human or womanly to them. In a society where adult, feminine status is evidenced by a portly form, I also appeared much younger than my twenty-nine years; though Azawagh Arabs do not keep ages, women's occasional suggestions that I marry their sixteen-year-old brothers reminded me of the less than adult impression I made.

It is difficult for the fieldworker herself to assess the way in which she was viewed by the community in which she did research. I was surely a strange asteroid to fall upon them unexpectedly, and I am sure speculation continues about my true nature and purpose. Try as I did to explain my "work" in Tassara to women who had hardly seen a book except the Koran, never been to school, and rarely left their desert villages and encampments, my task of writing a book about the history and customs of these people so that Westerners might know of them was a difficult proposition for them to grasp. Yet I was universally treated with kindness, respect, and generosity, even acceptance, and my attachment to this isolated corner of the world and its people only increased with time. When my mother visited in March 1992 people could see me in a new light, as connected to a woman who gave birth to me, a family who had not rejected me or given me up for an old maid. My mother, in fact, outshone me in many ways in their eyes. It was clear to women that she had been more beautiful than I, and her more respectable proportions threw forever into doubt my assertions that in America men had a penchant for bony women like me. Her ability to reach out and touch the hearts of people with whom she could not communicate linguistically except via my translations helped people to know that I, too, came from a community of warmth and caring.

I know that most men and women in Tassara viewed the Azawagh Arab position in the world as somewhat more significant than the unfortunate reality – that almost no Americans except my immediate family and friends had ever heard of them, and few had even heard of Niger itself. But I like to feel that at another level their society can be more important than their political obscurity suggests, in what it can teach us about the significance of beauty in social life, the different expressions of Islam, the nature of the body in culture, and humankind in general. While exploring these issues, I hope also to introduce to a wider audience a people whose courage, grace, and warmth impressed me beyond any expectations, and whose nomadic way of life and the particular insights it engenders may not last long into the new millennium.

Stasis and change

Understanding the Azawagh Arab world requires entering a landscape in which human life is both more fragile and more exalted than in a Western world of skyscrapers, cell phones, and twelve-lane highways. To live among Azawagh Arabs is to enter a world in which it often feels as if obedience to Allah and his plan is everything, even as people go about the most mundane tasks, and in which fulfilling one's duties in life as a good Muslim is often presented as the highest possible achievement. It entails letting go of the idea that individuals are self-contained entities acting on and above the world, and replacing it with a sense of the body's openness to and dependency on a world of subtle forces, hidden intentions, sneaky spirits, and secret desires. One must imagine a world in which the milk that flows from animals' udders and from women's breasts is all part of a cycle that breathes life into families, relating people to one another and to the tangible world. It requires understanding that in this Saharan emptiness, your kin are everything. And it requires granting, for a moment, that men and women were formed by God to be as different and complementary as possible, and that the tension between them is one of the principal driving forces of human life on earth.

Understanding this world also necessitates a leap of imagination that is increasingly unnecessary in anthropology today: envisioning a place in which the encroachments of colonial and modern states have been relatively slight. There are no paved roads, no television, no electricity,[5] and water only from a few public spigots in towns, and from simple wells out in the "bush." There were tetracycline pills to be had at the local clinic, but some people would not take them because they had been defined as "hot" in the indigenous humoral medical system (see chapter 8). The highest religious figure in the village, the qāḍi, had heard of the bloodshed in Yugoslavia, and attributed that year's bad winds to the chaos such violence was causing on the earth. In this way and hundreds of others, the global was incorporated into the local, little altering many longstanding assumptions about the nature of life and reality.

The men of this community, however, are moving much more quickly into a modernizing world than are the women. Men's travels take them far from the Azawagh to Algeria, Libya, and urban centers of southern Niger, places that are ever more connected to the rhythms of modernity. Meanwhile, women move less and less, as more and more Arab families give up a nomadic life to settle in permanent villages. Thus although most men were familiar with TV, listened regularly to the radio, and were at least passingly familiar with a life of paved streets and electricity, only a few of the women had ever watched a television, traveled on a paved road, or seen a magazine or newspaper. While many women were partially literate in Arabic from Koranic school, none read or wrote regularly and there was no news on the radio in a language they could understand. Only one Arab woman in the village where I did research had been to the capital of Niger, two days' drive away. They had heard of America, France, Saudi Arabia, and a place called "Africa." They asked me where this place "Africa" was, and wanted me to point in its direction. They also wanted to know whether people could ride on the kite I brought, as they knew people did on the airplanes that occasionally passed high overhead – shimmering, soundless, slow-moving specks in the huge vault of desert sky.

There is, then, an increasing divergence of experience between men and women in this quickly sedentarizing society. Whereas in the nomadic past women would be hoisted high on their camels for the seasonal migrations, and thus regularly see the landscape their menfolk traversed more often, today women's lives have become more confined, while men travel further into a modernizing outside world the women rarely see. Life at the still center of their gently arched tents is little changed for them, as they continue to do light chores, oversee the work of servants, and sit out their days immobile and proud, surrounded by children. And while the practice

of fattening is not as ubiquitous as it once was due to the decreasing avail-
ability of the necessary cow's milk and the necessity of doing work formerly
done by slaves, I talked to no one who questioned the practice's worth, or
the aesthetic which it aimed to achieve.

The current fashion in anthropology is to see change and inconstancy
everywhere in the societies studied, where once anthropologists saw only
tradition and stability in purportedly isolated village worlds. Underlying
the present study is the more middle-of-the-road conviction that what is
sociologically interesting is that some aspects of society and culture remain
stable in the face of other changes, be they economic patterns, ideologies,
or political structures. The present study examines a beauty ideal that seems
deeply entrenched, speaking of and to cultural convictions that have not
been easily swayed by changes in trade patterns, the presence of a nation-
state and its army, or the arrival of new technology and new foodstuffs.
While I focus, thus, on a relative constant in the Azawagh Arab world, the
point is not that everything in that world is and always has been the same;
the point is that amidst certain kinds of change, certain conceptions of the
body, beauty, and sexuality seem to have a particular tenacity. I suggest
that this is because these conceptions are grounded in deep-seated cultural
logics about what men and women are, how desire works, and the
perceived nature of the human body. These cultural commitments are also
in constant flux, but at a slower pace than more visible changes in the
society. Ideas about health and illness, men and women, and what constitutes beauty will no doubt undergo significant changes in the coming
decades, but according to the historical evidence that exists, the practice
of fattening and the ideas that uphold it have not changed markedly over
the past several centuries.

As Charles Piot has pointed out of northern Togo in his aptly titled
Remotely Global (1999), even among the seemingly most remote of peoples
the influence of the outside world is not necessarily new or insignificant.
Like the people he studied, the Azawagh Arabs have always been both
remote and global. They have always been part of a larger Arab and African
world with their trade routes, Islam, and multitude of diverse societies, and
are also increasingly part of a Westernized globalism, with pick-up trucks
from Japan, radio broadcasts from France, tomato paste and pasta from
Italy, and, not least, the armies, schools, and health clinics of a Western-
inspired nation-state. Nonetheless, even to Nigeriens from other parts of
the country the Azawagh region is considered isolated and remote, a back-
water that is a hardship post for civil servants assigned there.

Despite, or perhaps because of, this remoteness, Azawagh Arab women
struck me as comfortably grounded and surprisingly worldly-seeming. They
were warm and emotionally generous, ironic and tough, wise and knowing,
and unfailingly gracious and dignified. They had a confidence in themselves
and their understandings of the world that never ceased to impress me.

When the heat didn't bear down too hard or the winds whip too much sand in my face, I easily longed to be a part of these women's world: for their sureness, their earthy expressiveness, their loving relationships with one another, and their sense of their own self-worth. At the same time, I watched as they endured much suffering I would not have been able to bear: three days in labor with no relief from the pain, philandering husbands, beloved children who died, unending illnesses that resisted cure. The bodies to which women devoted so much attention and energy are inextricably intertwined with all these joys, struggles, and challenges, speaking to and of women's lives in a realm both before and beyond language. It is to this life-long "body project" that I now turn.

Plate 3 Young girl with her fattening porridge and accompanying bowl of water (Amassara)

2

GETTING FAT

The Moors have singular ideas of feminine perfection. The gracefulness of figure and motion, and a countenance enlivened by expression, are by no means essential points in their standard; with them, corpulence and beauty appear to be terms nearly synonymous.

-Mungo Park 1954 [1799]

Like the ever-shifting sands, the peoples of the Sahara have migrated, regrouped, and incorporated newcomers many times during the past several hundred years. Amidst the waxing and waning of trans-Saharan trade routes and the refiguring of alliances and ethnic boundaries, Islam, pastoralism, trade, and, according to the accounts of travelers and explorers, fattening, have remained constants of Saharan life. Below I survey the sparse historical record on female fattening, highlighting the extent to which descriptions from decades and even centuries ago coincide with contemporary practices among Azawagh Arabs, described in the second half of the chapter. That the practice has been so enduring and seemingly uniform across considerable distances in space and time suggests that a beauty ideal, and the means used to achieve it, can be more than a passing superficial fad.

Travelers and explorers, 1352–1936

The first reference to a practice resembling the fattening I observed in the Azawagh comes from as long ago as 1352, when the Moroccan traveler Ibn Battuta witnessed an earlier incarnation of the aesthetic among a Berber[1] group near what would today be the Mali–Niger border. Ibn Battuta, a Berber himself but from a different and distant ethnic group, seemed to appreciate readily the results of the women's efforts:

The women of the Bardama are the most perfect in beauty, the most extraordinary in their exterior, of a whiteness without

33

admixture, and of a heavy corpulence. I have not seen women as fat in any country. Their food consists of cows' milk and ground sorghum, which they drink, morning and evening, mixed with water and uncooked. He who wants to marry one of them must live with them near their own territory and not go beyond Gao or Walata.

(Ibn Battuta 1985 [1352]: 317)

Ibn Battuta not only noted the pleasing plumpness of the Bardama women, but also observed that they achieved this state by ingesting cow's milk and uncooked sorghum, a mixture virtually identical to the food which fattening Moor women eat today. Ibn Battuta even makes mention of a drink called *deqnu*, almost the same name as the *deghnu* that women fatten on today, although he refers to its use not in fattening among the Bardama but in the everyday diet of neighboring people.[2]

Although the Bardama no longer exist as such, they and their practices may have become incorporated into the Arab culture that entered this region as Arabs descended into the Sahara in the following centuries. The Bardama, then, may well be among the distant antecedents of the Azawagh Arabs.

The Sahara was little traveled by pen-toting Westerners in the following centuries, but in the late eighteenth century the Scottish explorer Mungo Park wrote a full account of his adventures there, including his encounter with Moors and their notions of female beauty. Among these Moors, the passage cited at the opening of this chapter continues,

[a] woman, of even moderate pretensions, must be one who cannot walk without a slave under each arm to support her, and a perfect beauty is a load for a camel. In consequence of this prevalent taste for unwieldiness of bulk, the Moorish ladies take great pains to acquire it early in life; and for this purpose, many of the young girls are compelled by their mothers to devour a great quantity of kouskous, and drink a large bowl of camel's milk every morning. It is of no importance whether the girl has an appetite or not, the kouskous and milk must be swallowed, and obedience is frequently enforced by blows. I have seen a poor girl sit crying, with a bowl at her lips, for more than an hour, and her mother, with a stick in her hand, watching her all the while, and using the stick without mercy, whenever she observed that her daughter was not swallowing. This singular practice, instead of producing indigestion and disease, soon covers the young lady with that degree of plumpness which, in the eye of a Moor, is perfection itself.

(Park 1954 [1799]: 116)

Unlike later European travelers in these parts, Park does not depict Moor women as confined and oppressed; rather, he seems to note their practices more as a detached observer. The Moor women did not, in any case, seem to be suffering too greatly from their "slavish submission" to their husbands' sexual appetites, for at one point a number of them accosted Park in his tent in order "to ascertain, by actual inspection, whether the rite of circumcision is extended to the Nazarenes (Christians)." Park, ever in good humor, offered to satisfy their curiosity only if all but one particular attractive young lady would retire. (Whether this particular young lady was unusually thin for a Moor or whether Park in fact shared Ibn Battuta's tastes in women we are not told.) Both the infidel (Park) and the Moor beauties got much pleasure and amusement out of his jest, and the women "went away laughing heartily" (Park 1954 [1799]: 100–101). It is easy to imagine this same brazenness among Azawagh Arab women today were they to come into the presence of a non-Muslim outsider with whom they could similarly let down their guard.

Twenty-five years later in the early nineteenth century the young French explorer René Caillié ventured across similar territory, and described the fattening of girls among the adjacent Brakna Moors, with less good humor but in remarkably similar terms:

> Beauty among the Moors consists in enormous embonpoint [plumpness]; and the young girls are therefore obliged to drink milk to excess; the elder ones take a great quantity of their own accord, but the younger children are compelled by their parents, or by a slave whose office it is, to swallow their allowance. This poor creature commonly takes advantage of the "brief authority" that is granted her, to revenge herself by her cruelty for the tyranny of her masters. I have seen poor little girls crying and rolling on the ground, and even throwing up the milk which they had just drank [sic]; neither their cries nor their sufferings making any impression upon the cruel slave, who beat them, pinched them till they bled, and tormented them in a thousand ways, to force them to take the quantity of milk which she thought proper. If their food were heavier, such a system would have fatal consequences, but it is so far from hurting their constitutions that they grow visibly stronger and fatter. At twelve years old they are enormous, but at twenty or twenty-two they lose their embonpoint; I never saw a woman of that age who was remarkably corpulent.
>
> (Caillié 1968 [1830]: 67)

Why Caillié saw no corpulent adult women I do not know; he may have been among people who did not have the necessary resources to maintain the promise of their young girls' "enormous" bodies; he may have been kept from seeing them; or pregnancies may have drained older women of their appealing size. In any event, the beatings, pinches, and pain that accompany fattening in Caillié's description are still very much part of the practice I witnessed.

In addition to the Moors, the other principal inhabitants of the Sahara, the Tuareg, have also practiced female fattening. In the early 1860s the French explorer Henri Duveyrier wrote about Tuareg women's desire for fleshy figures when he spent several years among them. While he does not write of encountering the forced fattening of girls, he recounted that abundant corpulence was "the supreme of beauty" for Tuareg women, and that they had learned to employ a plant used for fattening animals to season their meat and invite the corpulence they so valued. (Moors also have a number of plants at their disposal thought to enhance fattening.) After taking a small quantity of the plant, they lay under a blanket to induce perspiration, further provoked by drinking "by gulps large quantities of soured milk. If the medication succeeds, the skin dilates, and, after some time of this regime, embonpoint develops" (Duveyrier 1973 [1864]: 437).

With the arrival of the colonial powers in the Sahara at the end of the nineteenth century, the way was open for a greater number of Europeans to test their mettle on forays into this vast region. One of the accounts from this era that is most informative about women's lives is Odette du Puigaudeau's *Pieds nus à travers la Mauritanie* ("Barefoot across Mauritania"), written about the nine-month voyage this middle-aged French woman and her female companion made into the interior of Mauritania in 1933. Though laced with a French penchant for romanticizing the desert, her descriptions of family scenes, male–female interaction, and the fattening of girls also run surprisingly true to my perceptions sixty years later at the opposite end of the Moor world. At one point, for example, she describes a typical tent scene, of an old man and his luscious but shy pubescent bride, who is dressed in yards of thick, shiny indigo cloth:

> We sat down near Sidi to drink tea. His youngest son, a baby, played with his white beard. A little to the side, his wife, Fatimetou, who was barely sixteen, looked at us in silence. A new veil of *chandourah*, glistening with purplish-blue dye, enveloped her. Under the blue "make-up" [of dye that runs onto the skin], her face was the color of moonlight. She was pretty, with long voluptuous eyes, a secret air, and her delicate hands reddened with henna. But, at the slightest gesture, her *malahfa* [*hawli*] became displaced to reveal arms as fat as thighs, and her body had the grace of a goatskin sack full of milk. She was a very beautiful woman.
>
> (du Puigaudeau 1992 [1936]: 85–86)

Her choice of comparison indicates that du Puigaudeau understood much of Moor thinking. To liken an ample body to a goat-skin sack full of milk is a not uncommon, and not unflattering, simile that I heard said of plump children in the Azawagh. A full goat-skin sack has just the replete, fluid contours desired in a woman, and knowledge that the sack is full of milk and not just water only heightens its value, as well as its similarities to the properly fattened woman.

Children were clearly fattened at a young age in the Mauritania of du Puigaudeau's travels, for she describes girls younger than Sidi's wife with already Rubens-esque figures:

> A monstrous figure[3] came and collapsed near me. It was Toutou, the daughter of Ould-Deid, a poor little child of ten years, stuffed with milk, exhausted with fat, who could barely cross her fat little legs in Arab fashion under her stomach . . .
>
> The blacksmith had carefully shaved large circles on each side of her head where the skin appeared naked and white under tufts of hair stuck together with butter. Clinking glass beads embellished her frizzy hairdo. One cannot say that it was very becoming but, by this coiffure, one was immediately informed as to her caste, her tribe, and her situation as a young girl to be married.[4]
>
> Toutou remained there, without form, without looking, and without speaking, a tooth-stick of tact[5] in her half-opened mouth, given up to the lust of men, and to the envy of the women who filled up the tent.
>
> (du Puigaudeau 1992 [1936]: 132)

Later Toutou's mother shows off her daughter to du Puigaudeau, taking off her veils to expose a "torso covered in rolls of fat, and showing with pride the shoulders and sides where the distended skin was cracked with thin, pink chap-marks" (du Puigaudeau 1992 [1936]: 138). Du Puigaudeau goes on to describe her horror at watching the poor Toutou be tortured by a male slave into eating. Toutou clearly represented an extreme case, but du Puigaudeau also describes fattened women in numerous other contexts throughout her account.

French colonial officials in the Azawagh

Far to the east of where Park, Caillié, and du Puigaudeau ventured, in what is now Niger, Arab women were rarely encountered by French officials, but a number of colonial officers describe the fattening of Tuareg women (Abadie 1927; Nicolas 1950; Peignol 1907).[6] In the 1930s a French colonial officer named André Thiellement spent several tours of duty in the

Azawagh, and later wrote a romantic memoir in the colonial adventure genre about his years as a representative of the French empire in the Azawagh. Of the Tuareg he wrote:

> How charming the faces would be without the tallow that coats them! But the young, rich, marriageable girls fattened at the *gavoir* [funnel-like fattening instrument] are so heavy that they have to be carried on a donkey, supported on either side by servants.
>   As to the marabout women, not satisfied with being wrapped up in a triple thickness of dark veils, they conceal their steatopygic [with large behinds] forms behind a screen of mats,[7] and waddle on their huge legs, showing as they walk the soles reddened with henna of their fat feet.
>
> (Thiellement 1949: 63)

In addition to relating how difficult it was to get a good mistress at his post in the Azawagh capital of Tahoua, and the annoyance of having to beat one girl on several occasions until she would submit, Thiellement also describes his rare opportunity of meeting the wife of the then Arab chief. He asked permission to greet her, and it was given him, at least in principle:

> The interview took place under the chiefly tent: a partial interview, because Khadija [the chief's wife] remained squatting behind the tooled leather mat which separated the northern side, that of the men, from the *gynécéen* [women's quarters]. A hand, however, was held out to me from over the partition, a soft hand of red henna-ed skin. By way of heavy silver bracelets, this hand was attached to an arm that was very white, but monstrous, from which fatty rolls hung like fronds.
>
> (Thiellement 1949: 187)

When I was in the market of Tassara one day, a bright young man known for his adversarial nature once asked me why I thought so much had been written about the Tuareg, Hausa, and other local groups by Westerners, but so little about the Arabs of this region.[8] Not realizing he had an answer already in mind, I fumbled through my own reflections on the subject: their relative remoteness, the fact that they were not highly visible since the men often blended with Tuaregs in the public domain (at least to the outside observer), that they themselves were a closed society that had not opened its doors to nosy visitors. It turned out that the young man's answer was something altogether different: "The Tuareg let the French have their women, but we wouldn't let them have ours, so they didn't care to come study us," he proudly and defiantly asserted. After reading accounts like Thiellement's, it is hard not to suspect that there may be some truth in this hypothesis. Yet French accounts also suggest that Saharan Arab women were no more appealing to French colonialists than the idea of French inter-lopers was to Arab men. Certainly, though, Azawagh Arab women were kept from the prying, covetous eyes of the colonialists, as is testified by the silence of colonial accounts on Azawagh Arab women. As the record shows, Thiellement obtained three Tuareg mistresses while stationed in the region, but only managed to see one hand of an Arab woman.

Anthropologists on fattening in the Sahara

Several researchers have described fattening in post-colonial times. Edmond Bernus' *Touaregs: chroniques de l'Azawak* (1991) includes a photograph from the 1960s of a Tuareg girl lying on her back, her fingers holding her mouth open at either side, with a stream of milk dripping through her parted lips from a bowl held by the hands of an unseen woman. Bernus notes that fattening is said by the Tuareg to accelerate puberty and enhance the marriageability of girls, and he quotes from a Tuareg poem celebrating the beauties of folds of female flesh concealed behind fancy cloth.

Since my arrival in the Azawagh in 1985 I have not heard of any Tuareg girls being fattened, though the practice may continue among certain noble families in remote encampments. Because I am suggesting that Moor fattening is deeply embedded in structures that are particular to Moor life, the relationship of Moor fattening to Tuareg fattening deserves comment. Tuareg culture and Moor culture share Islam, a history of slave holding, and a dependence on herding and, to a lesser degree, trade. Although histori-cally matrilineal, the Tuareg have adopted Arab patrilineality over the past several hundred years. All of these cultural traits ground the practice of fattening for Moors, and, as the French anthropologist Aline Tauzin (1981) points out, have done so for the Tuareg as well. Tuareg culture differs vastly from Moor culture, however, in the relative equality between the sexes that characterizes it, and in the relative freedom of the women. While the two neighboring cultures shared the sexualized aesthetic that surrounds female fatness, as well as some of the foundational structures that undergird the practice, the crucial differences in constructions of maleness, femaleness, and gender relations between the two societies make it impossible to completely equate the two traditions of fattening, and may help to account for the practice's more marked decline among Tuareg in Niger.

In the Moor world, Aline Tauzin (1981: 45–64) has described how girls in Mauritania fattened until they were said to have a "dress of stretch-marks" on their bodies. They even ran combs along their skin in order to bring out the appearance of stretchmarks on the limbs. Tauzin's analysis of fattening's meanings coincides with my own among Moors in Niger: fat has an aesthetic value, a fat woman brings honor to her family, a fattened girl is made ready for marriage more quickly, and a girl undergoing fattening learns to subdue her own activity and sexuality. Tauzin (1981: 60) emphasizes the extent to which fattening quiets a girl and teaches her immobility: "it makes her docile" (*yeddebhe*) and "she sits and does not move" (*ga'da u hāmiye*), both phrases used in the Azawagh as well. The relationship between sexuality and fattening is also central to these Mauritanian Moors, for fatness in a female is said both to arouse male desire and to suppress a woman's own.

I have quoted from the historical record at some length in order to convey how stable and widespread the practice of fattening girls in the Sahara seems to have been. In addition, I find it remarkable that so many of the features of fattening described by these earlier visitors among both Tuareg and Moors persist among Azawagh Arabs today, with very little deviation from the practices witnessed thirty, seventy, and even 200 years ago. By contrast, during the two centuries since Mungo Park described a Moor woman's appearance in a way that could pass in a contemporary description of Tassara life, Western conceptions of beauty have been transformed many times over.

This does not mean that Moor society has been unchanging and stagnant. One hundred years ago Moors in Mali and Niger were hunting ostriches to send the feathers to women in Europe for their hats. Today the men trade black-market sugar and dried milk across nation-state borders. What the enduring character of fattening shows is that certain key elements of Saharan Arab life have remained relatively constant, and that the female aesthetic and the practice of fattening is in some way intertwined with these political, economic, and social constants. These constants include Islam, patrilineal social structure and endogamy, patterns of male economic activity, and conceptions of maleness, femaleness, the human body, and human sexuality. The Western counterparts to these social features – Christianity, extended patrilineal families, agriculture, and notions of sex and the human body – have all changed markedly over the past several hundred years, and with them, not surprisingly, beauty ideals and bodily practices.

Getting fat in the Azawagh today

When I came to Tassara in 1991, a number of girls were being quietly fattened in the corners of tents in scenes similar to those described above. The fattening process is in no way ritualized, however, and no public event marks the passage of a girl from unfettered childhood to her preparation for married adulthood. She loses her first baby teeth, and from one day to the next she begins to be fattened. To describe how the process of forced fattening begins and proceeds, I tell one girl's story here.

Aichatou

Little Aichatou (AY-sha-tou) was five or six years old when I first met her, and was being raised lovingly by her grandmother, Fatima. She was a quiet, peaceful little girl, who mostly stayed under the tent and clung to her grandmother's ample, indigo-swathed lap. One day in the hot season, however, some eight months after I had gotten to know the family, I entered Fatima's tent to find a rather different scene, and a changed relationship between grandmother and granddaughter. Aichatou sat in a corner, her head hung low, a disproportionately large bowl of porridge before her. Lazily and discontentedly she swirled a large ladle through the porridge. Every so often Fatima looked over and yelled, "What are you waiting for?" "Eat!" and "Swallow!" Later, after Aichatou had finally finished eating and got up to play, Fatima admonished the poor little wraith by exclaiming, "Cover your vagina and don't run around like a prostitute!" Over the next few months I observed Aichatou's easygoing if shy personality change quickly into one of true reserve and unhappiness, and she appeared constantly on the verge of tears. Although I never witnessed Fatima employ tactics commonly used against other girls being fattened – throwing household objects at them, pulling their fingers back to make them swallow, or pinching the back of their necks – clearly the emotional timbre of Fatima and Aichatou's relationship had changed drastically. From then on for the next six or seven years, under her grandmother's watchful eye, Aichatou's main purpose in life would be to fatten her body, and the loving indulgence of early childhood would be shown to her no longer. During the years to come, she would grow to "learn the value of fatness herself," as women said, and if she followed the path of other girls, would become a proud if shy, nubile bride by early adolescence.

The day of reckoning had been precipitated for Aichatou as for all other girls by the bodily transformation that signaled her readiness for this slow induction into female adulthood: her first two baby teeth fell out. Azawagh Arabs do not keep ages; instead, they watch the body, especially the female body, carefully for signs of maturation – the loss of the first two baby teeth means it is time to start fattening; the first show of pubic hair means it is time to take on the women's sari-like garment, the *ḥawli*; and first menstruation means it is time for a girl's first fast during the Muslim month of Ramadan.

Throughout these corporeal transformations girls continue to be force-fed; only the type of food they eat is altered with the onset of puberty. Then, after many years of drinking down milky porridge, girls switch to stuffing their mouths full of drier couscous, which they then swallow down with water. According to the indigenous humoral system (explained in chapter 8), couscous is a "colder" food. Since girls' bodies become "hotter" as they expand and especially when they become sexually potent at puberty, they eventually need "colder" foods to curb the possibility of a dangerous overabundance of "heat," which could lead to various ailments as well as to a too wanton sexuality.

As Fatima's treatment of Aichatou suggests and as my friend Sidi explained, fattening is about much more than body size:

> As soon as one says "this girl is being fattened," her behavior changes. She doesn't want to eat, she hangs her head and has her bowl before her but doesn't eat. She shouldn't go out, and if she does, she should walk respectfully. You must comport yourself as a woman. You are on the market now. It is an education.

Aichatou was of a chiefly family as well as the granddaughter of one of the most important women in the village, and thus was definitely "on the market" for marriage and would need to be fattened properly. Both Fatima and Aichatou were acceding to the behavior expected of them, based on the implicit understanding that Aichatou was now going to be "made" into a sexually mature and desirable wife.

Aichatou's grandmother Fatima was herself a paragon of Moor woman-liness, still full in body and demure in comportment. Although I had been in Tassara for eight months when Aichatou began to be fattened, and I visited Fatima often, I had never seen her stand, much less walk. Fatima complained, in fact, that she could no longer lift herself "even to pray," though she attributed this not to her fleshy, swollen legs but to some other as yet undiagnosed disease. "Our grandmothers were much fatter than this," she always told me patiently, "and they never had problems raising themselves."

Fattened as a girl herself, Fatima now spent her days seated cross-legged, swathed in her indigo *hawli*. Amidst an unending stream of visits from female relatives, she ran her household – or "tenthold" – from this seated position. She had borne at least eleven children, most of them to the former, now deceased chief, before she managed to secure a divorce from him and marry two other men in succession. At what I estimated to be about age forty-six, a grandmother and senior woman of the community, she became permanently a "divorcée," in fact a somewhat desirable situation for a woman as long as she had sons to support her, which Fatima did. She no longer had to cater to an old husband, veiling or sitting behind a mat parti-tion when any male visitors came calling on him, nor did she have to curb her own visitors in any way. In order to retain her respectable plumpness, and perhaps simply because she had so long eaten in this fashion, Fatima continued to eat as adult women do: stuffing every corner of her mouth with a type of couscous, and then swallowing each mouthful down with gulps of milk or water.

Fatima exemplified the type of body Azawagh Arab women spent all but the first few years of their lives trying to achieve and then maintain: a body marked by pendulous upper arms, rolls of fat around the waist, a protruding behind, and thighs that together form one vast expanse. Since women usually sit cross-legged on mats on the ground, their shape, particularly with their *hawli* pulled up over their head, grows to resemble a curvaceous pyramid, a form incarnated in the dolls little girls play with, like the ones I discovered on my very first day of fieldwork in Tassara. Made of rags or clay, these dolls usually lack legs or arms, but consist of a decorated head, elongated neck, and large lump of a body, with two carefully accentuated protruding buttocks (Popenoe 1997).

Together with my observations of Fatima, Aichatou and others, these dolls offered a useful tool for thinking my way into the local meanings of the female body. They encapsulated what seemed to really matter, and made the beauty ideal more concrete than changing, aging real bodies ever could. They also made me realize that for girls and probably everyone else in the society, those rotund dolls were simply what adult women should and often did look like. Albeit slightly formalized and "abbreviated" in their lack of anatomical detail, they were natural representations of human bodies that girls made unreflectively. Unlike Barbie dolls in the West, they were not manufactured by a large corporation to lure consumers, but were "designed" and made by girls themselves, occasionally with help from their mothers for the more sophisticated rag dolls.

Talking about getting fat: *leblūh* and *al-gharr*

The remarks of women to the girls entrusted to them, for example urging them to "keep their vaginas shut," suggests the extent to which the process of fattening was a process of sexualizing their bodies, and therefore not an appropriate subject for easy chatter. It was thus some time before I learned the vocabulary of fattening *per se*, and I never heard it used extensively. The terms used to refer to fattening and force-feeding girls are nonetheless telling in their apparent etymologies.

In Galgaliyya Arabic two words are used to refer to the practice of fattening. The overall process of fattening a young girl is called *le-blūh* (where *le* is the definite article). Although this word had no other meaning in the Galgaliyya Arabic spoken in the Azawagh, in the related Hassaniyya Arabic spoken to the west, *blūh* refers to "dates that are cut and exposed to the sun to make them mature more quickly" (Taine-Cheikh 1988).[9]

Despite the fact that people I asked in Tassara were not familiar with this meaning of the term, the association is evocative: girls who are fattened are essentially taken early from childhood and made to mature more quickly by feeding their bodies to plump womanliness.

The actual forcing of a girl to eat her fattening food, as Fatima forced Aichatou, is called *al-gharr*. Like *leblūḥ*, the term *gharr* has an interesting related connotation in both standard and Hassaniyya Arabic: "deception."[10] Although Azawagh Arabs I questioned were also unfamiliar with this meaning of the term, the "deception" of making a young girl into a woman faster than would be natural through fattening makes perfect sense.[11]

Even if the process of fattening itself is notable for its lack of ritualization, female corpulence is widely celebrated in conversation, song, and ritual. Stretchmarks are one indication of high beauty and, as Boukia explained, "any woman can get stretchmarks on her stomach; it is stretchmarks on one's arms that are really a mark of beauty." A song of a man celebrating his beloved's beauty tells how, through a hole in her garment, he glimpsed "stretchmarks from her waist to her knee." Another song celebrating the delights of a beautiful woman comments on the luscious "three folds" of her stomach. And although neither men nor women sat around comparing how fat different women were – such talk would have been tantamount to putting the evil eye on someone – comments on the appearance of women usually included subtle and indirect references to their relative plumpness. Indeed, one of the most common adjectives in Galgaliyya Arabic is *zeyn*, which means both "good" and "beautiful," and it went without saying that fatness in a woman was *zeyn*.

When does fattening begin?

As described above, girls begin to be fattened when their first two milk teeth fall out, a physical sign that their bodies are ready to be "ripened" into female adulthood. This is known as when a girl "changes," *tubeddel*, and is also accompanied by her first hair braiding. From being a relatively sexless child with "no heart" – no common sense or understanding of things – who has been able to run about and play quite freely, she is now ready to be made into a proper woman. The society has begun to form her body to its specifications, one might say.

Boys also follow a bodily calendar, and the loss of their first baby teeth signals that they should begin praying regularly, which girls also are expected to do from this time. Both girls and boys attend Koranic school before losing their first teeth, but girls' studying ends when they begin their new form of "education," while boys are expected to begin studying in greater earnest or, increasingly, go to the public school which almost no Arab girls attend. (The only Arab girl in Tassara who attended school was deaf.) Aline Tauzin (1981) noted that in Mauritania a boy was circumcised after the loss of his first two teeth, but the timing did not seem to follow such a strict bodily calendar in the Azawagh. Boys' maturing bodies do not receive much more attention until many years later when they begin to develop pubic, chest, and face hair, which in the past signaled that they could begin to wear a turban, and today, when turbans are less *de rigueur*, signals more casually an induction into the economic responsibilities of male adulthood as well as the accompanying freedoms.

The importance of a girl's apparent physical age and not her age in calendar years is also reflected in the ending point of formal forced fattening, dictated by the time of her first fast during Ramadan. This is determined by her achievement of secondary sexual characteristics such as pubic hair and breasts. Note that a girl's sexual maturity, not her reproductive capability, determines this point. A girl is considered marriageable when she attains sexual desirability, not the ability to have children. Hence the fact that Boukia's mother, and numerous other women I knew or heard of, had become pregnant for the first time before ever seeing their periods. That is, their husbands had begun having sex with them and they became pregnant at their very first ovulation. As many Arab women told me, of course fattening has nothing to do with fertility, since they have seen many thin women who have no problem having children. Instead, fattening has to do with making a girl into a sexually mature and desirable adult woman – something arguably harder to insure and more open to manipulation than getting a girl to reproductive maturity.

Who fattens?

Although all Azawagh Arab girls were force-fed (*tengharru*) in the past, according to those I spoke with, it is easier for wealthier families to spare the milk, grain, and servant/slave labor that is required for a girl to fatten. Today the practice is increasingly confined to the leading families in Tassara, although it is not uncommon for girls from less well-off families to be fattened, particularly, it appeared, when (1) the mother was herself of very ample size and (2) there was reason to think the girl might have trouble finding a husband, because her father was dead, the family was somewhat marginal to the community, or she was not particularly attractive. The other factor that played into decisions about whether or not a girl would be fattened was her planned marital future. If a girl was promised in marriage at a young age to a cousin, her family would fatten her so that she would be ready for the marriage to be achieved and consummated as soon as possible.

Like the reasons for fattening, discussions in Tassara of who fattened and why were muted, although women in the community could readily list on their fingers the girls in Tassara who were promised in marriage. Women told me that the ultimate decision on whether to fatten a girl or not rested with men, for it was they who supplied the food. In the past girls were even given a special milking cow by their fathers, a cow whose sole purpose was to supply the milk for fattening for the girl. Although I was never privy to any debate over whether or not a girl might fatten, I would hazard that while men may have had the last word, it was more often women who in fact exercised the power of decision, with knowledge, of course, of their husbands' financial capabilities. I knew several girls whose mothers were either widowed or divorced but who were being fattened, suggesting that women could decide how to use their own resources, including whether or not to devote a large part of them to the fattening of a daughter. Such women subsisted on the basis of support from their fathers, brothers, sons, or occasionally animals of their own that were herded by a male relative.

While I encountered little discussion about who supplied the fattening food or about the girls themselves who were being fattened, women had more to say about which female relative should be chosen to fatten the girls. *Ḥaraṭīn* (servant) women usually did the actual work of pounding grain, and *ḥaraṭīn* men the work of milking, but an Arab woman was always in charge of a particular girl's regime. The rule of thumb was to choose a woman who would have sufficient authority over the girl to enforce her eating, by physical means if words did not suffice. Because of this it is relatively rare for a mother to force-feed her own daughter, for a mother is thought to feel too much pity (*ḥāna*) to properly oversee what is necessarily an unpleasant chore for the girl. Instead, three categories of women tend to take on the role of "fattener": (1) a grandmother; (2) an aunt, especially a paternal aunt; and (3) a mother-in-law, if a girl is married young. As this implies, a girl is often sent away to be fattened, and many young girls who were fattening were essentially being raised by a woman not their own mother. Although one might expect paternal grandmothers to be a more likely choice than maternal ones in this patrilineal society, because women were close to their own mothers it was not uncommon for a young mother to send her daughter to her own mother to be fattened. Women did, however, tell me that paternal aunts exerted greater authority over their nieces than maternal ones, and of course more of their long-term interest was invested in this girl of their own immediate patriline.

Since it was believed that even among the most docile young girls physical inducements to fattening would be required at some point, the women who fattened girls were expected to be fit. Old women even said to me that they could not fatten a girl any more because they were too weak to hit anyone. While I cannot confirm the story old Kia told me of her wrist actually being broken by her mother while standing on her hand to make her drink her porridge when she was a girl, I did see many sandals, pots, and other objects lying around the tent go flying at dawdling girls (who usually dodged them easily), as well as the common practices of pulling a girl's hand back and pinching her throat and body to induce her to swallow her gruel. It is interesting to note that corporal punishment is also an integral part of teaching children to read the Koran, the other form of education they all undergo. It seems that not only in the case of fattening, but more generally in Azawagh Arab culture, the infliction of bodily pain is thought to enhance learning and development. This is not uncommon cross-culturally; initiation rites almost always involve some sort of physical pain for participants. The disciplining of the body is a powerful and expressive means to the disciplining of mind and soul.

What to eat?

It is possible to get fat on only two types of food, according to Azawagh Arabs: milk and grain, the latter almost always millet or sorghum. Of these, milk is preferable by far, because of its many desirable qualities – it flows into the girl's limbs easily, it is white as her complexion will hopefully be, and it is the most valued and healthgiving of foods. Grain, easier to come by these days, adds bulk, and, taken with water or milk to make it flow into the body's cavities, was an ingredient of all fattening I witnessed. A calorie-conscious Western reader may notice that Azawagh Arab women do not have an easy time, since neither grain nor the milk they drink has a high fat content. The women are essentially eating a carbohydrate-rich diet of nutritious foods, even if almost completely devoid of fruit and vegetables.

Although the fattening diet is bland, the simplicity of these ingredients can be misleading, for women make at least a dozen types of foods out of milk and millet. The decision of what to eat is based entirely on the elaborate humoral science by which foods and body states are categorized according to "heat" or "coldness," as mentioned earlier. Such humoral systems exist in many societies around the world, but there are considerable differences among them. The Azawagh Arabs' system is explained in more detail in chapter 8, but for now suffice it to say that most things of the natural world – bodily states, foods, diseases, plants, medicines – are by their nature "hot" or "cold," categorizations that have little to do with temperature. People strive to maintain a balance of hot and cold in their bodies, and if you get "heat" you need a "cold" food or medicine to treat it, and vice versa. As in the West, however, to be a little "hot" is also to be sexy.

Since young girls' bodies are cold and unsexualized, it is logical that they begin fattening on hotter foods that can swell their bodies, such as a milky porridge (*lhsi'*) as well as milk. As their bodies become fatter and hotter, they switch to the cooler grain-and-milk concoctions called *deghnu* (the term that closely resembles the name for the food Ibn Battuta discovered people eating in the Sahel almost 700 years earlier). There are at least seven different ways to combine millet flour and milk, like seven variations on basic oatmeal: with very fine flour or rougher flour; with soured milk or with water; cooked by steam, in the ground, or in liquid.[12] All of these vary on the hot–cold axis. (In brief, things cooked enclosed in a pot are hot, whereas when flour is sifted and a lot of liquid is used, the resulting preparation is considered cold.) Like Westerners on diets balancing their intake of carbohydrates, proteins, and fats, Azawagh Arab women are constantly engaged in determining the state of their bodies and deciding what to eat accordingly.

Even though liquid can bring on coldness, all fattening food must either be watery or be eaten with a lot of liquid in order to make it disperse properly into the limbs. (Recall that stretchmarks on arms and legs are a particular goal of fattening.) But *deghnu* porridge is not simply eaten by the spoonful accompanied by ample sips of water. Instead, it is always consumed by being stuffed into all the cavities of the mouth, and then swallowed down with large gulps of water (*tezwīz*).[13] Women always told me that they ate this way because they just wanted to get it over, but I suggest that by eating their food in a way that seems forced and uncomfortable, women avoid the problem of seeming to be voracious and lustful of appetite. As I will discuss below, this is one of the prime challenges of fattening: as a woman sexualizes her body, she needs to deny that sexuality ever more, and any sign of appetite and desire is readily perceived as sexual appetite and sexual desire.[14]

In implicit recognition of the fact that such eating to fatten is not eating for subsistence, fattening foods are always eaten at mid-morning and mid-afternoon, that is in between the times when "regular" meals are consumed by men and women not actively fattening. If a woman is fattening, however, she often skips the meals prepared for the rest of the family, because the heat of that thicker porridge (*l'aysh*) may "melt" her hard-won fat.

Why fatten?

As I searched for satisfying exegeses of the ideal of fat beauty, most people struck me as remarkably inarticulate about the reasons for fattening. Asked directly why Azawagh Arab women like to be fat, people invariably answered in one of three ways: (1) because it is beautiful (*zeyn*); (2) because men like it; or, less commonly, (3) because it makes a girl into a woman. Their answers were usually delivered with a hint of exasperation; the question itself seemed too stupid to require an answer.

The frequency with which I was told that fatness in a woman was a good thing because it was beautiful underlines the extent to which this aesthetic value is, in some way, "enough" to explain the practice indigenously. Unlike contemporary Western society, where catering too closely to society's beauty ideals may be considered morally suspect, or where bodily values like thinness are increasingly framed in terms of biomedical virtues, the Azawagh Arabs I spoke with considered it adequate explanation for a practice that it achieved beauty. It went without saying that beauty was desirable.

As the second reason people gave suggested, if men like a girl's appearance she will be more likely to make a good marriage, which is to her advantage. I also came to realize that the beauty which female fatness represented was a highly sexualized beauty. Once when I raised the issue of why women like to be fat, a lively Tassara woman replied immediately, "Would you rather sleep on a flat board, or on that mattress over there?" The beauty of a fat, "cushioned" body and its sexual desirability were closely linked. The voluptuous, weighty, "closedness" of the fattened female sparks the erotic imagination. "So men like fat girls?" I once remarked playfully to Boukia, my friend from my Peace Corps days. "Oh yes!" she answered. "They say 'Oh my, what a girl!' They squeeze her breasts and stomach, and her pubis becomes like a woman's, big, like that teapot over there."[15] When young men referred to making love to a woman (only very bold young men would dare to do this), they squeezed their hands together in the air to imitate squeezing flesh.

The third answer, "because it makes a girl into a woman," refers more to the process of fattening than to the appeal of the beauty ideal itself. On close examination, the comment reveals an array of underlying assumptions about the world that help an outsider make sense of the practice. First of all, this statement assumes that girls need to be *made* into women; they will not necessarily become women naturally, or at least will not become proper women without these human interventions. Combined with the early age at which girls start fattening, the statement also indicates that it is a desirable thing to become a woman, and to become one as early as possible. The statement also assumes that fatness = womanliness. To be fat is to be a woman, and to be a woman is to be fat. This equation is supported by the fact that although some older, wealthier men in the community became stout in later life without attracting any comment, a younger man who showed signs of chubbiness was teased for being like a woman; and women who are "like a board," without curves and love handles, are denigrated for being like men. "Eat, so that you will become a person!"[16] old Kia once yelled at me as we played that she was going to force-feed me, as she was doing to her granddaughter. A certain degree of fatness is nothing less than a consequence of being a fully human female.

These, then, are the facts of fattening among Azawagh Arabs, including their own attempts to explain the practice. As I hope has begun to be clear, a series of tropes and oppositions are central to the logic of fattening and how women generally handle their bodies: open and closed, cold and hot, wet and dry. These binary pairs that are so essential to the logic of fattening also pervade domains of Azawagh Arab culture from Islamic belief to the curing of illness to the sexual imagination. Of these the most important is the negative value placed on that which is open and porous versus the positive value placed on that which is closed and contained. Akin to the value on "interiority" that Janice Boddy (1989) describes among Sudanese Arabs, Azawagh Arabs strive to achieve what I will call "closedness" in many ways: by marrying close relatives, by remaining remote from other ethnic groups, by closing off the female body through veiling, by numerous practices aimed at shutting off bodily orifices, and of course through fattening, which "swells" a woman shut and grounds her in immobility. In this way fattening is about much more than simply being beautiful or being womanly; it also represents a physical expression of central cultural values that go beyond the aesthetic and the sexual. These values emerge not only in care of the body, but also in the practice of Islam, the reckoning of kin relationships, and the structure of Azawagh Arab economic strategies, which I will turn to next.

Part II

SELF-REPRESENTATIONS

Plate 4 Girls learning to read the Koran (Tchin Tabaraden)

3

IN THE NAME OF
ALLAH, MOST BENEVOLENT,
EVER MERCIFUL

Have you not seen how your Lord
lengthens out the shadow?
He could have kept it motionless if He liked.
Yet We make the sun its pilot to show the way.
Then We draw it back to Us, withdrawing it little by little.
It is He who made the night a covering for you;
and made sleep for rest, the day for rising.
It is He who sends the winds with auspicious news
in advance of His benevolence;
and We send pure water down from the sky
To quicken a region that was dead,
and to give it as drink to animals We have created
and to men in plenty.

Koran 25: 45–49

The above passage from the Koran conveys the all-encompassing power God has for Azawagh Arabs: he "lengthens out the shadow," pilots the sun, brings rain, and created mankind. This particular passage from the Koran was not regularly recited by Azawagh Arabs, but it nonetheless captures the centrality of Islam in Azawagh Arab daily life. Islam is so foundational to Azawagh Arabs' sense of themselves as well as to everyday life that after having discussed fattening itself, I open the rest of my ethnographic account with a description of Islam's meanings and practices. No arena of life is without the felt presence of God and Koranic teachings, and this includes care of the body.

Arguably there is a general way of understanding the body, sexuality, and the sexes that, while not explicitly outlined in the Koran, nonetheless is widespread across the Muslim-Arab world. While I do not mean to claim that there is one unvarying way of understanding the human body or one "Muslim sexuality" (Abu-Lughod 1997), it is common across the Arab-Islamic world to see sexuality and sexual desire as pervasive, powerful, and potentially disruptive forces, and to regard men and women as radically different – and often opposed – kinds of beings. These views correlate with particular perceptions of the body – women's bodies inherently attract, and men's bodies are inherently attracted. None of these ideas are unfamiliar to Western, Judeo-Christian thought, even if they have taken different forms historically and come under challenge in the modern era. If Islam colors how Azawagh Arabs understand bodies, men and women, and sexuality, it is not surprising that Islam also has much to do with the meanings and logic of female fattening. In this chapter I argue that even though Azawagh Arabs did not bring up their religion directly when I asked about fattening, the beauty of fatness is in fact deeply embedded in and shaped by Islam.

The centrality of Islam in Azawagh Arab life

After I had been in Tassara less than a week, a village man who had taken me under his wing suggested that, since I professed to be interested in "customs and history," I should go to meet a respected religious teacher ('ālem) who lived in the desert and was very knowledgeable about the history of the Arabs of this region. I readily agreed, and was soon bouncing over the roadless desert in my jeep with three accompanying men who would show me the way and introduce me when we reached the encampment several kilometers outside of Tassara.

We arrived at a spare cluster of tents in an otherwise uninhabited stretch of undulating sandy savanna. The blue Suzuki made a most incongruous splash in the serenity of the scene, which was all variations of sand in color, except for the white and indigo of the men's jellabas, and a few tufts of light green in the desert vegetation. With time I became used to the utter incommensurability of the two worlds – the technological complexity of the world I brought with me, and the material simplicity of the one I encountered – but at this point in my stay it all still seemed surreal.

When we approached the tent where the 'ālem lived, I thought of what I already had been told by the men I was traveling with: the 'ālem would not shake a woman's hand, as is otherwise the custom even between people of the opposite sex throughout Niger. I therefore carefully did not offer my hand to the old, turbanned man who greeted us, and did my best to affect what I took to be humble feminine comportment. The women seated in the back of the tent erected a sort of cloth partition to keep themselves out of view of the visiting males, while I sat down with the men on mats just inside one tent edge, veiling somewhat clumsily. Once my escorts had explained what they had come for, the 'ālem Bai began his story, with one of the other men translating his words into French.

I expected to hear a more elaborated version of the story I had heard from other men and women about the Azawagh Arabs' descent from Algeria into Mali and then into Niger about a century ago, with possibly some interesting information about a significant drought or battle. Instead I found myself listening to a very different tale. It began with the first four Islamic caliphs, the earliest leaders of Islam after the Prophet Muhammad's death in 632. When I expressed interest in "history," I began to realize, this could not only mean memories of the arrival of the French in 1900 or of the 1984 drought, but could equally well apply to their history as Muslims, connected through a line of worthy men to the Prophet himself. It was this history, in fact, reaching back some 1300 years, that defined who they were in a way that the travels and travails of the past mere 200 years or so never could.

Bai, it turned out, was a Kunta, a different tribe from that of most inhabitants of Tassara, and one more common in Mali and Mauritania, from where he had originally come. His version of history, however, was clearly considered relevant to my interests because both the Kunta and the tribes in Tassara were thought to be descended from men who were close to the Prophet. Bai's account of Saharan Arab history went on to describe the struggles to spread Islam in Egypt and elsewhere, and the role of the valiant *lieutenant de guerre*, Uqba bin Nafi, in the seventh and eighth centuries. After this point the story converged more directly with Bai's specific tribe's own history, and, unfortunately for me, was also where he found it appropriate to stop. The next thousand years or so, I guessed, merely witnessed the disintegration of the original Muslim unity and glory, and though Bai was no doubt proud to be a Kunta, there was no point getting into petty details about what tribe went where.

In order to elaborate on what he seemed to consider the relevant and important history – the time of the Prophet and the few centuries following – Bai called on a servant to bring his own manuscripts of Kunta and Islamic history. From the back of the tent emerged a package of dusty plastic, tied in string, in which was wrapped a series of thin notebooks of the type used by Nigerien schoolchildren. As Bai leafed through the books in search of what he was looking for, I saw that each was filled with line after line of neat Arabic handwriting. Finally Bai found the notebook he sought, one in which on every page or so a name was written in red against the black ink of the rest of the writing. These, it turned out, were the names of the descendants of Uqba bin Nafi, the early leader of the Muslim army in Egypt and a fellow tribesman of the Prophet Muhammad. They represented the patrilineal ancestors from whom Bai traced his descent, ultimately back to the birth of Islam itself.

At the time I was rather disappointed to hear this textbook recital of Islamic history and the names of a few old men, instead of stories of what I thought were more recent and relevant events, even while somewhat surprised that Bai's story so precisely coincided with the "official" histories of Islam. In retrospect, however, I realized that the fact that interest in Azawagh Arab history could so easily be interpreted as an interest in the history of Islam said something profound about the way in which the Arabs of the Azawagh conceived of themselves.

As I was to discover in countless additional conversations during my time in the Azawagh, the story of Islam and the story of twentieth-century Azawagh Arabs were inseparable from one another. When on occasion I asked people what they would like me to tell those in my home country about themselves, Islam was usually the first thing mentioned. That I was not a Muslim was a barrier to intimacy and acceptance that was always present in my interactions with people, whether spoken or not. Friends constantly begged me to accept Islam and convert, and I believe many thought it their duty to bring me to this salvation by the end of my time there. Near the end of my stay the chief's prominent nephew, Mohamed, told me in front of a gathering of men that the women in Tassara liked me, but that if I would only convert (and marry an Arab man – these two things went hand in hand), then they would hide no secrets from me. Boukia once dreamt that I converted to Islam and was to marry a Muslim, and she told me of the deep joy she had felt; even though my intended husband was a former slave, at least he was a Muslim. Their professions of allegiance to Islam were not mere formality. Almost all Azawagh Arabs pray the requisite five times a day, pepper their talk with references to Allah and the rewards of the next world, and do not conceal the fact that they consider Islam to offer all humans the only path to salvation.

Islam and Islams

Talal Asad (1986), among others, has noted that Westerners either treat Islam as a monolithic faith with an unvarying inner logic or analyze it in terms of simplistic dichotomies between the orthodox and non-orthodox religion or a Great and a Little Tradition (Gellner 1981). Since the Azawagh Arabs themselves speak as if one and only one Islam exists, it is easy to fall into the trap of essentializing the religion. But when I write here of "Islam," I want to emphasize that I refer only to Islam as practiced by the Azawagh Arabs. Unlike many other nomadic Arab peoples, for whom Islam has been described as something of a backdrop to more immediate tribal or ethnic concerns (Lancaster 1981: 90; Abu-Lughod 1986), the Azawagh Arabs, both men and women, asserted their Muslimness above all other aspects of their identity. This may be due to the fact that Moors have been messengers of Islam to surrounding peoples, and continually want to mark their own Islam as purer and more original than that of these same surrounding peoples.

Believing that they are descendants of the companions of the Prophet himself, Azawagh Arabs hold their Muslimness to be of a higher, truer standard than the Muslimness of the peoples around them: the Wodaabe who have only recently begun to convert to Islam, and are still often thought of as pagan; the Tuareg with their spirit cults and non-Arab roots; and the Hausa (the largest ethnic group in Niger) with their perceived allegiance to the ways of the infidel French colonialists. Azawagh Arabs also have Islam's language as their own, although the Galgaliyya Arabic they speak is so far removed from Koranic Arabic that people do not necessarily even understand all the parts of the Koran they can recite. For the Azawagh Arabs, Islam is not something they converted to at some point in the past but is something in their blood, as Bai's story attests. Their very heritage insures their Islamic orthodoxy, even if their practice sometimes departs from what is decreed.

And indeed it sometimes does: for example, although Azawagh Arabs pray dutifully, they do not always adhere to the fast during the month of Ramadan with the same fervor that people of neighboring ethnic groups do. In large part this is because they understand and follow the Koranic injunctions against fasting when ill or traveling, as well as when pregnant. But I also perceived a sense in which following the precise letter of the law was less vital for those who had such worthy claims to Islamic heritage than it was for more suspect recent converts. For the most part, however, adherence to Islamic orthodoxy was the unquestioned ground of everyday existence.

The world Allah made

While, in the terms of modern social science, Azawagh Arabs, like all other peoples, are continually "making" their world through their social activity, to them themselves the world was profoundly "made" when they were born into it. As Ernest Gellner has pointed out, daily life for practicing Muslims unfolds largely according to a blueprint that Allah spelled out to mankind in the Koran:

> Islam . . . holds that a set of rules exists, eternal, divinely ordained, and independent of the will of men, which defines the proper ordering of society. This model is available in writing; it is equally and symmetrically available to all literate men, and to all those willing to heed literate men. These rules are to be implemented throughout social life.
>
> (Gellner 1981: 1)

For those who stray from this divine blueprint of life, for example Westerners and other infidels such as Chinese and Indians, hellfire and damnation await. "Do you know how hot the fire is?" people would ask me, forever hopeful that I would see the light and convert. "Hotter than that fire over there; hotter than anything you can imagine," they would answer their own question, surprisingly literal, as indeed the Koran is, in their depictions of the pain of hell and the rewards of heaven. For those who follow the path that Muhammad laid out, women explained to me on numerous occasions, a paradise awaits where all women are beautiful, milk flows from faucets, and all desires are fulfilled.

Coming from an American academic milieu of perpetual doubt and disillusionment, I found it difficult at first to grasp how very real was the Muslim vision of this world and the next for Azawagh Arabs, and how alive their faith. Islam in this part of the Sahara is supremely confident and I never witnessed anyone who doubted the absolute truth and rectitude of their faith. Indeed to call it "faith" seems misleading, for their belief in Islam was really knowledge, not faith: an understanding that the world was ordered, right and wrong defined, and life's path ordained, by an indomitable and unquestionable power.

The Koran and Hadith (sayings of the Prophet Muhammad) were the first and last authority not only on subjects addressed directly in the sacred texts, but also on subjects they do not in fact speak of. Women believed, for example, that using hair extensions was wrong because Islamic law forbade it. Similarly, a chemical product used to enhance the effects of henna was said to have been forbidden for being against Islamic law. These proscriptions were probably related to Koranic injunctions against women flaunting their charms but there is, as far as I know, no specific injunction against hair extensions in the Koran or Hadith. Such proscriptions illustrate how deeply Islam has reached into the most mundane of everyday activities.

Although all Muslims are technically equal before God according to Islamic theology, some have learned more of the holy books than others. Muslim scholars, known collectively as 'ulama (sing. 'ālem, from the word for "to know"), administered Islamic medicine, pronounced on subjects such as the permissibility of hair extensions, and interpreted the Koran to the community. They were also called on to interpret more worldly mysteries, such as dreams. Once when I dreamed that my father died, a friend assured me that the 'ulama say this means he will have a long life. In daily commentary such as this, Islam was the ultimate guide to life's meanings. At any moment, conversation could turn from mundane topics to Islam. One night I sat up after dark with a group of young unmarried girls and boys, who were giggling over the latest gossip and whispering about a scandalous affair, when suddenly the topic changed, effortlessly, to a discussion of the unparalleled goodness of Muhammad and the nature of heaven.

Islam punctuated daily discourse in other ways as well. The title of this chapter, "In the name of Allah, most benevolent, ever merciful" ("Bismillahi ar-rahmana ar-rahīm")[1] is both the opening of every sura (chapter) in the Koran, and a common expression of amazement. While such appeals to Allah were judged inappropriate by many, refrains of

"*MānnAllah!*" ("No way") and "*Allah!*" ("I swear!") and "*La ḥawla wela qūwat illa billahi!*" ("There is no possibility and no strength other than Allah!") and even the confession of faith "There is only one God and it is Allah, and Muhammad is his prophet" ("*La illaha illallahu Muhammad, Resullelahu*") were uttered many times a day by young and old at moments of excitement or frustration. To be fair, threats and insults were even more common, though often issued with a certain degree of light-heartedness: "May your father burn", i.e. in hell ("*Ya ḥarag bouk!*"), "May I never see you again!" ("*Ya ḥaram shoftek!*"), and "May you be struck by lightning!" ("*Y'aṭik rezza!*"). The mere refusal of a child to run and get some chewing tobacco from a neighbor could invoke a lively volley of such exclamations.

Even the creative imagination and the arts are largely centered on the Prophet. Apart from at marriages, drumming and singing only take place on Islamic holidays. Furthermore, many songs and poems focus on some aspect of Islam. At the wedding in Tchin Tabaraden of my old neighbor and friend, Asseghiyera, some young women sang beautiful, mournful, intense songs. Rather than a moving tale of marital bliss or unrequited love, as I first sat dreamily imagining, the repeated refrain turned out to be "Oh when I get to see the Prophet's face, how beautiful it will be." Although this disappointed my own fancies at the time about more earthly desert romance, it was, of course, about love of a sort, and indeed reflects the fact that the purpose of marriage has as much to do with adherence to Islam as with individual emotion and love.

Islam and the body

An incident that occurred in my first weeks of fieldwork brought home another aspect of Islam to me: the salience of the body and ideas about it in everyday Muslim practice. While making a rest stop on a trip, I pricked myself on a thorn, and quickly sucked off the drop of blood that emerged. A teenage boy in the pick-up truck we were traveling in turned and said to me immediately: "Muslims don't do that. Things that come out of one's body are not pure." In the chapters that follow, much of what I will discuss about how women manage their bodies is grounded in a particular Muslim understanding of the body's forms, openings, and doings in the eyes of God. Here I want to introduce those understandings of the body that can specifically be linked to Islam.

It has often been noted that Islam is a religion that seamlessly links faith and social life, belief and practice (Combs-Schilling 1989: 73; Delaney 1991: 25; Denny 1987: 7; Esposito 1988: 68; Gellner 1981: 1). While this could be said to be true of certain forms of the other major monotheisms also, Islam's linking of faith and salvation to the body makes it impossible for a practicing Muslim to allow religion to become a matter of "mere" belief, set apart from everyday life. Islam suffuses the bodies as well as the minds and souls of the faithful not only because of Islamic understandings of how the body works, but especially because of the regular corporeal devotion it demands – prostration toward Mecca five times a day amidst a series of ritualized bodily postures that accompany prayer. In Tassara both men and women drop whatever they are doing to pray; it is not unusual to be in the middle of a conversation with someone who suddenly moves a few feet away, turns to the east, and launches into prayer. Carol Delaney, who has studied Turkish Muslim notions of the body, cites Abdelwahab Bouhdiba's assertion that Islam is "a constant attention paid to one's own body" (1985: 55); she comments that it "prescribes in minute detail how the body in its myriad activities must be presented; indeed, every aspect of bodily existence has been discussed at length in a voluminous literature both legal and erotic" (Delaney 1991: 25).

Prayer not only involves bodily actions, but must be performed with the body in a state of purity, wiped clean and emptied of any "dirty" contents. It is always preceded by ablutions that are performed according to prescribed Islamic ritual. Hands, arms, feet, face, and orifices – mouth, nostrils, ears – are each cleaned in turn. In addition, the bladder should be emptied and any traces of sexual fluid cleaned away. Since menstruating women cannot empty their bodies of what is seen as a polluting substance, they do not pray at all, or fast during Ramadan, although they have to make up the missed fasting days later. The euphemism commonly used for menstruation is "lack of prayer" (gillit aṣ-ṣalla).

Although sand can be used for these ablutions if water is not available – more often than not the case in the Azawagh – the purifying force of these ablutions rests not so much in any Western notion of cleanliness, but more in the purifying force of adhering to Islamic rule. The injunctions to empty the body of all compromising substances also speak to the concern with inner purity that is reflected in the protection of the inner spaces of the tent and of women in general. Menstruation puts women in an impure state not only because the blood itself is conceived of as unclean, but also because in menstruation a woman's body is opened and uncontained. Following a similar logic of closed body = pure body, women also do not pray during the forty days of confinement following childbirth, when their bodies are open and leaking inner fluids to the outer world.

Islam is a highly embodied faith in the bodily obedience it demands of adherents – prostration and fasting; it is also a faith that speaks to the body in the implied meanings it bestows upon the body's forms, particularly female forms. By requiring ablutions, the emptying of all bodily wastes, and the cleaning of all sexual fluids from the body's surfaces before every prayer, Islam sends a strong message to its faithful: that the body as the physical icon of the person is most holy and most valued by Allah when uncontaminated by the flows, accretions, and processes of regular physical life. By forbidding prayer when there is any kind of discharge from women's bodies, Islam portrays the uncontained, unbounded, leaking body as problematic, and holds up the whole, "closed" body as pure and desirable. That is, while the body in many ways constitutes a vehicle for religious expression (ablutions, prayer, wearing of amulets), some aspects of bodily nature, especially women's bodily nature, are perceived as profoundly contradictory to the body that Islam upholds as pure and virtuous. The widespread Islamic practice of female veiling, while not an explicit Islamic teaching, obviously has appeal in part because it allows women to close off and protect bodies that are prone to offending Allah by their "openness." In short, by making the soul's salvation largely dependent on what the body does, Islamic practice lays a solid foundation for Azawagh Arab concepts of the body.

Islam, gender, and the social fabric

Islam has come to be associated with oppression of women by many in the West, but the lived reality of Islam in the many different societies where it is practiced, as well as in many Islamic writings, paints a more complex picture of what is expected of and destined for the two sexes. Perceptions of sexual inequality are at least in part misreadings of the fundamental ways in which women and men are understood simply to differ in Islam. For in orthodox Islam, as in orthodox forms of Christianity and Judaism, men and women are considered to be profoundly different types of creature. The Koran attributes the creation of new life, for example, only to the male's contribution of semen. While one woman in Tassara supported this view, explaining that women merely held male "water" inside them, others in Tassara told me that both men and women contribute to gestation. All were agreed, however, that male fetuses mature twice as quickly as female fetuses, so that a miscarried fetus at four months, for example, will have much greater development and differentiation if it is male.

While the differences between men and women are exemplified concretely in their bodies, Islamic writings treat women and men differently in many ways that extend beyond the body. To begin with, the Koran is written to and for men, not women. It instructs only men on whom to marry, how to treat their spouses, and the ways in which heaven will cater to their every sexual wish. No equivalent information is imparted to women.

The Koran is equivocal over the relative status of men and women, undercutting numerous statements that privilege male control with statements elsewhere that seem to censure practices such as polygyny, divorce, and men's power over their wives (Ahmed 1992: 63). Nevertheless, the overwhelming implication of both the Koran and other Islamic writings is that women and men are not only radically different types of beings, but that a woman is generally considered to be worth half of what a man is worth.[2] In a criminal case, for example, two female witnesses are required to equal the weight of one male witness. (I never saw this ruling applied, however; today cases have to be tried in a Nigerien government court, which follows French legal practice.) The Koran also establishes that a woman's inheritance should be only half of what a man receives. (I did not witness this practice in Tassara either, but people quoted the rule to me.)

The most formative moment in a girl's life is her marriage, and this occurs in Tassara in close obedience to Islamic scripture. Unlike some forms of Christianity, in which marriage traditionally has been seen as second best to celibacy, Islam has no tradition of celibacy. Islam not only expects but encourages men and women to seek sexual fulfillment in one another (Bouhdiba 1985). As people in Tassara told me, one of the principal reasons that girls marry young is that God smiles on those who marry. Even though men marry much later, in their twenties usually, they too should not delay, for to die without producing a son is to risk God's disfavor. Marriage, then, is both much discussed in Islamic writings, and a central concern of Azawagh Arabs.

Islamic societies are ideally endogamous, with preferred patrilateral parallel cousin marriage; that is, the best possible match is between the children of two brothers. Numerous instructions about whom, how, and why to marry and divorce are laid out in the Koran. I quote at length to give a flavor of its tone:

> If you want to take another wife
> in place of the one you are married to,
> then even if you have given her a talent of gold do not
>   take back a thing.
> Would you take it away by slandering
> and using unjust means?
> How could you do that having slept with one another
> and when they had taken a solemn pledge from you?
> And do not wed the women your father had wed.
> What happened in the past is now past:
> It is lewd and abhorrent,
> and only the way of evil.
>
> Unlawful are your mothers and daughters
> and your sister to you,
> and the sisters of your fathers and your mothers,
> and the daughters of your brothers and sisters,
> and foster mothers, foster sisters, and the mothers
>   of your wives,
> and the daughters of the wives you have slept with
> who are under your charge; but in case

you have not slept with them
there is no offence (if you marry their daughters);
and the wives of your own begotten sons;
and marrying two sisters is unlawful.
What happened in the past (is now past):
God is forgiving and kind.

The Women 4: 20–23

As this passage suggests, the cautions over whom one should marry concern those who might be too closely related rather than too distant; the implied worry is that, in striving for endogamy, one might marry too close. Indeed, the *qāḍi* himself in Tassara had been married to two sisters, though not simultaneously. This is not a violation of Koranic law, but it did raise a few eyebrows. (He had divorced the once much sought-after Aichata years before, and soon thereafter married her sister Bakka; he divorced Bakka after years of her asking for a divorce, during my stay in Tassara.)

The Koran also allows polygyny, though it is rarely practiced by Azawagh Arabs:

If you fear you cannot be equitable to orphan girls
(in your charge, or misuse their persons), then marry
women who are lawful for you, two, three, or four;
but if you fear you cannot treat so many with equity,
marry only one, or a maid or a captive.
This is better than being iniquitous.

The Women 4: 3

Some Arab feminists claim that since the Koran requires a man to treat all his wives equally, which is impossible, Islam implicitly forbids polygyny. This was not, however, the reason for the absence of polygyny among Azawagh Arabs. Azawagh Arab women told me that they would not permit their husbands to take second wives; since a woman's husband was often her father's brother's child, it was not as difficult as one might suspect for her to make her voice heard. One of the chief's wives (he had been married several times) had simply left him when he married another wife, and he was forced to give her a divorce. One possible reason for the lack of polygyny among Moors is the strong influence of Berber culture, such as that of the neighboring Tuareg, who have not traditionally been polygynous.

Structures of Islamic life

Women and men professed their Muslim faith to me with equal fervor; indeed the women were probably the more adamant that for me to be a truly integrated and accepted part of their world, I should convert to Islam. Although women could not be Islamic healers or hold positions of Islamic leadership, they could be as "good" Muslims as their male counterparts since Islam is fundamentally about an individual's relationship to God. People need no priestly mediation to have access to God, and anyone can read and recite the most important parts of the Koran for their own edification. All Arab girls and boys in Tassara were taught to read the Koran, but boys tend to study longer. In Tassara, unlike more urbanized areas of Islam, there were no weekly sermons at the mosque, and no publications about Islamic thought, so there was no official Islam to which men and women had differential access, even if men in practice learned to read more of the Koran and probably discussed its contents more. People's relationship to Islamic leaders and scholars in the community and surrounding desert tended to be a personal one; that is, these leaders offered help or guidance to individuals, not to the community as a whole.

This said, although women always and men usually pray alone, men could also pray together at the mosque, which women never did (as it would have involved a foray into the public world otherwise largely off limits to them). Older men especially often recited the late afternoon prayer together by one of the mosques. Like the houses in Tassara, the village's three mosques were simply mud buildings with very little special adornment, and their interiors were rarely used. Instead, men used the space around them to pray as a group and occasionally, in the case of older men who did not go to the market, for simply hanging out and talking to one another. At desert camps there were no mosques, but sometimes an outline of one was made with stones in the sand.

Although there were few physical markers of Islam's importance in Tassara comparable to the clinic, school, and mayor's office, for example, as markers of the government presence, the Islamic leadership comprised the most respected and revered members of society. My experience mostly with women may have weighted my understandings of religious vs. secular authority, since women talked constantly about things Islamic but very rarely about tribal politics. Had I been able to spend more time with men, the role of the secular leadership might have seemed more significant. In any event, the authority of religious leaders seemed unquestioned, even if the scope of their power was being eroded by the increasing presence of Nigerien government authority.

The highest position in the Muslim hierarchy is the *qāḍi*. While this literally means "judge," the *qāḍi* traditionally has done much more than adjudicate legal issues. The *qāḍi* is the supreme authority on Islamic knowledge, and leads prayers on the high holy days. He has the last word on questions of Islamic law and teachings, which govern secular as well as religious life; indeed the distinction between secular and religious makes little sense in Muslim society.

The Arabs of the Nigerien Azawagh were blessed for forty years with a man who lived up to the calling of the *qāḍi*-ship with exceptional erudition and grace. Sidi al-Mokhtar was in the twilight of his life when I met him, but his wisdom and dignity still shone from his watery eyes and gruff but gentle voice. He sat out his last days in a tent of no special proportions or elegance, still sought out by people from far and wide for his advice on questions over inheritance or divorce, or simply for wise counsel. Once when I was interviewing him about Azawagh Arab history, a poor man arrived from the desert with a letter, and we interrupted the session while Sidi al-Mokhtar dealt with the man's request. After honoring the letter by touching it to his forehead, Sidi al-Mokhtar read it through (it was written in Arabic), and then advised the man on how to proceed. The question concerned a marriage, though I was not told the specifics. The man departed quietly as he had arrived, seemingly satisfied.

Azawagh Arab Islam resembles Mauritanian Islam in its separation of juridical and mystic functions (Stewart 1973). The *qāḍi* is the supreme arbiter of matters to do with divorce, marriage, inheritance, etc. and is the highest religious authority, but the more numerous *'ulama* (men learned in the Koran) are consulted for training in the reading of the Koran, for treatment of illness, and for their wisdom on a host of issues. They have memorized much or all of the Koran and can be divided into two groups: (1) those who teach the Koran; and (2) those who treat ill-being caused by spirits. Most *'ulama* are old, but a handful of younger men were on their way to achieving the respected title. My friend Sidi Mohamed was one of these. In his early thirties at the time, he had memorized the whole Koran and was occasionally sought out by friends and relatives for aid. Once a cousin of his, for example, lost a key to a trunk, and asked Sidi to help her; he said a prayer over some sand which she then tied in a corner of her *ḥawli*. If someone requested his help in diagnosing an illness, he would read the Koran before going to bed, and then see what he dreamed – a common way of gaining insight into the cause of disease.

Bai, whom I was taken to visit in the bush and who described Arab history to me, did not treat illness, as far as I know, but was respected for his Koranic learning and teaching. Boys were regularly sent from all over the desert to stay several months or even years with him in order to learn to read the Koran. All Azawagh Arab children attend Koranic school, though not usually away from their village or camp, starting as early as age four. Koranic schooling does not take place in any building appointed for this purpose, but in the teacher's compound or tent. The teacher is compensated by the parents with gifts of grain or animals. The children are given small boards on which the teacher writes with ink that can be washed off, and after learning the Arabic alphabet they begin to learn the shortest chapters (*suras*) in the Koran, the ones used in daily prayer. The teacher writes them on the child's board, he or she goes off and learns the passage by chanting it over and over again to him or herself, finally chanting it back to the teacher. If students show aptitude or their parents are eager for them to become learned in the Koran, they continue until they have memorized a significant part of the book. More rarely, a child memorizes the whole book.

Tassara had several Koranic teachers, but the most popular was an old woman of the artisan caste (m'allem). Early every morning the cacophonous chanting of a dozen or more children could be heard over the walls of her compound, as they sat against the wall in a row working their way through as much of the Koran as they could.

Although girls never chant the Koran publicly in the Azawagh, boys grow up to have many opportunities to do so. On the holiday for the Prophet's birth, men sit up all night out at a desert camp, under the yellowy light of a kerosene lamp, chanting from the Koran. The women, meanwhile, sing and dance as one woman plays a "drum," a big mortar covered with moistened goat skins. These songs are mostly about the the Prophet and Islam.

Men also chant the Koran when someone dies. They each take a section and sit together, chanting their sections at the same time, on top of one another, as it were. At the death of old Maya, a woman in Tchin Tabaraden who was a wonderful storyteller and came from a family of 'ulama, men came down from Tassara and in from the distant bush to sit in a house across the street from Maya's and chant the Koran seven times, three times the first day, and then twice on the two succeeding days. As women prepared food and greeted new arrivals, the pile of sandals built up outside the door of the house where the men were chanting, and the low, melancholic voices of the twenty or so assembled there floated out the door and windows into the hot, sad afternoon. As one young man who took part in the chanting said to me in French, Maya had been "une dame de classe," a woman of class. "She never said ill of anyone," women told me. Although not all deaths were followed by days of chanting, when someone old and revered died, man or woman, people dropped everything to help send the deceased on his or her way to Allah's paradise.

Spirits

To fully appreciate Azawagh Arab perceptions of the world Allah made, including how they shape understandings of the human body, requires knowledge not only of canonical Koranic teaching but also of the nature of the ever present spirits that impinge regularly on daily life (sing. jinn, pl. janūn, whence the English word "genie"). In many parts of Africa spirits constitute a counter-world to Islam, offering an alternative vision of morality and causality, as well as an arena in which groups outside of the hierarchies of established monotheisms exercise a certain kind of power (see for example Boddy 1989; Masquelier 2001). For Azawagh Arabs, however, spirits are experienced as internal to Islam, and they are dealt with not by female-led possession rituals but by learned Islamic scholars. According to the knowledgeable Aichata in Tassara, spirits are created by God – indeed they are referred to in the Koran – and they can be men, women, or children. They are invisible, human-like beings, some of whom are good, but most of whom operate counter to Allah's wishes. They are held responsible for causing many sicknesses and for various interpersonal problems, including that of wives who cannot get along with their husbands.

In the Azawagh spirits are said to dwell largely to the north, but they are always lurking nearby. In this world that values wholeness and boundaries, it is not surprising that moments that are "betwixt and between" are the most dangerous: dusk is the time of day when one must be especially careful to guard against spirit interference. Not only do they swarm about during this liminal time, but they seek out bodies that are somehow compromised in their wholeness: vulnerable little children, women who are "open" from childbirth, people weakened by disease, or those with open wounds on their skin.

Spirits are almost never spoken of, for they might hear and be angry or consider the words an invitation. When I naïvely asked about spirits early in my stay – "Do you do that to keep away spirits?" – people lied to me and said no, pretended not to hear, or, if I was lucky, whispered a hurried answer. Myriad activities, I soon came to realize, are performed with the sole aim of deflecting spirits' unwelcome presence. The most visible is the wearing of amulets (aḥjāb) around the neck, and occasionally elsewhere, that consist of pieces of paper with the Koran written on them, sewn in small pouches. Virtually every Arab I knew wore at least one of these, usually hidden under clothing, and many wore more. In old photographs taken by the French, the Arab chiefs can be seen with several huge ones hanging on their chests, one on their turbans, and, I am sure, one hidden under their sleeves around the upper right arm as many men wear today to give them strength and protect them against swords and guns. Amulets can be encased in beautifully tooled silver, dyed leather, or in simple pouches of cloth or even plastic. When an epidemic of meningitis threatened, suddenly all the children in town appeared with emergency amulets in small pouches sewn out of old dusty plastic bags tightly secured around their necks.

People also guard against spirits by saying prayers at times when spirits are likely to slip in. One always says "in the name of God," bismillah, before opening the mouth to eat food, and before going on a journey. Once when Boukia was teaching me to stuff myself the way Arab women do during fattening, she said a little prayer before I began inserting the fist-fuls of grain into my mouth. (The prayers did not help to make it a more pleasant experience.) Inaugurating a new item, especially if it will be worn or contain food, is also a time when a prayer to ward off spirits is advisable. Pouring milk from one bowl into another, unfolding and preparing to wear a new *ḥawli*, and leaving an empty compound all merit a quick prayer to keep the spirits at bay.

Although they are responsible for what Westerners classify as mental illness, a designation that does not exist among Azawagh Arabs, spirits' main port of entry into the person is through the physical body, whether or not they go on to affect the individual's desires, physical health, or capacities of reason. They have a special talent for perceiving when a body is less than whole and not adequately "closed," allowing them a way in. For this reason, any body that is unusually "open" – from childbirth, diarrhea, a wound, or other disease – is carefully protected from the threat of spirits. Menstruating women not only do not pray but also do not wash because their bodies are "opened" by the blood flowing out of them and spirits could therefore get in.

Being more open than men, women are far more susceptible to spirit "infection." "Women are more scared of spirits than men," Aichata told me. "Spirits like women the way men like women. They want them, they go to them, they make them give birth [i.e. impregnate them]." She cited the old *ḥaraṭaniyya* in Tassara who was made pregnant by a spirit a long time ago, and therefore has never been able to conceive a human baby. Indeed, spirits seem to have as strong desires for women as men do, and therefore particularly desirable women such as the newly divorced should not wear perfume, I was told, to avoid attracting what one might call the wrong kind of guy.

Childbirth is a particularly perilous time for women since it "rips" their bodies wide open, as Azawagh Arabs say. When her daughter was going through a painful labor, Bettu sat facing east and began quietly praying for protection (*teḥajjam*) while making small circles with her finger in the air to scatter the spirits. Since I was about to go out to the bush to visit a renowned *'ālem*, Bettu asked me to bring back some water that he had blessed, so that her daughter might drink it and gain further protection. Once a woman has given birth, she spends forty days in confinement while she heals from her tear, resting on several layers of mats, wrapped in cloth and blankets, in a separate enclosure in the tent to protect against the entrance of spirits.

To become an *'ālem* who "knows" the spirits requires years of work. It is these *'ulama*, of whom there were only a few near Tassara (they tend to live in the desert), who are generally sought out to treat serious diseases as well as problems potentially caused by the ill wishes of others. Such problems include women who are unable to gain weight.

Unlike many of their Islamic neighbors, the Azawagh Arabs (and Moors in general) shun spirit cults. "We don't invite spirits as the Tuareg do," one woman told me with a tinge of self-righteousness. "We fear them." Although spirits possess people from time to time, they are dealt with by "quieter" Islamic medicine – usually amulets. Azawagh Arabs seemed to consider the practices around spirit possession that neighboring Tuareg and Hausa engage in as tantamount to cavorting with the devil, and they keep their eyes focused on more canonical Islamic practice. And the best protection against spirit "infection" is proper maintenance of the body's openings and general state. For women this entails not only veiling and controlling body openings, but also maintaining the proper balance between hot and cold in their bodies. All of these activities are associated with female fattening, as I will discuss in later chapters.

Heaven, and heaven on earth

The visions of sex, gender, and embodiment that I have described find particularly vivid expression in Azawagh Arab fantasies of heaven (*al-jenna*). In contrast to the heaven of Christianity where humans will finally be free of desire, Islam's paradise is one in which every desire will be fulfilled.

> The semblance of Paradise promised the pious and devout
> (is that of a garden) with streams of water that will
> not go rank,
> and rivers of milk whose taste will not undergo a change
> and rivers of wine delectable to drinkers,
> and streams of purified honey,
> and fruits of every kind in them, and forgiveness of their
> Lord.
>
> Muhammad 47: 15

Food and wine will flow freely for all, but when it comes to sexual desire, only men's are addressed in the Koran: "They would recline on couches set in rows, paired with fair companions (clean of thought and) bright of eye" (52: 20). These female companions, called "houris," are "undeflowered by man or by jinn [spirit] before them" (55: 74), and will serve men's every whim. As old Moussaysa told me in more prosaic terms, in paradise men will be able to have sex with an unlimited number of women, all virgins.[3]

In keeping with my own observations in the Azawagh and in contrast to some stereotypes of the Islamic world, Abdelwahab Bouhdiba (1985) and Elaine Combs-Schilling (1989: 94–95) have pointed out that Islam celebrates sexuality on earth as in heaven. Even if the chief beneficiaries of sexual pleasure according to the Koran are men, other Islamic texts portray sexuality as "a divine prerogative that enables man to go beyond nature and to achieve a veritable sexual mission which, Islam teaches, should be carried out in the joy, exaltation, and intoxication of creation" (Bouhdiba 1985: 91). Bouhdiba (1985: 104) notes that sexual pleasure is itself "an essential prefiguration of the pleasures of paradise." Even though Bouhdiba declares that the Islamic vision of sexuality has been degraded in contemporary Islamic practice, the difference he paints between the fundamental attitudes of Christianity and Islam captures something of the significance of sexuality in Azawagh Arab society. In accordance with this, I suggest that even the sensuous, sexual connotations of fattened female bodies have their roots in Islamic ideology.

Like the above Koranic descriptions of paradise and like their faith on earth, Azawagh Arabs' vision of heaven is also concrete and practical. Although women did not foresee sexual experiences in heaven, or at least never articulated that they did so, they envisioned the full satisfaction of their own particular desires. One boisterous and imaginative young mother, Kia, described heaven to me as a place where "all the houses are nice, and all the food is good." She went on to explain that in heaven,

> your body becomes very good, there will be milk flowing through your body, and you will be white. The men's bodies will be like glass; you will be able to see yourself in a man's body. You won't defecate, or have mucous, or be sick.

Reflecting their concerns in this world, women often expressed similar depictions of paradise to me, as a place where all corporeal worries and scars would vanish. All women would be beautiful, the body would be whole, pure, and "closed," and milk would be plentiful. Most interesting in Kia's description is the fact that men come to mirror women's beauty, rather than consume and use it. Kia, who herself was frequently annoyed by her humorous knave of a husband, had on an earlier visit acted out a hilarious pantomime of a man making love to a woman, squeezing her flesh and groping and snorting all over her. Clearly she sought not so much sexual pleasure in heaven, as release from men's unwelcome demands.

This is not to say that all women perceived male sexual desire as a burden. Some women also described heaven as a place where women were wanted, and were free from the worldly worries of not getting or keeping a husband. After first announcing that heaven could not be described (*ma tgid tuwāṣif*), an adolescent girl went on to say that "you will see a man who wants you very much." In both male and female visions, the sexes are no longer each other's enemies, but at peace in their desiring. Their divisions are not erased, however; rather, the achievement of the pleasure the two sexes promise each other is rendered pure and fulfilled, voided of the impurities, unsatiated longings, frustrations, and tensions that plague their passion-filled opposition in earthly life.

Abetting God's order

Bouhdiba prefaces his argument about the nature of sexuality in Islam with a description of its vision of the two sexes. "The bipolarity of the world rests on the strict separation of the two 'orders,' the feminine and the masculine" (1985: 30), he explains. As I have begun to describe, this vision is played out in numerous domains, including marriage practices, inheritance, and the perceived realities of male and female bodies. Fattening can also be seen as a way of acceding to this God-given order, for it constitutes an active embrace of sexual difference, and an assumption by women of a femininity that leaves no room for ambiguity between the sexes.

To recent arguments in the West that male/female dualism is "merely" culturally constituted (Butler 1993) – even that there are really three sexes or five (Hubbard 1996) – Azawagh Arabs would cry sacrilege. Even male homosexuality, often denied but in fact practiced, was described to me not as two men having sex with one another, but as one man acting like the woman. Stories of hermaphrodites provoked fascination, puzzlement, and disgust, as they represented to Azawagh Arabs a complete confounding of the most basic fact of nature on which the order of the world is founded.

The polarity of maleness and femaleness is encoded in the ways in which men and women exercise their Islamic faith as well. The fact that women always pray singly and in private, whereas men may pray together in public, further legitimates and reinforces the association of women with inner spaces and men with outer spaces. Men are also the sole actors involved in the religious aspects of marriages, birth naming ceremonies, funerals, and prayers on holidays.

Given the fundamental difference between men and women encoded in Islamic scripture, it makes sense that women's path to fulfillment will be very different from men's. It follows, as Janice Boddy described of Sudanese Arabs, that "women do not achieve social recognition by behaving or becoming like men, but by becoming less like men, physically, sexually and socially" (1989: 56). For the Sudanese women, their achievement of social recognition included "enclosing" their bodies through the most radical kind of female circumcision, infibulation, exaggerating the contrast to their male counterparts' exposed sexual organs. For Azawagh Arab women, who do not practice female circumcision, their physical differentiation from men is brought on by fattening. (In Mauritania, a mild form of clitoridectomy is practiced by some Moors [Zainaba 1990].)

In sum, since Islam (1) understands men and women to be profoundly different types of beings; (2) believes that men and women should fulfill each other sexually, and women should especially provide for male pleasure; and (3) holds that it is women's God-given destiny to bear future Muslims, it is logical that a woman should attune her life and being toward fulfilling these purposes. By fattening herself to a supremely differentiated vision of femaleness she achieves the first of these Islamic ideals. In the Azawagh Arab sexual imagination, inspired by this vision of sexual difference, this same fattened, decidedly non-male, female form also sparks the greatest male desire and provides the greatest sexual satisfaction. And since women's most noble purpose is to bear sons and Muslims to populate God's earth, it is logical that they should reach the age of childbearing and marriage as soon as possible, a process they believe fattening accelerates. For a girl to fatten, then, is for her to embrace and abet her God-given destiny and purpose.

Lived Islam

In her description of the Egyptian Bedouin, Lila Abu-Lughod (1986) underscores how important their identity as Bedouin is; in Janice Boddy's work on Sudanese village women, she notes that they refer to Islam rarely (1989: 4). Although both of these societies have many parallels with that of the Azawagh Arabs, Islam is decidedly the most defining feature of Azawagh Arabs' own self-image, for both men and women. Islam connects them not only to the promise of life after death, but to the wider Arab world and all the prestige it confers, as well as to their own past by their putative descent from companions of the Prophet Muhammad. Furthermore, it grounds in Allah's unquestionable truth the constituting oppositions of their world – closedness vs. openness and male vs. female – as well as particular visions of embodiment and sexuality.

No one who knows them would doubt that the Azawagh Arabs consider themselves part of God's chosen people, holier if not wealthier than most others they come in contact with. They believe that Christians/whites/Europeans (anaṣāra) are descendants of the Quraysh tribe of Muhammad, but that they went astray. One young man in the market had a big poster of Saddam Hussein in his store, and another with pictures of George Bush and other "enemies" crossed out in red pen. We had many spirited and, fortunately, good-humored conversations about the Gulf War, but they were never swayed to support the United States as the country of Niger did, for their Arab brother had a far greater claim to their support by his membership in the Islamic community.

Islam could be a self-righteous, intolerant, and demanding religion as I saw it among Azawagh Arabs, but it was also a religion carefully tuned to rhythms of desert life, caring and generous toward its own, beautiful in its expression, and compelling in the confidence its adherents held for it. And though Azawagh Arabs take their faith very seriously, most seemed to feel that strict adherence to the formal performance of prayer and ritual allowed them some leeway both in less publicly visible behavior, such as adultery, and sometimes in the seriousness or purpose they brought to religious ritual. I remember in particular the biggest Islamic holiday of 'Id-al-Fitr, when people ask one another forgiveness for any wrongs they may have committed during the year. With what struck me as considerable irreverence, many young men making the rounds of their aunts and sisters strung the ritually uttered "Forgive me" to another almost ritualized, very frequent phrase in these regions: "Give me tobacco" (for chewing). The two phrases are structured similarly in Arabic so they made a cute little duo: "*Semhili wa gememli!*"

A more serious and striking scene that captures something of the power of Islam in this community remains with me from Tchin Tabaraden in 1986. All in town were awaiting the change of month, marked by the new moon's rising, that would signal the start of the fasting month of Ramadan when no food or water is consumed between dawn and dusk. At Boukia's compound one still, luminous evening as we searched the western horizon for a glimmering sliver, a cry went out from a neighboring compound, and suddenly from over every wall came the shrill, joyous ululating of women, celebrating the moon's sighting. Hard to pick out with the naked eye, the moon then showed itself to us – hanging like a thread of silver low in the darkening sky only briefly, before disappearing into the horizon's dusty haze. The naked eye read the cosmos' sign that the body was now to begin obeying God's word by spending a month alternately depriving the appetites and indulging them, striving for salvation by a holistic form of devotion in which the body and the mind cannot be pulled apart.

Plate 5 Moussaysa (on the right) and his nephew (Egawan)

4

TIES OF BLOOD, TIES OF MILK, TIES OF MARRIAGE

You do not betray your blood or your Lord.
  -Arab saying about kinship recorded from Sidi

For the purposes of understanding fattening, perhaps the most revealing kinship relationship is the marital one. It matters that a woman be fat, both to her and to her family, because by being attractive she will enhance her chances of getting a good husband. Fattening also expedites a girl's eligibility for marriage, Azawagh Arabs say, by hastening the onset of womanliness. Perhaps because I was myself of marriageable age – really beyond it, at twenty-nine – and yet was frustratingly unmarried, talk of marriage filled many of my discussions. Though my particular age and position may have led this topic to arise more often than it would have done for a researcher at another life stage, marriage is in many ways a topic of unceasing interest for everyone in the society. Young men joked with the mother of a newborn girl that they would marry her new daughter, and the octogenarian *qāḍi* joked with me, when he gave his third wife a divorce, that he could now marry me. Since women often marry first as young teenagers, and since divorce and remarriage are common, getting into marriage, getting out of marriage, and getting into marriage again take up a lot of time and a lot of conversational space. I bracket my account of patrilineal kinship, thus, with discussions of the logistics, sentiments, and challenges of marriage for Azawagh Arabs.

Kith and kin in daily life

If Islam gives life its ultimate purpose for Azawagh Arabs, relations with kin are what structure the ebb and flow of day-to-day existence. Most of the Arab villagers of Tassara were really members of two large extended families, with a few more distantly related "satellite" families, so that village life, like desert life, is really life lived among one's mother, father, sisters, brothers, aunts, uncles, grandparents, cousins, children, and

75

grandchildren. The only people women spent time with to whom they could not somehow trace a relationship were those of other castes. Men encountered a wider social circle in their travels, but blood kin were the people they too depended upon. As in other kin-based societies, the idea of getting away from your family in order to "find yourself," and the possibility of "not getting along with" members of your own family, are both quite unthinkable. I once explained to Boukia how teenagers in the West often turn against and even profess dislike for their own parents. This was impossible for Boukia to imagine. "We know girls whose mothers beat them, and even they love their mothers more than anyone else in the world," she explained.

As all of this suggests, for Azawagh Arabs the bigger one's kin networks, the more kin living nearby, and the more relatives one regularly interacts with, the better. And as the saying that opens this chapter intones, to betray your "blood" – your kin – is as unacceptable as betraying your faith in Allah.

Even marital relationships are essentially blood relationships, since Azawagh Arabs prefer to marry first cousins, ideally the children of two brothers. Nonetheless, marriage relationships are in another way in fundamental opposition to blood relationships. Ties of marriage produce the sons (and daughters) who will carry on the family and tribal line and ideally overlap with ties of blood, but they also present a challenge to social ideals because of the sexual antagonism and tensions that naturally exist between men and women. How the structural and emotional tensions between ties of blood and ties of marriage are resolved is a large part of the story of the Azawagh Arab cultural world. In fact, marriage is in a sense the fulcrum on which society turns: it is the institution in which blood ties are reaffirmed and reproduced; but also in which dramas of sexual antagonism and desire are expressed. This tension between the normative, official social order and the undeniable, vital urge of sex that so often transgresses the constitutive order forms one of the central tensions around which life is lived.

In this chapter I will explore this crucial ground of Azawagh Arab daily life, beginning and ending with two vignettes of marriage – a marriage breaking apart and a marriage forming – because it is in marriage that many of the meaningful aspects of kinship for Azawagh Arabs are laid bare. In between these two vignettes I will discuss how blood relationships through men and women, and "milk" relationships through women, form the underpinning of Azawagh Arab social structure as well as of their emotional worlds. Throughout the account I will emphasize cultural logics that emerge in numerous spheres of Azawagh Arab life, as well as in how kinship is imagined and lived: social exclusiveness and closedness as a way of guarding honor and maintaining power; the opposition of maleness and femaleness; the tensions of sexual attraction; and the power of milk and blood to connect human beings irrevocably.

All of these themes are expressed in fattening and the ideal of fat beauty, as I will discuss at the end of the chapter. Fattening hurries a girl toward eligibility for marriage by endowing her with attractive womanly curves and, it is thought, hastening the onset of puberty. She can begin bearing children earlier, and her desirability is enhanced. Hence the logic behind why Ketti, the female Islamic teacher, did not fatten as a girl: to fatten is to ready oneself for marriage, and as long as Ketti was studying the Koran, she was engaged in an activity not compatible with marrying, having children, and taking care of a family. To fatten is to ready oneself for one's role as wife and mother, and in this way to fulfill one's duty to family and patriline.

Ahmed and Aminatou

To illustrate something of how the values named above operate in practice, I want to relate an unusual incident I witnessed one afternoon – an instance of what might be described as Moor marriage counseling. It brings to the fore many of the understandings of kinship and relationship that shape Azawagh Arab society. The couple receiving the "counseling" had been married for about two years, were in their early twenties, and had a child on the way. It was the man's first marriage and the woman's second. His name was Ahmed and hers was Aminatou.

One quiet December afternoon in the "cool" dry season while I was writing notes in my compound, three young men came knocking at the door. After the appropriate greetings, one of them announced, "Ahmed has come in from the bush and says Aminatou is angry and threatening to leave. We need to go out and talk to her. Can you take us to their camp?" Dubious about this strange explanation, I nevertheless acquiesced. (I had once been duped into taking a perfumed and beautifully robed man out to "look at his herds," which turned out to be an extramarital lovers' tryst.) I threw on my *ḥawli* (I wore Western skirts and dresses in my house) while they went to get Ahmed. The three young men, all in their twenties, were (1) Aminatou's brother and a second cousin of Ahmed, named Moussa; (2) Ahmed's younger brother, Sa'id; and (3) a more distant relative, an age-mate (*ntij*) and old childhood friend of Ahmed, named Najim.

We took off eastwards, quickly veering off from the tire tracks in the sand that constitute the road into Tassara. It was the usual navigation challenge for me: the men gently pointed the direction every few minutes as I continuously wavered off course, unable to differentiate one sandy swelling in the distance from another. After twenty minutes or so of bouncing over the bumpy desert we arrived at a camp of a few low, widely spaced tents.

I parked the Suzuki, as glaringly anomalous and intrusive as ever, next to Ahmed's tent. The men swished their robes out of the car and seated themselves on mats so that Ahmed's tent stood between them and a tent some way off. Moussa's in-laws lived in that distant tent, so he wanted to avoid being seen at all costs. Men and their in-laws always avoid one another, and in this case the situation was especially charged for several reasons: Moussa had married his thirteen-year-old wife very recently (after divorcing his previous wife); his wife's pretty young mother Zahara was about the same age as Moussa himself; and his wife's father was a respected '*ālem* in the area, an old man who was much sought after for Koranic treatment of illness.

Since I was a woman and Sa'id was Aminatou's husband's younger brother, we could both greet Moussa's mother-in-law Zahara and Aminatou (women don't veil for husbands' younger brothers), and so we walked the short distance to the tent where they were sitting to greet them. Husbands and wives never sit together in a tent during the day – Zahara's husband was either away or at another small tent where men spend the day when not traveling or looking after their animals. The plump, smiling, and placid Zahara sat cross-legged on a low platform bed, enveloped in her blue cloth, cradling her latest child in her arms. The normally shy Aminatou sat on a mat on the ground, and was especially subdued in her greetings. "*Labās*," we announced quietly to the two women (literally, "Nothing wrong"). "*Labās*," came the answer. "How are you?" ("*Sh'hālek?*") "*Labās*." "How are the children?" ("*Sh'hāl at-terke?*") "*Labās*." The greetings went back and forth for a few minutes, before Sa'id abruptly broke in with a vague explanation of why we were there, and asked Aminatou to come over to her husband's tent. Aminatou seemed to understand what our visit was about, though it was never stated directly.

We then returned to the men and waited for Aminatou. After a few minutes she emerged, walking slowly, swaying from side to side, her veil over her face, as befits womanly comportment. When she arrived she greeted everyone in a low voice, looking away, and sat to one side, not quite facing the others.

Moussa, Aminatou's brother, began the proceedings. "Tell us what happened," he asked Aminatou. Aminatou had always seemed to me rather inarticulate in the past, but she became a new person as she began to talk, speaking confidently and smoothly. "He spoke bad words to me," she re-iterated many times in her story. "He looked for other women." She described at some length fights that had occurred and Ahmed's generally unseemly behavior. As the conversation went on, she slowly let her veil drop; as I have explained, her brother, her husband, and her husband's younger brother were not people she needed to veil before.

Her husband Ahmed, who, to be frank, had always struck me as a some-what immature young man, went next. "I have always given her food and clothing and water, and she has never wanted for sugar or tea or tobacco or sandals or anything." He accused her of having a bad character, and of going off visiting other tents too much.

Najim, the one young man not closely related, took over. "Supplying Aminatou with clothes and so on is not the issue." Ahmed was not going to get away with this weak appeal to a very by-the-rules version of marriage. Supporting one's wife was a *sine qua non* of marriage, but it was not enough.

Najim then voiced the principal refrain that was addressed to Ahmed and Aminatou again and again over the next hour by all the young men: "You are brothers, and such behavior shouldn't happen. It is not necessary." He used a well-known Hausa expression, "*baikamata ba,*" for a little added emphasis: "You are her brother and she is your sister."

Indeed, there were only "three men between them," as the Azawagh Arabs say. Aminatou's great-grandfather was Ahmed's grandfather, so the couple were closely related through men. They were not literally brother and sister, of course, for that would have been incestuous, but they were classificatory siblings, that is they were not "real" biological siblings but were classified as siblings in the Arab kinship system. As important perhaps, Aminatou's grandfather was the *qāḍi* and Ahmed's father was a revered *'ālem* in the region, so they were a politically propitious match. However, though the men later tried to convince me that Ahmed and Aminatou had chosen each other, Aminatou was not a very attractive woman by local standards and I feel quite sure that their marriage was largely arranged. It was her second marriage and his first as far as I know, and they were about the same age – an unlikely scenario for a chosen marriage, which usually occurred between a man and a woman with a considerable age difference between them. Even young men may marry previously married women, since many girls are married very young but divorce as teenagers, but it was more problematic that Aminatou was Ahmed's age – not a young bachelor's marital dream. Ahmed's remarriage several months later to a considerably younger, very pretty, never-married girl only confirmed my suspicions.

Najim and the others had numerous other lines of advice to offer: "Be patient – increase your patience." Najim directed his urgings to his age-mate and childhood friend Ahmed, and Moussa reiterated them to his sister Aminatou. Ahmed kept answering, "I have increased my patience, over and over, but it does no good." Although marriages should not be bitter, it is understood that they require considerable reserves of patience. Husbands and wives never overcome the distance and tensions between them caused by the inherent differences between men and women, sexuality, and the fact that each spouse considers his or her natal family the primary object of allegiance. An old couple I knew still sat with their backs to one another in respectful avoidance when they were at their compound together, and it was this same old woman who once teased me about sleeping with her husband when I drove him to Tchin Tabaraden.

Another concern was that they had let their fighting become public knowledge: "Everyone has heard about your fighting, and this is not good. Women, men, slaves, everyone has heard it." Najim said to Ahmed, "You are not children – you are a man and she is a woman. Men younger than you, like Ibrahim uld Mohamed, are married and manage; they're patient."

When it came out that Ahmed had actually hit Aminatou, Najim began a long series of "shame on you's" to him that the others took up as well: "'Ayb 'aleyk!" For Ahmed to have treated his own "sister" in this manner was truly inexcusable.

Toward the end the men turned to the old female servant (ḥaraṭaniyya), Dije, who had been sitting on the sidelines all the while. She welcomed the chance to tell her side of the story. "Early on I intervened when they fought," she explained, "but I was told it was none of my business, so I have kept out of it ever since." When asked who was at fault, she asserted that she was on neither one's side because they were both her children: "Ahmed is the son of M'hamed" whose ḥaraṭaniyya she was, and "Aminatou is the daughter of Sherif," with whom she must have had some other connection I am unaware of. She also explained that they put their mattresses on opposite sides of the tent, and that Aminatou spent every day with Zahara at Zahara's husband's tent (a woman can't be said to have a tent, so it was not "Zahara's tent").

When we drove home later in the afternoon, leaving Ahmed and Aminatou in stony silence, the men expressed confidence that all was repaired, but their moods suggested otherwise, and indeed from witnessing the scene myself I assumed that a divorce was on the way. Sure enough, Ahmed was remarried by the time I left Tassara ten months later, and Aminatou was a divorcée (ḥajāle) again. Although being a divorcée while still a teenager is an enviable state for a woman – for she has the experience to express some choice in her next marriage and, of a mature adolescence, is generally courted by men – Aminatou was already well into her twenties and thus less likely to remarry easily.

The challenges of marriage

Primary among the many facets of Azawagh Arab marriage practices that this incident illustrates is the significance of blood relations to a marriage's strength. There was no implication by any of the "counselors" that Aminatou and Ahmed needed to make their marriage work because they were husband and wife; what made their disagreements other than ordinary, expected, and perhaps even acceptable was that they were related through men. The story of Ahmed and Aminatou also shows that, emotionally, marriages are stressful affairs. Husbands and wives are expected to be at cross-purposes: in the crudest, most simplistic terms, husbands want sex and compliance, and women want material things and at least relative faithfulness. "Women don't care whether a man's face is attractive, only whether he has money and can work," a group of women once explained to me.

Men and women hope that they will be attracted to and have affection for their spouse, but it would have been utterly taboo for Ahmed and Aminatou's relatives to take up the issue of sex or attraction in the marriage. Like the veil shrouding women's sexually charged bodies, silence or at least indirectness shrouds the subject of sex in daily conversation, especially in mixed company. Nonetheless, I think it was clear to all that simple lack of attraction between Ahmed and Aminatou, especially in his attitude to her, was at base the problem in their quickly disintegrating marriage. It was both easier and more appropriate, though, to address the issue on the higher plane of kin relations than to confront the unspeakable. One might say that in one Azawagh Arab version of reality marriage is about kin relations anyway, even if this nobler vision must constantly struggle against another version of marital reality, that of sexual and emotional attraction. I discuss this fundamental tension in Azawagh Arab life further later in the chapter.

Since sexual attraction is thought to arise out of distance rather than closeness, women are caught in an emotional bind of encouraging men's loyalty and respect by displaying reserve and constantly pulling back. As one rather outspoken woman explained to me, in reference to a cousin who was known for blowing up at her husband periodically:

> It isn't good for a woman to yell at her husband during the day like that. Then at night he won't respect you; he won't care – he'll just have sex with you and you can't say anything. It is better to wait until the night, when it is just you and he on the mattress. This is when husband and wife talk about everything – politics, the home, the children, everything. If you are mad about something this is the time to tell him, because he can't refuse you.

The idea here seemed to be that because husbands want sex, and yet should not force themselves on their wives, a woman should use her greatest leverage – her sexuality – in order to get what she wants from her husband.

Husbands are expected to provide amply for their wives, but in order to do this, it is expected that men will be away for long stretches of time, engaging in trade or looking after their herds. During this time period the woman is a grass widow (*masteghiba*) and should not dress in fine clothes, do her hair, or wear make-up. "If you are putting on eyeliner (*kohl*) and you have finished one eye and not the other and your husband goes out, you should not put *kohl* on the other until your husband returns," Minatou informed me. I could always tell the day after a woman's husband had returned even if I had not heard the news, because she would be dressed in her finery and have her hair newly braided. Women's charms should be for their husbands only, even if in fact there is a fair amount of infidelity by both men and women in the community.

When Najim declared that "supplying Aminatou with clothes and so on is not the issue," he made clear, however, that marriage is not merely a business relationship, but should be based on respect and affection befitting kin: literally, "love according to Allah," *hubb 'ala Allah*. In fact, despite the tensions inherent in the relationship, many marriages are marked by genuine affection.[1] I inquired about several couples who were childless and asked why the husband did not divorce the wife and try to remarry, since children are so important. On each occasion, people answered me by stating something to the effect: "But they like each other," as if it were obvious that this would override other concerns. (To be fair, in at least one case the man was known from previous marriages to be infertile, so he had little motivation to divorce his very rotund and much admired wife.)

I observed that when a couple had had some choice in their marriage, and often when the two were not too closely related, marriages tended to be much more affectionate. A marriage such as that between Ahmed and Aminatou seemed unlikely to succeed: he had never been married but she had already been married once and was no longer young by Azawagh Arab standards; they were close in age, rather than the preferred situation of the wife being much younger; Aminatou was not particularly attractive; and Ahmed, in his early twenties, was still quite young to settle into a lasting marriage.

Since blood ties are what define who you are, the potentially fleeting and always fragile ties of marriage never define a person's identity. I was constantly laughed at because, knowing the women of the community better than I knew the men, I referred to men as "so-and-so's husband," a highly inappropriate way to label a man. Men are "so-and-so's son" and women are "so-and-so's daughter," no matter how long her father has been dead and even after fifty years of marriage. Once when I referred to a young man named Ijid as "Taime's husband," his younger cousin scolded me: "Ijid's mother is sitting right there and you say whose husband he is? He isn't Taime's; he belongs to his mother."

The fact that a man does not "belong to" his wife, and vice versa, has certain advantages for women. A woman's blood relatives will be there throughout her life to support her, while husbands may come and go. If a woman is married to an unrelated man or distant relative, her brothers will be unable to look out for her interests as they can if she marries a close cousin, as Aminatou had. So although patrilateral cousin marriage (marriage between cousins related through their fathers) embeds women ever deeper in a web of relations defined through men, it also gives them a position of greater strength in their marriages by keeping the men who will support them close at hand.

Day-to-day male–female relations can only be understood in the context of marriage prohibitions and prescriptions. That is, women and men act in one way with each other if it is even remotely conceivable that they could ever marry, and act in another way if they are unmarriageable. If a woman is not marriageable to a man, she does not have to veil for him and they can chat openly as brother and sister; she is *meherima* to him.[2] Otherwise, not only should the woman veil, but the man should keep his distance and show reserve as well.

Although most people in a community know who is *meherima* to whom, from time to time discussion arises about the topic, as when my young bachelor friend Sidi suddenly charged in and shook young Anebu's hand. Sidi then explained that he had just learned that they had both been nursed by the same woman when they were children, making them the equivalent of siblings. Another time, a feisty young woman named Nennou walked over and very openly greeted a man who had come in from the bush. Another woman present asked how she was *meherima* to him, and they got into a lively discussion about it. They were also "milk kin," i.e. nursed by the same woman. Nennou seemed to relish her display of openness around this man, before whom others did not realize she could go unveiled.

I will take up the discussion of veiling later, but as this account of Moor marriage shows, the potential for sexual relations governs all male–female interaction. Since the only legitimate, public resolution of these longings and tensions is marriage, marriage is at the center of Moor life emotionally, as it is at the center politically and socially for purposes of reproduction and increase of the patriline. If, as Emrys Peters (1990) noted of Arabs in Libyan Cyrenaica, Arab marriage is about relations among men, not between men and women, this is the case only if one considers the political aspect of marriage. In the Azawagh, both men and women talked about marriage as a sexual and emotional bond as well.

For a thirty-year-old female anthropologist interested in women's daily lives, marriage loomed large, but blood ties, especially those through men, are the primary links in Azawagh Arabs' own mental maps of their social worlds. Even if the vicissitudes of marriage occupy a large place in daily life, it is ties of blood that last, and that ultimately define one's place in the world. It is to these that I now turn.

Ties of blood

Like all Arabs and most pastoralists (Goody 1976: 4), Moors are devoutly patrilineal. Although (or because?) physically it is women who do the bearing and rearing of children, ideologically it is men who are the connectors among people, the threads that tie people to one another. Women don't count in official genealogies; relationships are calculated through men if at all possible.[3] "There are two men between us," both men and women might say to describe their relationship with a cousin, referring to the two brothers who link the cousins.

Blood is the central metaphor of relationship in Moor society. Blood ties exist between people related both through men and through women, although their paradigmatic form is through men. While "blood" refers primarily to genetic relationship, it is also used metaphorically to refer to identity and group affiliation (see Abu-Lughod 1986). Upon meeting my mother many people told us happily, "Your blood is one!" ("Demmkum wāḥid"), meaning that our biological connectedness could be read in our similar appearance, a fortuitous demonstration of the strength of our relationship. After I had been a few months in Tassara, some young men asked me if I could tell an Arab from a Tuareg by asking if I had learned to "tell someone's blood."

That blood is more commonly a metaphor of connection through men reflects an Azawagh Arab belief in the active role of men and the passive role of women in conception. Azawagh Arabs abide by the traditional Muslim understanding of conception, described at length by Carol Delaney (1991)[4] for Turkish Muslims, in which only men contribute substance to the fetus. As Minnou explained to me, the woman is only a container in which "a man's water forms a ball and then differentiates and becomes a baby." Another woman, Aichata, known for her expertise with local medicines, described it this way: "The man's water becomes strings of blood; they keep assembling until they become flesh." As sons and brothers "coagulate" to form a family, tribe, and people, so does a man's sexual substance differentiate and congeal into the stuff of human physicality.

On another occasion Minnou elaborated on the woman's role in the process:

A child comes from a man's "urine" drops [i.e. semen].[5] [And the woman?] She does not put anything in; she has no part in it. She is like a sack, like that sack that you put money in [pointing to the fanny pack on my waist]. That's the way it is with the urine that a man puts in a woman. She hides it for you. That's why the child is the man's, not the woman's. And if a man divorces his wife, he gets the children.

Minnou connects the facts of gestation further to the stipulation of Muslim law that children belong to the father. If a couple divorces, the children go to the father as soon as they reach the age of five or six. (They often end up being raised by the father's mother, the children's paternal grandmother.) So although Azawagh Arabs recognize that there is a genetic connectedness through women as well as through men, cultural ideology attributes the ultimate powers of creation and growth to the male element, and therefore ownership of offspring to men.

Reflecting the fact that relations through men and relations through women are of a fundamentally different order, the terms for relatives in Arabic distinguish between those related patrilaterally and matrilaterally. A father's brother is an *'am*, and all relatives related through a father are referred to by some version of this term, whereas a mother's brother is a *khāl*, with all maternal relatives referred to by a version of this term. The *'am*, the paternal uncle, is a person one can depend on for support and protection, whereas the *khāl*, the maternal uncle, will be more demonstratively affectionate but less significant in terms of support, marriage arrangements, and long-term alliances. As the saying goes: "If you are hungry go to your maternal relatives, and if you need protection go to your paternal relatives."[6]

In keeping with the patrilineal mindset, the general term for a relative of any kind is an *uld 'am*, literally "a son of a father's brother." I was always asked if any Westerners who visited the Azawagh were *ulād 'am* (pl.) of mine; it was unimaginable that all these Westerners gallivanting about the desert so far from their own people were unrelated to one another. They also found it odd that we married people who were not *ulād 'am* but pure strangers.

All people who share blood are referred to as one's "people" (*nās*), brothers (*khūt*), paternal relatives (*ulād 'am* – literally children of a father's brother), or relatives (*ahel*).[7] People described in any of these ways are people of whom it can be said that "our blood is one." If a relationship can be traced, it is cited – "he's an *uld 'am* of mine," "she's a *mint khāl*" (maternal relative's child), or "her grandfather and my grandmother were siblings." There is a special term for a relative distanced by only one man, *uld 'am shugga*,[8] i.e. a literal and not simply classificatory paternal uncle. If the specific relationship is unknown, people may say "there is blood between us" (*bainna ad-demm*). Again, if you can emphasize closeness, you do; otherwise, citing shared blood is the next best thing.

The body also plays its part in the way in which kinship ties are imagined. As my friend Boukia explained one day:

> The relatives of the father, they are the back, and the relatives of the mother, they are the stomach. [How's this?] It's as if they come from the stomach. Your paternal aunt comes to you from the back, from your father.

The fact that women's stomachs and breasts are such powerful images of relationship (and creators of relationship through breastmilk, as we will see below) suggests an alternative vision to the official patrilineal line.

Indeed, at least one feisty woman challenged the ideology of Muslim law by declaring to me that women actually have a greater right over their children than men do, because they bear and raise them.

The contrasting significance of kinship through men and kinship through women underscores the way in which men and women are imagined to be fundamentally different in this society. In fact, children do belong to their father and his family, and if a couple should divorce, the children go to their father or his relatives. Whatever women's powers for creating connection, and however warm relations are between matrilateral relatives, religious doctrine, social ideology, and historical tradition all make it clear that ties between men are those that shape the official histories as well as visions of the future, even if not always the lived, everyday world.

Ties through men

At the opening of the last chapter, on Islam, I told the story of my visit to the ʿālem Bai during the first weeks of my stay in Tassara. I noted my initial surprise that a history of the Azawagh Arabs should be synonymous with a history of Islam in local eyes. But this story also revealed how the story of the past, and the story of Islam, are stories of ties through men. The image of the red names standing out against a sea of black ink, traced in a careful hand into notebooks that have been carried across the desert, wrapped in all manner of protective layers, copied again and again over decades and centuries, the names indelible and perennial, offers a striking metaphorical illustration of the importance of men as markers of time and identity.

Turning each page Bai read out the names to me: Aqbata bin Nafi (Uqba bin Nafi), al-Aqeb, Yaqub, Shaker, Yahiss, and so on, through twelve generations, to the founder of the Kunta line and finally to his grandson, Sidi Ahmed al-Bakai, called Budamʿa.[9] In a world where tents only rose a few feet from the ground and the mosque was a mere outline of stones in the sand, this line of ancestors rose up tall and proud into history, tying Bai to a glorious past, establishing his dignity and place in the world not in material structures or goods, but in men.

As striking as the genealogy reaching back a millennium, and the male nodes of connection standing out on the pages, was what Bai told me next. "None of these men had brothers, except for half-brothers by their mothers. Each was his father's only son." While normally Arabs want large families and many sons, the version of his history that Bai told kept his vision of his past free of any ambiguity – an unbroken, clear line of men extending back to the Prophet's own tribe. It would be unfortunate if each man had only one son, so the story allows for sons by other, presumably later, wives, but keeps each man's eldest son without brothers with whom familial division might have taken place. Only the last man in the

86

genealogy, Sidi Ahmed al-Bakai, had three sons, who then presumably went on to found different branches of the Kunta. It was with those three sons that the story ended, the perfect containedness and wholeness of the male line broken, mythical simplicity giving way to real-world complexity. The story also points to the unspoken significance of women, for clearly the sons by later women were not deemed as important, although Bai did not say whether this was because their mothers were not of as high rank or because they were not as close cousins.

I return to this story because it demonstrates both the "official" importance of ties through men and the reverence accorded such ties. It also points to the fusing of kinship, Islam, and history that characterizes the self-representation of Azawagh Arabs: they consider themselves to be connected by blood through worthy men to an honorable and lengthy past and, ultimately, to the very roots of the Islamic faith.

While the lack of brothers in Bai's genealogy keeps identity and ancestry free from the threat of fission, in real life the bond between brothers is as central to social life as the bond between father and son. To fight with one's brothers is very shameful, as emerged in the story of Ahmed and Aminatou and as I was told many times. The colonial archives record that when, in 1938, there was fighting between the chief and his cousins, many other men intervened, asking them to stop their disputes "which covered them in shame" (Brachet 1938b). It is one's brother who, one hopes, will produce a suitable marriage partner for one's own son or daughter; and it is he whom one will depend upon for economic and political support. A person's father and his or her patrilateral uncle ('am) are as one. When I once showed surprise that a woman's 'am and not her father had given her gold jewelry, she answered, confused at my surprise, "but my 'am is my father." Men decried the individualism of Westerners, for instance how we would eat alone, and not share everything we had with relatives. "If I am eating," one man explained to me, "I can't enjoy it if my brothers aren't eating too." This is not mere rhetoric. When one son of Tassara made his fortune in the construction business in the capital, he paid for no fewer than ten of his classificatory brothers to go on the pilgrimage to Mecca, and bought several of them cars as well.

Sons are important not only because they carry on the family line, but because they support their mothers when their fathers, husbands, and brothers have passed on. When my mother came to visit, the most frequent question she was asked was why she had no sons. Azawagh Arab women were fully aware of the utilitarian necessity of sons, and understood my mother's explanations (developed after several days of less acceptable ones) that she did not need a son to support her since she could work. When I professed a desire for daughters over sons once, a group of women told me that if their girls could go around and be educated and work as I could, they would want daughters too.

to lament (mourn over) loudly & shrilly.

Accordingly, when a son is born women ululate; when a daughter is born, women quietly thank God that mother and child are all right. Boys are given larger name-day ceremonies on the seventh day after birth than girls are, and their mothers tend to stay in confinement longer. When I told Mayghania once that Aminatou had given birth to a girl, she responded in mock disgust. "We are afraid of our girls," she said, in half-jest. "They shame us; Tuaregs and Blacks 'take' them," meaning that outsiders can have sex with them, thus destroying not only their own honor and purity but that of their family as well. I knew of no cases where this had happened, but the fear of it loomed large. The entire society depended on women and their bodies for the production of sons and patri-lines, and yet women's bodies were all too vulnerable, too "open," and could thereby as easily bring disruption of the social order and its continued proper reproduction.

In keeping with the tremendous weight put on ties between men, patri-lateral relations are less warm and loving than they are respectful and strict, especially in public. While a matrilateral uncle will lovingly kiss and play with his nephews and nieces, a father or patrilateral uncle will retain a much stricter and more distant demeanor. I once encountered a particu-larly taciturn new father at the small local pharmacy. We chatted a little and he finally got around to asking the shop owner about cough medi-cines. "Who is sick?" I broke in, since visiting and inquiring after the ill was a major part of women's daily routine in Tassara. "A child at our house," he answered curtly. Knowing his wife had recently given birth to their first child, I started to catch on. "Is it *your* child?" I asked, in my usual nosy fashion. He broke into a big, embarrassed grin. Simply to buy medicine for a first-born child (in this case a daughter) was to publicly demonstrate a level of attachment that caused considerable discomfort for this new father.

It was not, however, that men were not affectionate with their children, especially young daughters, merely that its expression had to be carefully governed in public. Once I took a woman and her new daughter to a desert encampment, where the woman was going to spend a few weeks fattening. Her husband, whom I had never seen so much as touch his adorable daughter, came with us and, to my surprise, he held her for the entire ride, bouncing her on his lap and cooing at her. Without others around, it was permissible to show the affection that he felt for his daughter. While I occa-sionally came across men in quiet domestic moments showering great love on their children, in public they always retained the strict and distant mien befitting the father–child relationship, the relationship that carried the highest expectations and heaviest responsibilities in the society.

I should also mention that for men and women to display affection toward their children was problematic in its implication that they cared more for their own offspring than for parents, siblings, and other relatives.

For this reason, despite the child-loving nature of this society, people displayed their love publicly for children not their own much more frequently than for their own. Especially around first-born children, parents were expected to show great modesty, partly in deference to the fact that the child implicitly announced their sexual maturity and activity. When a woman gives birth to her first child, this also signals several implicit challenges to the role and authority of the elder generation: between the woman's husband and his father, whose authority until then defined the son's role in the world; between the woman and her own mother, whose emotional claims over her daughter have now been to some extent superseded; and between the woman and her mother-in-law, who now witnesses the beginnings of the weakening of her position as well, even while in the short run she presides over a larger domain.

Tribes

Above the day-to-day, close kin bonds of men and women sits the tribal structure of Azawagh Arab society. Like other Moor and Arab societies, Azawagh Arab society is divided into genealogical groups which each claim descent from one eponymous male ancestor. Although I would argue that the tie between two brothers or between a father and son is the strongest and most significant social bond for Azawagh Arabs, tribal affiliation forms an important aspect of individual identity as well as a means of furthering one's interests, be it watering herds at a well or setting up trade relationships. In the Azawagh today there are seven major "Arab" tribes (qaba'il, sing. qabīla) and many other smaller ones. People generally marry within their tribe, and side with it in any political conflict. The tribes of the Azawagh are all subsumed under the leadership of a ṣulṭān, a member of the Deremsheka tribe who for the last forty years has been a wiry, clever, somewhat elusive man named Oumada. In addition to the salience of tribal affiliation in marriage and battle, tribes are also each said to have their own particular character: the Yaddess are known to be business-oriented and high-spirited; the Turshan haughty and independent; the Bin Haida brave and fiery; the Twaij quarrelsome and belligerent.

Although traditional analyses of social organization in Arab societies and much research on Mauritania have focused on the level of tribe (for example Bonte et al. 1991; Evans-Pritchard 1949; Gellner 1969; Peters 1990), recent studies have demonstrated that social organization in Arab societies is often more fruitfully investigated by focusing on individuals and the multiple ways in which they reckon and create different types of relationships (Eickelman 1989; Geertz 1979; Rosen 1984; for a non-Arab society, Comaroff and Roberts 1981). My understanding of kinship among Azawagh Arabs is that however set in stone kin relations may be, individuals draw on them with considerable leeway, and thus inject a good deal of agency into an otherwise seemingly circumscribed social world, and this is especially true of tribal affiliations.

Tribes are mostly significant to Azawagh Arabs in Niger to the extent that they reflect the widest possible extrapolation of the very closest, brother-to-brother ties. Rather than constituting the model of social organization, tribes constitute the inner kernel of Arab society writ large, a useful magnification of the closest blood ties that matter most.[10] As Combs-Schilling (1985), Abu-Lughod (1986), Barth (1973) and others have suggested for diverse Middle Eastern societies, tribal affiliations are called upon in certain instances but are not the stuff of daily or even regular, routine social relations. Consequently, a consideration of lived social organization among Azawagh Arabs should work from the inside out, as I have done here by beginning with a discussion of ties through individual men.

While some have suggested that tribal affiliations are shifting and ambiguous, this is not the case in the Azawagh as far as I could tell. People know to what tribe each person belongs and I never heard the validity of anyone's tribal affiliation debated, nor saw evidence of any shifts in histories I collected. The names of the tribes that exist in the Azawagh today extend back over centuries: the earliest mention of the Deremsheka, allowing for some vagaries of spelling, is from 1478 (Martin 1908: 119); the Yaddess and Deremsheka are mentioned in a document dating to 1755 (Nicolas 1950: 69; Norris 1986: 233); an apparent ancestor of the Twaij was a figure of some renown in the 1500s (Batran 1979: 125); and the Taggat seem to date at least to the seventeenth century (Hamet 1911: 161). This is not to say that in even the recent past these "fixed" tribes did not coalesce out of different sorts of affiliations, but that at present they are not in an observable state of flux. Indeed, their historical trajectories seem quite certain: while the Deremsheka, Yaddess, and Twaij seem to have roots in the Touat region of Algeria (Nicolas 1950), the Taggat seem to have migrated from eastern Mauritania (Hamet 1911).

Azawagh Arabs can name the tribe of any individual, and are also likely to know if he or she has any forebears of a different tribe, but in day-to-day interaction reference to tribal affiliation is rare. Although men especially enjoyed testing me on my knowledge of the names of different tribes, and delighted in adding distant, obscure ones to my repertoire, when the questions became more personal, people drew back from discussing which tribe someone belonged to, or tribal relations in the recent past.

In part this reflected a wish not to risk sowing resentment between tribal groups, where tensions lay but cooperation was necessary for large-scale political purposes. More importantly, however, I believe that people were not used to identifying themselves or other members of their tribe as, for example, Deremsheka, because naming a specific relationship of shared blood was a preferred way to express closeness. In other words, to identify someone as belonging to your tribe appeared to imply that you did not know your actual relationship to that person, and therefore connoted distance rather than closeness. In Tassara there was a particular reluctance to designate someone by the name of one of the two dominant Deremsheka subtribes that most belonged to, the more humble but religiously powerful Haj Hamma or the chiefly Muhammad Lamīn. In addition to the fact that each subtribe had colonized different areas of town and married mostly within its membership, there had obviously been tensions between the two that people were trying to keep under control, and whose precise nature I was never able to discover. Given the contrasting nature of each group's power, one religious and one secular, it seems reasonable that there were tensions over leadership and control of resources among men that were also felt by the women I spent my days with.

In keeping with my interpretation of the sense of discomfort people felt around tribal identification, it made sense that people more readily used tribal membership to identify those outside of their own tribe than those within it. A Deremsheka friend spoke of having a grandmother who was a Turshaniyya, a man we ran into on the road was labeled a Taggati, and for most of my stay in Tassara a very popular paramour of a series of philandering men was known simply as "the Towjiyya."

Not only in connection with their love lives did men have cause to mention tribes more often than women. Barth (1973) has suggested that descent groups are about politics, not kinship, and while I would say the distinction is a fuzzy one in the Arab world it is true that tribes come into play mostly for large-scale, strategic purposes. Combs-Schilling has suggested that both models and ideologies may be operative and available to individuals on different levels (cited in Abu-Lughod 1986: 279, n.16), and since it is men who negotiate relations at levels beyond the family, it is not surprising that they should evoke tribal identity more often.

Because I was relegated to the female world, I had little opportunity to see tribal politics in action. When there were meetings between the leaders and adult male members of all the tribes in Niger, like other women I was kept decidedly in the dark about details of the proceedings. Two intertribal matters were, however, under discussion during my time in Tassara. The first was the organization of resistance to Tuareg rebels, who had been attacking Arab cars and camps. The Tuareg waged a separatist struggle from the mid-1980s until 1997, and engaged in tactics remarkably similar to those of raids that were the norm when the French arrived at the turn of the century. In the endeavor to defend themselves, the Arab tribes banded together to form a militia (which apparently received covert military supplies from the Nigerien government) that engaged in defense and sometimes aggression against presumed Tuareg attackers.

The other intertribal issue that was under debate during my time in Tassara was a division that had been smoldering for some time: the desire of the Yaddess tribe to break free from the leadership of the Deremsheka chief, Oumada. The Yaddess were the largest and richest of the tribes in Niger, and wanted to be free of direct control by the dictatorial Oumada. They did not, however, achieve this split while I was there, and I have not heard of a definitive rupture since.

Tribal affiliations, I have suggested, are brother–brother bonds writ large, an extrapolation of the unbreakable ties between closely related kin. From this highest-level incarnation of the principle of agnation, I will now turn to the less official but equally important ties that structure everyday life: ties through women.

Ties through women

Although men constitute the patriline and form the ideological underpinning of lived social organization, it is women who insure the family and the tribe's purity by never marrying non-Arabs, by bearing sons, and by safeguarding family prestige in their fattened, swathed bodies at the center of the tent. Relationships to and through women are significant for their rich emotional warmth.[11] There is also a degree of comforting genetic certainty to relations through women that is not present in relations through men; that is, you can always be certain who the biological mother of a child is, but never completely certain of the biological father. Since who your father is defines your identity, it makes sense that women's purity and honor must be so carefully guarded – it is crucial that one can be certain whose "blood" they carry in their womb. An Arab saying expresses this in the broader terms of matrilaterality and patrilaterality: "The *khāl* [maternal relative] gives birth and the Lord is witness." In other words, if a man's sister gives birth, he knows positively that he is the uncle, whereas if his brother's wife gives birth, he can never be positive that his own blood brother really inseminated the woman. Azawagh Arabs also acknowledge that, emotionally at least, the ideal situation is to be connected to and cared for by both mother and father. As another saying has it, the optimal situation for a child is "to lie before your mother's *garfa* [a decorated leather bag in which women kept their belongings], and to be covered by the pants of your father."

It is also worth noting that, although women are to some degree pawns in a system of male-dominated kinship organization, in daily life they experience and perpetuate the strength of kin ties perhaps even more strongly than do men. Azawagh Arabs are patrilocal and children "belong" to the father, but a woman returns to her mother to give birth and have her confinement, even on an eighth pregnancy, even if the mother is divorced and remarried. And while men engage frequently with non-kin and occasionally marry outsiders, women engage almost entirely with kin and never marry outside Azawagh Arab society.[12] It is women, then, who ultimately insure the purity of descent that is ideologically represented as running through men.

Without the burden of duty attached to patrilateral relations, maternal relatives are free to show much greater affection to children. As Boukia said, "We, the Arabs, say that there is more liking from maternal relatives (*akhwāl*). . . . Caring and attachment to a child are stronger in the *akhwāl*." In a society where it is unusual and frowned upon to be too emotionally expressive, mothers and daughters cry when they must leave one another. The strength of the mother–daughter bond is present in other ties through women as well. Supporting Boukia's statements, Sidi explained,

> Maternal uncles (*akhwāl*) love their children more than paternal uncles (*'amām*). If you see two children, one raised at his *khāl*'s and the other at his *'am*'s, the first will be spoiled. The *akhwāl* can't refuse anything to a child. Paternal uncles will hit and scold.

Children, especially first children, are not infrequently raised by grand-mothers, and it is commonly understood that those raised by a maternal grandmother have an easier time of it.

The expected strictness of paternal relatives explains the slight prefer-ence for having girls fattened by paternal grandmothers or aunts. As I have said, mothers themselves rarely fatten their daughters because a mother's love for her own daughter is too great, and maternal relatives carry the same disadvantage. For fattening, you want someone who can be strict with a girl, and since *akhwāl* can "like a child too much," a paternal relative who will not be afraid to force the girl to eat, by yelling and beat-ings if necessary, is often the first choice. Of course it is also the girl's patriline who will be responsible for her marriage, and it is they who there-fore have a greater interest in her becoming a plump and appealing young bride.

Milk kinship

The most significant way in which women affect official social relations is through breastfeeding children not their own, and the particular Arab notion of milk kinship (*ridā'a*) this creates.[13] Soraya Altorki (1980) discusses this highly significant but underexplored aspect of Arab kinship, explaining how the Hadith (sayings of the Prophet) stipulate that a rela-tionship created by a woman's nursing of a child is tantamount to a blood relationship.[14] She also notes that in the past in Saudi Arabia, milk ties were considered as binding as blood ties. As my own research, as well as that of Tim Cleaveland (1993) in Mauritania, has shown, milk kinship rules are still followed strictly among Moors.

Women nurse children not their own under several conditions. Like many peoples in Africa, Moors believe that colostrum[15] is not good for newborn infants, who are therefore breastfed by women other than their mothers for several days after they are born. Since women breastfeed their children for up to three years, stopping only when they get pregnant again, there is ample opportunity for other women to give a child their breast. This may happen because the mother is away momentarily and the child starts crying, because a woman wants to establish a particular bond to a child, or because the mother does not have enough milk (see Boddy 1989: 100).

While I did not see women openly calculate the long-term consequences of creating a milk-kinship tie, certainly the potential for influencing marriages and family relations exists. Altorki (1980) notes that Saudi Arabian men and women encouraged the creation of milk ties to prevent unwanted marriages, to broaden the circle of kin support, and to relieve women of having to veil before non-blood kin in the household. It remains an open question to what extent Azawagh Arab women's nursing of children not their own is motivated: that is, do they calculate that they do not want a son to marry a certain girl, and then offer her their breast? As Janice Boddy points out, milk kinship restricts marriage possibilities for the newly created siblings, but extends such possibilities for the following generation. Although women in the Azawagh never spoke openly of manipulating kinship, I noticed that a certain degree of thought and caution went into choosing who should nurse newborn children. Moreover, women have a more or less clear memory of whom they may have nursed as children. But knowingly to marry someone who is a milk sibling is, as Sidi told me gravely, to go against Islam.[16]

Sidi himself had been put in very difficult straits by a loving and generous paternal aunt of his. Wanting to give her children, nephews, and nieces a wealth of siblings, so that everywhere they went "people would be glad to see them," she nursed what he said (I hope hyperbolically) were one hundred children, including himself. Now everywhere he went, he complained, although there were many women who did not need to veil for him and whom he could freely "greet" and "chat with," many marriage possibilities had been ruled out. Often people learn of these relationships when they are already grown. As I described above, for example, one day Sidi strode confidently up to a veiling young woman, Anebu, and said "give me your hand," explaining to all around that he had just learned she was a milk sister. Now he could shake her hand, and she no longer needed to veil for him.

A milk tie is almost as binding as a blood tie. One exception is the reckoning of kinship for marriage: I am unaware of any marriages considered to be between the children of brothers where the fathers were brothers by virtue of a milk tie rather than a "real" blood tie. Put another way, milk ties seem to be more important for what they prevent one from doing than for what they allow one to do. In general, however, for Azawagh Arabs milk ties are not so much an alternative to blood ties as an alternative way of creating them. Accordingly, in daily discourse, people usually did not distinguish between the different types of bonds unless I asked specifically. Although I never heard a physical explanation of how milk creates a blood tie, Altorki (1980) notes that Arab notions of milk kinship are based on the belief that the man a woman is sleeping with contributes his bodily fluids to the generation of her milk. Whether this understanding was prevalent in the Azawagh or not, in practice milk indeed seemed to "become" blood. For example, when Asseghiyera and I were joking once that I had a baby, she said that she would nurse it so that its blood would become one with hers. In contrast to Altorki's model, however, this transformation of milk into blood seemed to be worked solely by women and their own physical powers of creating connection. In the face of Arab-Islamic orthodoxy that makes patrilineal ties so central, the on-the-ground reality of milk kinship creates a strong counterbalance to this male-centered model.

Milk kinship also points to the centrality of milk in Moor society, which I will discuss further in the next chapter. Animal milk is the most valued form of nourishment, esteemed for its qualities of taste, whiteness, healthiness, and ability to fatten. Several people described heaven to me as a place where milk would be abundant; even running from faucets, as one woman envisioned. Women's breastmilk, sustained by fresh animal milk, is a similarly powerful substance, creating ties equal in strength and significance to those embedded in male-governed descent. While blood is a largely metaphorical connector among people, the milk women produce connects them in a literal way by its very materiality. It is not coincidental that it is a female substance that has such literal "weight," for it is women who mind the material world, in their domestic life as in their fattening. The fact that women's bodily substances hold more weight than men's reflects the reality that women's fluids, bodily orifices, and their flesh itself are central to the expression of Moor values and the maintenance of social order.

This brief examination of different sorts of kin ties has underlined, I hope, several key values of Azawagh Arab society. First of all, it begins to explain the logic of the male–female opposition, and its embeddedness in an ideology of relationship that makes ties through men and ties through women profoundly different sorts of connections. Second, I have stressed the emphasis placed on unity and containedness, and the way in which men are as bright stars in the constellation of relationships that define the group, and, implicitly, those who are not inside it. Third, I have underlined the importance of honor and purity in kin relations, both in the inviolability of the kin group, and in traceable connections to Islam's roots.

And lastly, I have tried to paint a picture of the contrast between kinship ideology, based on patriliny, and kinship on the ground, where women play a dominant role in "nursing" kinship relations, both literally and figuratively.

Kinship and sentiment

Arab kinship is a matter of duties and rights, but it is also a matter of sentiment. In daily discourse, kinship was invoked as often in conversations about sentiment as in conversations about roles and rights; indeed, it is hard to separate the two.[17] The husband and wife who were told not to fight were expected to fulfill the duties of patrilaterally related relatives, but also to express the sentiments of respect and caring befitting such kin. Patrilateral and matrilateral relations also differ in emotional disposition: as I noted above, relations through men are characterized by strictness, duty, and loyalty, whereas relations through women are characterized by warmth and gentleness.

Crosscutting these differences in emotional bonds is the contrast made between the pure, companionate affection modeled on the bond of male friends and the more troublesome erotic passion that can arise between members of the opposite sex. Azawagh Arabs distinguish between two types of love that people can feel, one modeled on love between brothers and the other modeled on love between members of the opposite sex. "Love according to Allah" (ḥubb ʿala Allah) is a love of companionship and loyalty between friends, family, and people of the same sex; "love according to Satan" (ḥubb ʿala Shayṭān) is an erotic love for the opposite sex. The term "Satan" (Shayṭān) has several uses in Galgaliyya Arabic, and its use here, along with the invocation of Allah, is best regarded as what Michael Jackson (1989: 142) calls "quiescent metaphors"; that is, they do not consciously evoke the religious imagery to which they refer, but are general terms for types of emotional attachment. Thus "love according to Satan" does not literally connote "Satanic love"; it connotes love inflamed by erotic desire, and therefore tinged with sinfulness or at least the risk of sin.

Love according to Allah is easy, straightforward, controllable, and righteous; love according to Satan is not under one's own willpower and control, and is tinged with danger. As Sidi explained it to me,

> When a man is attracted to a woman, or vice versa, it is Satan acting. Love according to Allah is like love for a man [i.e. by a man]. If you have this kind of love for a woman, you want the same thing from her as you want from a man. Love according to Satan, however, is different. . . . When a woman has strong attraction, if a man gets near her his body will rise up.

In other words, if a man feels the first type of love for a woman, he wants only friendship and loyalty from her – what a friendship with a person of the same sex would offer. If he feels the second type of love, however, he wants a sexual relationship, and he loses mastery over his own sentiments and bodily reactions. This opposition between "pure" love of kin and the troublesome love of sexual attraction is key to the sense that kin relationships are the most noble type, and will be discussed further for its implications about the economy of desire in chapter 9 below.

Of course in an endogamous society most people are kin in one way or another. While *hubb 'ala Allah* should govern all kin relations, one hopes to feel some of the other kind of love for the person one marries, kin or not. One young man explained to me that he had only felt *hubb 'ala Allah* for his last "girlfriend," a distant cousin, and it wasn't enough. He had started courting another girl, also a distant relative, for whom he felt both types of love, he said, a much more satisfying situation.

The lived feeling of kinship ties in a kin-oriented society, particularly preferred cousin marriage, was one of the hardest things for me to comprehend as an American from a land of individualism, anonymity, and supposedly freely chosen marriage partners. I used to sit and reflect that when many women I knew lay with their husbands at night they looked into the eyes of not only a spouse but also a close cousin, one of their own family, features they may have known since childhood, if not in their own husband's boyhood face then in that of his mother, sisters, brothers, or cousins. (In fact, after the birth of their first child husbands and wives sleep not together but separately, and the husband comes to where the wife is sleeping only to have sex.) However much young people in fact resisted marrying cousins they had known in childhood, the fact that they expected their spouses to be of their own family certainly imbued the ideology of patriliny and endogamy with emotional attachment and weight.

How does one work out the balance between *hubb 'ala Allah* and *hubb 'ala Shaytān*? How does one insure and nurture the perfect closeness of ties through men when dependent on tension-laden, potentially uncontrollable relations between the opposite sexes to reproduce those ties? How does one maintain the ideal closed wholeness of the family and tribe, when inescapable sexual urges draw one in other directions? And how do women negotiate a life that socializes them to unquestioned attachment to and love for their mother and the home of their birth, but requires that they sit out most of their adult days among in-laws? These are some of the challenges for Azawagh Arabs that marriage both poses and seeks to resolve.

Marriage

From the day I arrived until the day I left, discussions about how Westerners marry, what kind of bride-price we receive, and whether we divorce were topics of unending interest to the women of Tassara. It was so anomalous and clearly discomforting to people that I claimed adulthood and yet was unmarried that both men and women suggested seriously that I marry just for the time I was in Tassara. I once read that American films always have a car chase scene; French films a scene at a lavish dinner table; and Arab films a wedding (Langewiesche 1996: 140). In fact, this generalization seemed to be borne out when a crew from the Nigerien television station came to Tassara to film a short piece on this little-known ethnic group: the townspeople staged a wedding for them to film. (A brother and sister shyly played the bride and groom.)

Why does marriage excite such unending interest among women? In large part, of course, because marriage is perhaps the most significant event in a woman's life, with vast consequences: on the wedding day proper she is celebrated and made the center of attention as at no other time in her life, and after the wedding her life may take a radical turn, away from her mother and birth family and to a sometimes distant home among demanding and expectant in-laws, not to mention a husband whose ways may be largely a mystery to the new bride.

But marriage's centrality for both men and women has deeper roots as well. Except for the contingency of milk kinship, to whom you are related and how are givens for Azawagh Arabs. Whom you marry, however, is not. It is in marriage that the family's honor and increase are assured, the patriline strengthened, alliances made, individual desires fulfilled, and the central tensions and challenges of Azawagh Arab culture played out, especially those of sexuality. In her analysis of the meaning of marriage ties in Morocco, Hildred Geertz concluded that marriage was "an opportunity to build a zone of predictability and control, a framework of obligations and expectations that will provide slightly surer footing in the quicksand of personal relationships" (1979: 377). My observations of Moor marriage suggested precisely the opposite, that marriages were the "quicksand": fragile and impermanent bonds set against the "predictability and control" inherent in blood relationships.

Marriage encapsulates a driving tension of Azawagh Arab society – that between an ordered, controllable world of cooperative ties through men, and the lusts and pleasures of sexuality that both threaten and ultimately reproduce that world of male–male relationships. As John Comaroff and Simon Roberts have noted, "the constitutive order and the lived-in universe exist in a dialectical relationship, and it is in this that the historicity of any system resides" (1981: 230). For Azawagh Arabs, the "constitutive order" is the patrilineal, tribal ideology, and the "lived-in universe" is one of sexual passions that demand expression, sometimes within marriage and sometimes without. By bringing the "constitutive order" into communion with the sexual drive, marriage forms the stage on which the fundamental existential concerns of Azawagh Arabs are expressed and, to some extent, resolved.

Another part of the conscious ideological conception of proper marriage for Azawagh Arabs involves the fundamental opposition between in-marriage and out-marriage, where marrying in is what is desirable. This opposition, I suggest, constitutes a version of the opposition between closedness and openness, now in a social register, that structures other domains of Azawagh Arab life. "Blood" should be concentrated and kept "closed off," one might say, retained within the family and not dispersed to outsiders. Marrying close cousins, as is preferred, allows this "enriching" of Azawagh Arab stock and pride to be achieved. In this way marriage practices among Azawagh Arabs express and reinforce some of the deep cultural categories that make life meaningful. Thus the concentration of relationship and sentiment inwards by both endogamy and the value placed on those of the same blood encapsulates a central trope of Azawagh Arab life. The opposition between things "outside" and things "inside," between that which is porous and open and that which is guarded and contained, arguably finds its root and most powerful expression in the system of marriage and reckoning kin.

Even in a physical, genetic sense, in-marriage is thought to create stronger children. Although I occasionally heard the idea expressed that Arab–European (white) matches produced beautiful children (largely because of their light skin),[18] it was much more common to hear that marriage with outsiders was deleterious for the children and the family as a whole. "When people who are patrilateral cousins (ulād ʿam) marry," a haratāni told me, "their children are smart, strong." Women, who are less directly affected by the political and economic advantages of in-marriage, have their own reasons to resent men marrying non-Arabs and non-family members, for such marriages deprive them of potential spouses.

Mayghania, the chief's daughter, who suffered greatly because of her own husband's incessant philandering, explained to me: "In the past, before we entered towns and were ruined (yukhassar), we didn't marry Hausas, haratīn, and Tuaregs. We used not to marry with them. We began mixing with them in the towns."

The idea of mixing has negative connotations here, for it connotes the opposite of concentrating purity inwards, and Mayghania said it with derision. To mix with outsiders is to deplete the society's very core and vitality. For women especially, marrying out constitutes a rejection of all that they stand for.

Although the ideal marriage is one between the children of two brothers, only a few marriages in Tassara fit this ideal, and they tended to be marriages among the most important families. At the other end of the spectrum, only a few marriages were among people who were not related at all, and these were all cases where either a local woman had married a

man from a nobler tribe than her own or a man who had moved away
had married a non-Arab.[19] Both men and women desired to marry someone
they liked, and most divorces were made in an attempt to move on to a
marriage of true affection. Thus one of the never-ending challenges
to marriage was to create a match that was both close in terms of blood
relationship, and also desired by the couple themselves.

Although political purposes to marriage seemed always to be overridden
by affection in the long run, men talked in the abstract about marrying for
political reasons, and there were numerous marriages in Tassara that
were clearly the desire of the parents, not the married couple. (Most of
them were unhappy.) As I sat with a group of relatively powerful men one
evening, the chief's nephew Mohamed expounded on marriage strategies
to me:

> We like to marry *ulād 'am*, and, if that's not possible, then someone
> from a noble family, with money, and with a long history. Now I
> have a daughter, and I want her to marry an *uld 'am*, and, if that's
> not possible, someone from a good family, a big family, a "free"
> [noble, *ḥurra*] family. Even if they aren't rich, their status and
> nobility matter more.

Mohamed's daughter was only four months old at the time, but he was
not the only one thinking ahead. Just a few weeks earlier I had been visiting
with his wife when some young men came by, both cousins of varying
degrees, and, playing with the cute little girl, they began to discuss who
had the better claim to marry her. One of the men, although married to a
thirteen-year-old who was then pregnant, playfully tied a string around her
neck as a way of "reserving" her. The mother laughingly went along with
the game.

Divorce

Despite the unceasing interest evinced in marriage, the seeming strictness
of Islam, and the seriousness with which the arranging of marriages is
undertaken, no discussion of Moor marriage can ignore the subject of
divorce. Divorce is the rule rather than the exception in Azawagh Arab
society, and both men and women are likely to marry more than once
during their lives.[20] Indeed, when women talked to me about marriage they
inevitably also talked to me about divorce. No matter how politically desirable a particular match may be, the sexual attraction and emotional
affection sought by the individuals themselves often ultimately hold sway.
And this, in many cases, means that divorce occurs. And while the first
marriage is usually arranged, later ones often involve greater choice on the
part of both men and women.

100

Just as only men "marry," only men "divorce." That is, the verbs "to marry" (*yujowwez*) and "to divorce" (*yukhella*) can only take a male subject. Women "are married," just as they "are left" or "are divorced." (Only in the metaphorical expression for marriage "to make a tent" (*'adel al-khayme*) are women the active subjects, getting married. By Muslim law a woman can only demand a divorce if a husband does not support her or does not have sexual intercourse with her, but even in these rare cases *he* must divorce *her*. Although I witnessed no instances where wives claimed explicitly that men were neglecting their provider or sexual duties toward them, women nevertheless frequently wish to be released from marriages. They had numerous, usually unstated reasons for wanting to leave a marriage: they wanted to marry someone of their own choosing, perhaps a man who had been courting them before the marriage; they felt their husband mistreated them by not giving them enough things or by his behavior; they disliked their mother-in-law; or they simply wished to return to be near their own mother. In such instances, a woman goes about obtaining a divorce by more or less indirect means – making her wishes known to her husband, acting out before her mother-in-law, acting relentlessly sullen around her husband, and so on. Finally, the husband generally gives in and grants the divorce. If a woman asks for a divorce her family must return the bride-price (discussed below); if a man initiates the divorce, the bride's family can keep the bride-price. Usually, however, women manage to orchestrate the divorce so that their family can keep the money.

When Boukia's daughter Tetou, for example, resolutely refused to cooperate in a marriage to a rich Algerian by continually "escaping" from her husband to a neighbor's house, her family did not return the high bride-price, for it would have been considered in very bad taste for the rich and much older groom to demand it. He realized the relationship was untenable and divorced her after a few months, marrying a slightly older cousin of Tetou's just a few months later. In another case, however, a young girl in Tassara waited some four years for her stubborn husband to grant her a divorce, even though she had moved back home three years before and her family offered to return the bride-price. Marriage among close relatives only complicates the situation: on the one hand, a man may be more easily persuaded to divorce a girl when her father, the man's uncle, brings pressure to bear, but on the other hand families have a greater investment in seeing family marriages succeed, and often exert pressure on the couple to stay together, as in Ahmed and Aminatou's case.

Weddings

I began with a story of a marriage breaking apart, and I end with the story of a marriage beginning. Even if the unraveling of an institution makes bare its internal workings with a spare kind of clarity, weddings also tell a story about the foundational structures and values on which a society rests. And if marriage is the fulcrum on which the social order of Azawagh Arabs turns, as I have argued, then weddings are the rituals through which this social order achieves its most articulate expression and dramatization.

In conformity with general Islamic practice, Azawagh Arab weddings consist of three distinct stages:

1   the contract (*'aqd*) when the marriage is made official and bride-price decided upon;
2   the wedding proper (*'ers*), including a big celebration; and
3   the "separation" (*'azūl*), when the girl is finally taken to live with her new husband, and thus separated from her own natal family.

These stages highlight three of the central themes of Moor marriage in their three stages of celebration:

1   the first, the contract, speaks to the concerns of the patriline with its exchange between men of a daughter for bride-price;
2   the events of the wedding celebration highlight Azawagh Arab views of sexuality and male–female relations;
3   finally, the "separation" of the bride from her natal home brings into focus concerns over reproduction, the creation of a new shoot to the family tree, and the tensions between close matrilateral ties and dutiful patrilineal ones.

Just as they involve very different aspects of marriage, the three stages can be separated by a number of years in practice, though the contract is often signed on the same night as the wedding.[21]

The women of Tassara used to tell me with great regret, "People don't marry anymore," referring to the fact that it seemed harder for girls to find husbands, perhaps because of more out-marriage by men and the increasing time men spent away, trying to make a living, before getting married. Indeed, although twelve children were born to Arab parents during my time in Tassara, there was not one wedding. I did, however, witness a wedding in the winter of 1990 in Tchin Tabaraden, and since the bride was my good friend Asseghiyera, a neighbor from Peace Corps days, I was able to participate fully. Although she was only about eighteen, it was her second marriage. She had been married very young to a man from a different tribe (a Turshani), but with the girlish stubbornness that new brides often suddenly evince, she refused to stay in that first marriage, and was now marrying an *uld 'am* more of her own choosing. He was related both through her mother and her father; men cited the patrilateral relationship to me, and women the matrilateral.

Asseghiyera's wedding began as most do, at the home of the bride's father. One dark evening in the dry season, when word had gotten out that the wedding would be that night, people began assembling at the home of 'Omar, Asseghiyera's father. The women sat quietly, whispering, under the tent in the yard, while the men assembled out in the open, around the Muslim learned man ('ālem) who would perform the formal part of the marriage. The contract stage is clearly about the patriline and the way in which marriages create and reinforce ties among men, and accordingly only men are involved in this part of the marriage ceremony. Due to the intense sensitivity of the negotiations and the implicit acknowledgment that a man's daughter is about to have sex, the fathers themselves do not attend. Instead, representatives of the bride's and groom's fathers carry out this brief ceremony, arranging the contract and partaking in the Koranic benediction that is pronounced over the marriage. Usually the bride-price has already been decided, but it is announced at the contract and at least some of it is paid. Women regularly asked me how much bride-price women fetch in America, and evinced few illusions about the practice among themselves: "It is like selling a woman; a man buys her and she becomes his."

After the hushed, dense circle of men rose from their negotiations and Islamic prayers, a cry went up from the women under the tent, and they broke into ululation. With the contract agreed upon, the couple is considered joined in marriage. Whispers circulated about the amount of the bride-price, and the women began only now to convert a big wooden grain mortar into a drum, by stretching a goat skin over its opening, securing it by a rope wound tight around long, heavy pestles. Like singing and dancing at Muslim holidays, the wedding celebration was run entirely by women and included drumming, dancing, and singing. It lasted almost until dawn, and culminated in theory with the bride and the groom sleeping together for the first time, although I think that circumstances in fact delayed this event for a few more nights.

Where are the bride and the groom in all of this? Like their fathers, the bride and groom themselves are kept away from the actual festivities, underscoring both the extent to which marriages are about the wider family, and the extent to which sexuality hangs in the air, requiring that the couple exhibit reserve, if not shame. While the groom was off somewhere with his friends, the bride sat in a back room of the house, being washed, henna-ed, and perfumed by her age-mates. She was dressed in a new ḥawli that the groom had sent her – henceforth her husband would take over her upkeep from her father. Asseghiyera remained completely passive and silent throughout; after all, to show excitement would, again, have been tantamount to expressing desire to have sex, and might perhaps have mocked the seriousness of this occasion whose significance went so far beyond changes in her own life circumstances. It was strange to see

Asseghiyera, usually so lively and so modern seeming, with such an expression of deadly seriousness on her face, and acting so helplessly as her cousins did everything for her. As van Gennep (1960) described of rites of passage generally, the bride retreats to a childlike dependence: she is not herself, but in a liminal stage of betwixt and between before she gradually takes on her new status of wife.

Even from within the mud-walled house, the deep beat of the drum resounded as the women pounded out intricate rhythms that surged forward and broke; a complex, lulling pattern that seemed to me to encapsulate the game of marital and sexual indulgence and restraint that the new bride would soon enter into. Above the drumming, women sang songs, of the Prophet or events of the Arab past, in an intense, almost mournful tone, one woman singing verses while others joined in the refrains, again creating a back and forth of isolated emotion and then a surge of communal energy.

Once Asseghiyera had been prepared, her body made new, fresh, and fragrant as on no other day in her life, she was carried to a separate place where the groom awaited her. She still conveyed utter indifference, almost as if she were in a trance. In the past she would have been heaved onto a camel to travel to a special tent erected for just this moment, but now in the town she walked, dragged and supported by her age-mates, to a small empty house nearby that was not being used. As she was led out into the sandy lane, excitement mounted with shrieks and yelps from the crowds of young women who accompanied her and the children who flocked around. Much to my surprise, otherwise demure young women began snorting and jumping on one another in not so subtle allusions to goats having sex.[22] At the separate residence, the *marwa*, where the bride and groom would sleep together for several nights in a row, Asseghiyera was finally pushed struggling through the door, thrown together finally with her new husband. In contrast to the solemn formality of the signing of the contract, and the deep emotionality of the drumming and singing, now a carnival atmosphere seemed to prevail. The celebrations were moving into phase two, where the matter at hand was consummation of the marriage.

Before the new couple could consummate their marriage, however, a number of further obstacles were created by their age-mates. First of all, the *marwa* was full of young men and now young women, who began avidly chatting, playing cards, and listening to taped music, while the groom remained quiet and restrained and the bride lay silent and veiled. This continued most of the night, leaving the newlyweds only a few hours toward dawn in which the groom may or may not have "gotten on top of" his new bride.

Whether or not the groom and bride had yet had sex, the wedding proper was still by no means over. The next day, as the couple still lay silently in the *marwa*, and as the rowdy guests returned, somewhat refreshed from sleep, the bride's age-mates searched for a way to "steal" her, a common custom. The young women succeeded finally in stealing her and hiding her for over twenty-four hours, during which time the young men searched valiantly from house to house. In the end an all-out battle of the sexes broke out. The men ended up paying the equivalent of about 50 dollars for Asseghiyera's return, but managed to throw pails of muddy water all over the young women along the way.

As this charade suggests, weddings are the time not only when a man and a woman forge a bond with one another, but also when the tensions and opposition between men and women explode. The bride's own reluctance to leave her natal family is acted out by the collectivity of her female age-mates; the groom's desire to possess the new bride is acted out by his age-mates, who "hunt down" the stolen bride and ultimately make clear their dominance.

When, finally, the bride and groom are allowed to consummate their marriage, people explained to me that the bride continues to act entirely passive while the man "talks to her gently" before "getting on top of her," as one woman put it. While men should not force young women to have sex, men and women told me that some men were gentle and slowly came inside their young brides just a little each night, while others forced themselves upon them. There is no displaying of a bloody sheet as in some other parts of the Arab world, though people had heard of this custom.

Asseghiyera's uncle, a man full of melancholic but good-humored irony whom I also knew from Peace Corps days, talked to me about his own marriage and marriage in general on a long trip we took to a distant missionary hospital. He had sex with his wife even before she had her first period, he admitted. "If a girl is small and thin, her husband waits for her to get her period to touch her. But if she is fat, he can touch her before that." "Didn't Allou [his wife] cry?" I asked. "Yes, sure," he said with a smile, "but it has to be that way. Afterwards she gets used to it. You have to force her in the beginning, no matter what."

Although young brides must demonstrate passivity, they are fully aware of what the wedding night promises and occasionally make their feelings apparent, embarrassingly so for their family. Boukia's daughter Tetou, as I mentioned, was married off when she was only twelve years old to a rich and rather sleazy Algerian for a huge sum of money – a sure sign of her family's poverty and low social standing, and fear that no cousin would step forward for her hand. Tetou, however, was not one to be pushed into a marriage against her own choosing. She first ran off on the night of her wedding, and later locked herself in the house where she and her new husband were to spend the night. Although people knocked on the doors and windows all night, Tetou claimed to me later, she spent the whole night inside alone without letting anyone in.

Later when the Algerian took her off to the capital and set her up in a big house where he would leave her for long days, she ran away several more times and, she also claimed, resisted all sexual advances on his part. After about four months he granted her a divorce. Boukia and her family maintained that another family, who wanted the man to marry their own daughter, had bewitched Tetou to make her act that way. Tetou herself was rather proud of her behavior, it seemed, and I secretly suspected that Boukia did not mind too much either. They got to keep the large bride-price, and since the man was not a relative, no family rifts were created. For her part, Tetou was now a desirable *hajāle* (divorceé), who once laughingly told me that there was no man in Egawan (her encampment) who had not tried to court her in the secret nightly visits that are the "dating" custom among adolescents. (These visits, as far as I could determine, do not involve sexual intercourse, but involve much fondling, mostly of the girl by the boy/man, and may even involve "thigh sex," where the man brings himself to climax between the girl's thighs.)

The last stage of the marriage, the "separation," marks the separation of the bride from her natal family. Note that what the term signifies is the breaking of the blood relationship between daughter and mother, not the forming of the new marital relationship. The separation, *'azūl*, is almost always traumatic for the bride, and something she tries to put off. When she does move in with her new husband, it is almost invariably to the home of his parents, where the couple are allotted their own special tent or house, a *ṣiniḥ*, to sleep in for the first several years. The existence of this special tent or house seems to indicate the importance of not just reproduction but sexual activity, since this otherwise takes place while children are sleeping, and rarely in a completely separate space. The newlyweds may start sleeping together in a *ṣiniḥ* even before the "separation."

After three days of festivities with music and general merriment, Assegheriya returned to her parents' home, and her new husband left town for a time. Only on his return, some months later, did the couple begin spending nights together in yet another house converted to just this purpose, their *ṣiniḥ*. Asseghiyera was extremely lucky not to be taken from her mother and her relatives in Tchin Tabaraden to the far-off village where her new husband's parents lived. Instead, Asseghiyera trekked over from her father's house every night to the appointed nearby house where she and her husband slept together for several years, even after she had borne their first child. There was nothing there but a bed; Asseghiyera ate with her family and the husband with his relatives. Although the marriage was official after the signing of the contract, there are degrees of marriedness, and Asseghiyera and her husband would only become a truly established couple when they either moved in with his family, or established their own permanent household and had the children to populate it.

Even if a new bride is already living in her husband's household when she becomes pregnant for the first time, she will return to wherever her mother (or grandmother) lives to give birth, and will try to stay as long as possible. The "separation" is a very hard time for girls, who see no advantage in moving away from a mother to a husband who will often be absent and to a potentially demanding and judgmental mother-in-law who will be their most constant company.

Fattening and marriage

Some of the connections between fattening and marriage have begun to appear in the above account of marriage and weddings among Azawagh Arabs. Indeed, one of the few explicit answers people gave to the question of why they fattened girls had to do with marriage: because fattening made a girl grow up faster, and therefore able to be married all the sooner.

Since families' honor and power lie in their ability to create many offspring, it makes sense that girls should be encouraged to start reproducing as soon as possible. Biology proves what Azawagh Arabs intuitively realize: that fat on a girl's body correlates with the onset of puberty and the start of ovulation (Frisch *et al.* 1973). Azawagh Arabs believe that it actually hastens the start of menarche, as well as the emergence of secondary sexual characteristics like breasts and pubic hair. Thus fattening expedites girls' ultimate purpose in life, enabling them to fulfill their destiny as soon as possible.

But fattening is only partially about hastening reproductive ability. It is just as significantly about hastening sexual attractiveness. As Asseghiyera's uncle pointed out, a man will not have sex with a young bride if she is thin, but a fat one has the womanly allure that will draw him to her. If a girl's marriage has been arranged when she is still a small child, as is often the case, then the family has good reason to want to make her attractive to her husband-to-be, as well as to hasten the date when she can be given over to her promised spouse. If a girl does not have an arranged marriage, then the family is equally or more interested in making her as nubile and voluptuous as possible, in order to draw potential mates.

The nature of husband–wife relationships and the sequence of marriage rites illustrate how the inherent opposition between men and women is both that which heightens sexual attraction and that which makes marriages tension-laden. For females, to differentiate their bodies from men's as much as possible is to emphasize their physical contrast to hard, upright, mobile male bodies. In this act, they simultaneously draw men to their own soft, fleshy, seated immobility, and establish themselves in their own right – not as pseudo-men, but as Women. Since sleeping with a thin woman was like sleeping on a board, how uncomfortable and pointless that would be! It would be like a man sleeping with a man. Or, as Zheyra once noted of the idea of two women sleeping together, it would be like two spoons nestled in one another. How would that work? Sameness is useless; it is difference between men and women that Allah intended and that creates both the spark and the biological conditions for pleasure and fulfillment. By fattening, girls and women abet God's plan on several levels.

Even though Azawagh Arabs express a preference for marrying close cousins, both men and women occasionally told me that they did not like to marry someone they had known through childhood. The practice of fattening speaks to this dilemma of spouses who are "too close" in two ways. First, when girls fatten they are effectively separated from future spouses as they stay inside the tent and are expected to be quiet and reserved. Second, by conforming to their society's aesthetic and erotic ideal they enhance the chances that their husband will be attracted to them. Thus in women's maximal differentiation of their bodies from men's and their simultaneous withdrawal from public male space, women provide a distancing counterweight to the intense closeness of kinship that is most desired in a marriage, but unappealing sexually and emotionally to the couple.

The non-negotiability of blood relationships creates both great security and warmth in daily life, and a potential for tremendous stress and constraining insularity. Weaving one's way between these extremes – for women, making a marriage with a man they like, for example, as well as managing to stay close to their own female relatives – is a pivotal challenge people face in life.

Plate 6 Aichata, Selama (an artisan), and Khira (a *ḥaraṭaniyya*) at Aichata's tent
(Tassara)

5

"THE MEN BRING US WHAT WE WILL EAT"

Herding, trade, and slavery

Boys' work is head work; girls' work is stomach work.
-Casual statement by an Azawagh Arab woman in
Tchin Tabaraden complaining that children at
school, including girls, were made to carry sand on
their heads as part of a construction project

In chapters 3 and 4 I discussed two pivotal contexts of meaning and sustenance for Azawagh Arabs: their connections to Allah, and their connections
to kin. Azawagh Arabs are also, of course, connected to the material world
on which their physical survival depends. From a land of searing heat, vast
distances, and little vegetation, they wrest their livelihood with considerable tenacity and even ambition. They have managed to convert the
hardships of this environment into a means of capital accumulation not
only by following careful herding strategies but by occupying an economic
niche few others in the area seem interested in: long-distance trade. In this
chapter I want to explore these subsistence strategies, and ultimately the
relationship of these economic practices to constructions of gender and
female fattening. In doing so I want to confront one of the "commonsense"
explanations for fattening that Westerners readily invoke: that a woman's
fatness is a sign of men's wealth.[1] To read fatness as a crude "sign of
wealth," I will argue, is to misunderstand both Azawagh Arabs' own
conscious readings of the fattened female form and the social symbolism
tacitly embedded in that form, even if, as I will discuss here, there is a vital
connection between the Moor predilection for female fatness and the
material realities of Moor life.

Material value and aesthetic values

To express the subject of this chapter another way, I want to attempt to
reconcile two seemingly opposed truths about fattening and Moor life in
general: (1) the beauty and allure of the fattened female form are read

111

almost entirely in aesthetic and sexual terms by Azawagh Arabs themselves; and yet (2) the aesthetic is necessarily grounded in the material realities of Moor subsistence. The line of reasoning that I will develop can also be applied to the West, where rich women tend to be thinner and richer men to have thinner wives on average, but where no "native" would claim that thinness is a sign of wealth. Neither would any Westerner perceive going on a diet as an attempt to show off her own or her husband's wealth. Yet just as a preference for plumpness tends to occur in societies that experience scarcity, so the ideal of a slim body has been mostly confined to societies with overabundance (Powdermaker 1997). There is a general correlation, thus, between economic circumstances and bodily ideals, but it is reductionist and misleading to explain the latter as a mere result of the former. After all, many societies experience scarcity more acutely than Azawagh Arabs do, but have not developed an ideal of female bodily obesity. And there is also the complication that Azawagh Arabs themselves do not necessarily perceive themselves as living in a land of such scarcity, for it is the only world they have ever known.

This argument will be spelled out in more detail in the exposition of Moor subsistence and economic logic that follows. I will begin by describing the ultimate "good" that Arabs seek to accumulate, honor and prestige, as well as by noting their economic position vis-à-vis other peoples in the area. I will then describe the socioeconomic hierarchy on which Arab honor largely rests – the caste system which is also the context of all labor and economic activity in Moor society. The largest caste comprises the former slaves, who still perform much of the hard labor in Nigerien Moor communities. Without a tripartite division of labor in which former slaves are depended upon for all household and much herding labor, "white" men would not be free to engage in trade, and "white" women would not be free to devote themselves to their own corporeal pursuits. Before turning to Arab men's work, I will discuss briefly the role of Arab women in this economy, and the kind of cultural work that they perform. As the offhand comment at the beginning of this chapter suggests, the only "work" Arab women are expected to perform is a kind of pseudo-work – "stomach work."

Having laid out this groundwork, I will turn to the two-pronged economic strategy of Nigerien Moors – herding and trade – and discuss what the telos of these economic practices seems to be: neither subsistence nor the production of surplus value *per se* (as a Marxian interpretation would argue), nor the reproduction of men as a precondition for successful production (Meillassoux 1972), but the accrual of (1) honor and prestige, measured in sons, worldly success, and other-worldly devotion, and (2) earthly comfort and pleasure, attainable at least in part through sexual satisfaction.

I will conclude with a discussion of how the flow of milk, indigenous notions of value, and women's bodies work together to constitute a type of "consumptive production" (Gregory 1982). That is, by the very act of consuming, Arab women produce something valuable, even if it is not in the tangible form of milk and grain that men's work produces. Men's production alone does not fully encompass the culturally embedded economic system of Azawagh Arabs, because ultimately it is in women's fattened bodies that the honor, prestige, and earthly pleasures of Azawagh Arab society are guaranteed.

Honor and pride

The outside observer must not be misled by the Moors' lack of material possessions or the general bleakness of the dry desert scrub that they call home. Azawagh Arabs have a general sense of themselves as reasonably well off (though never quite well enough off), and they certainly consider themselves to be of a higher station than all neighboring peoples. When toward the end of my fieldwork I once asked a group of assembled men from the chiefly family what they would like me to write about their society, they mentioned, after Islam and family, that Arabs don't like to be lower than anyone else. They said this of themselves in neither a boastful nor a defensive tone, but as if they were stating some valueless fact about some other people, as if this were merely a fact of nature. To be free, *hurra*, was a matter of great pride, encompassing the concepts of superiority and purity in addition to freedom from any earthly master or overlord.[2]

The French found the Arabs of the Azawagh to be "independent" and "difficult to control" (Thiellement 1935; Untitled document 1944), and their neighbors, I think it is safe to say, frequently find them haughty. Azawagh Arab elitism grows out of their claimed Islamic heritage but also out of the caste system of Moor society, in which "noble" "white" Arabs stand at the top of a set of essentially racial categorizations of human beings. In the presence of this immutable hierarchy of an ingrained caste system, wealth differences *among* Arabs are downplayed. Though some in Tassara wear finer cloth and eat meat more often, the gradations in affluence are minimal to an outside observer. Wealth measured in material possessions – fine robes or a bigger house – matters, but wealth in people and in prestige matters more (and indeed is often essential to achieving the former kind of wealth). The man who is well off is the father of many sons, and the son himself of a great man. Women, too, achieve status by the men from whom they come and the men to whom they give birth. Thus, once again, to interpret women's fattened bodies as "a sign of wealth" is to imply a Western concept of wealth akin to "money in the bank" that does not exist in Nigerien Moor society. To the extent that women's bodies do connote affluence and well-being, it is an affluence of people and of honor. The early marriage of girls and the hope for many sons reflect not so much a need for reproduction as a precondition for production, a desire for men in their own right. The value and honor of "free" men, and the way in which this value is made, must be understood against the social grid of Moor society – their caste system.

Caste in Moor society: slaves, freed slaves, artisans, and Arabs

The caste system as a whole, including not just "whites" and former slaves but also artisans and musicians, forms the scaffolding on which "noble" Azawagh Arab pretensions to honor and prestige rest. While the castes are not considered to be divinely ordained and do not have the explicitly polluting potential that castes in India do,[3] members of the Moor castes are considered to be fundamentally different sorts of people, and inter-marriage is strongly discouraged. Although the caste system is not dictated by Islamic texts, Moor folk beliefs find the roots of the system in tales of early Islam. The slaves are said to be descended from Muhammad the Prophet's faithful slave, Bilal, while the artisans are said to be descended from those who refused to accept Allah.[4]

The former slaves of the Arabs, known in Mauritania and sometimes in Niger as *ḥaraṭīn*, are as numerous as their former masters. There are two other castes in Moor society: artisans and musicians. Niger has only a handful of members of the musician caste, *iggāwen*, none of whom live regularly in Tassara. The *iggāwen* play traditional instruments, sing and compose songs, and safeguard the oral history of Moor society. The arti-sans (*m'allemīn*) are more numerous, and there are several families of them in Tassara. Also known as blacksmiths in the Western literature, the artisan caste exists in a number of West African societies and has traditionally been responsible for metalwork, leatherwork, and the fabrication of numerous everyday items. Members of the Moor artisan caste in Niger tend to be relatively well educated and well off. With their traditional training in crafts, they have skills that have remained in demand through changing economic circumstances. Odd as it may seem to the outsider, however, the artisans are considered the lowest of all castes, despite their apparent prosperity, because of their ignominious ancestry. "If an Arab woman were alone on earth and there was no Arab man for her to marry," I was once told, "better she marry a slave than an artisan."

The existence of artisans and *ḥaraṭīn* effectively frees Arab men from engaging in certain types of physical work, and forces them to focus their energies on herd management and trade. In particular, "white" Arab men have no part in working with the earth and raw materials – the making of bricks, the tanning of skins, the forging of metals, the working of leather. Instead, Arab male "work" centers not on the creation of value through

114

production of goods or services, but on overseeing the reproduction of animals, and by accruing value to goods by transporting them over long distances. Before I discuss these logics of male subsistence, however, I must discuss slavery in more depth.

Slavery

Moors have been a slave-owning society for centuries, and according to many human rights groups slavery is still widespread in Mauritania today. Slavery was formerly widespread among all peoples in Niger, "black" and "white," but in Niger, as in Mauritania, slavery has been officially abolished on several occasions, first during French rule and then by the newly independent Nigerien government. Archival records in Niger show that while slave raiding was successfully stopped by the French in the first decades of the twentieth century, the trading and selling of slaves still continued surreptitiously among Azawagh Arabs into the 1930s (Brachet 1938a). Sidi al-Mokhtar, the *qāḍi*, said that the Arabs' slaves had been "bought, stolen, or sold by Tuaregs who were hungry; they also were given to a Koranic specialist in exchange for the writing of an amulet. The Blacks (*as-Sūdān*) also sold them." When he was young (he was born in 1908 according to Nicolas 1950: 74), however, there was only a little selling of slaves because the French didn't allow it.

There was one *haraṭaniyya* in Tassara who remembered being captured as young child. In her eighties by my calculations, Tekelentet was the oldest person in Tassara except for, ironically, the *qāḍi*. It seemed gently amusing to both of them that the other was their only surviving age-mate. They were, of course, at opposite ends of the social spectrum, he one of the most revered men in the Azawagh, she a withered, nearly blind, and toothless old slave. As a sign of how things were changing, however, Tekelentet's daughter Shanay was one of the most prominent *haraṭīn* women in town, respected for her skills as a midwife and appreciated for her barbed sense of humor.

I met Tekelentet by accident one day, when I had gone to look for the voluble Shanay. Instead of finding Shanay I found her mother in a little shrunken heap in the dark hut. I described her thus in my fieldnotes: "She is all wrinkles – it's as if her body has receded and receded until it is almost gone and there is only her spirit left." She punctuated all her talk with praises to God that she was still alive, and periodically inquired "where that slave has gone," referring to her daughter Shanay.

Tekelentet came to the Arabs when she was very small. Her hair, she said, had been in the style small children used to wear. "It was the time of Hama and Iyada, those first people; the fathers of Ibrahim who 'left' [was the father of] Dᶜī and Alᶜalia and those people." She did not know if she

115

had been bought or not. But she remembered playing with some children one day when a man came and took her hand and they left. They were somewhere to the west at that time. Later, she explained,

> when I "woke up" here [i.e. was old enough to have sense], some Iwillimedden [Tuaregs] came and stayed with us. Moul'id, Boudari's mother [another slave], and I went to take them their porridge and I asked them, "have you seen my parents?" But they said no, they didn't know them.

Despite this tragic tale, Tekelentet looked on the past with great nostalgia as almost all Azawagh Arabs did. She elaborated at length about how good the people were then: "They were good, and their land was good and what they possessed was good, and their slaves and their artisans." Now, she said, "there is only refuse left of that world."

Although slavery technically does not exist any longer even in the most remote corners of Niger, a master–serf relationship still survives between many Arab "masters" and their former slaves. For example, while all laborers and servants now receive a wage for their work, the former slaves continue to work for the families that once owned them, receiving relatively little compensation, and more in kind than in cash. Arabs will only perform certain types of work if no *haratin* are around: pounding, cleaning pots, drawing water. If a *harataniyya* (female) so much as walks into a compound where Arab women are seated, she is often asked to do some little task, and, amazingly, she usually does it without showing much resentment. In the case of a naming ceremony, marriage, or death, former slaves tend to show up at the homes of their old masters to cook and participate and receive payment in kind, and at Muslim holidays former masters generally fulfill the expectation that they give gifts of sandals, clothing, or food to their former slaves.

One couple of the former slave caste even explained to me that when they married in around 1980, the man had paid bride-price not to his wife's father, but to her Arab master. They said, however, that even this practice had ceased in the intervening decade, though former masters still exerted considerable influence over whom their former slaves might marry. Women of the chiefly family in Tassara explained to me that if a slave marries without his or her master's consent, then the child of that union is like a bastard.

Even *haratin* who work regularly for Arabs do not live in the same compound, nor did they in the past. In the desert they often pitch their tents out of sight of the Arab tents, and in Tassara, the *haratin* all lived on the north side of town. They had their own small mosque, with their own muezzin to chant the call to prayer.

Although I regularly use the term *haratin*[5] in this work, to a Westerner's consternation the terms for "slave" were still in wide usage, both by "slaves" and by "free" Arabs. The old "slave" Tekelentet who recalled her own capture or sale into slavery as a child referred not only to her own daughter as "that slave," but once demanded of me, "Where is that *khādem* [female slave]? She never comes to see me any more," speaking of her niece who carried water for me. "I was out in the desert," a *haratāni* might say, "and ran into that *'abid* [male slave]," referring to a friend or relative. Sometimes I would ask *haratin*, "Why do you call yourselves 'slaves'? You aren't slaves any more!" They would commonly answer: "Oh, yes, you are right. But, oh well, we are still *'abīd* [pl.]." This indicates that the term *'abīd* has connotations going far beyond ownership of one's person. It is also a status, class, or ethnic term, telling something about one's background and one's position in society. It was only outside of the Azawagh Arab world, for example in the capital of Niger, that all who spoke Arabic would be called simply "Arabs." Otherwise the term was reserved for the highest caste, and caste or skin-color terms were used for others.

To be fair, the terms *'abid* and *khādem* have somewhat different connotations from their most common English counterpart, "slave." In addition to referring to an indentured worker of sorts, the Arabic terms represent a relationship to the Almighty, a term of endearment, and a designation almost akin to an ethnic label. First, the term *'abid* can be used of any human being in reference to his or her relationship to God; as the Koranic phrase goes, we are all "slaves of Allah." Since Allah bore no children, enslavement is the most common way of expressing humankind's relationship to Allah. (I once got myself in a tight spot by commenting that we were all "sons of Allah," a sacrilegious and infidel way to express humankind's oneness under God.) Second, the terms for "slave" are also used daily by women, especially Arab women, to refer to their own children and other young relatives. "Come here, *khādmi* [my slave]," a woman might call to her daughter, or "*Ya 'abeydi* [my little slave], stay away from there," she might admonish a mischievous nephew. Third, all "black" Arabs are referred to as *'abīd*, even when they live entirely independently of any former "white" masters, suggesting almost ethnic status.

The use of *haratin* was reserved for those former slaves who had been explicitly freed by Arabs themselves, not the government, such as Boudari the horse-trainer. Even when slavery was widespread, there were always *haratin*, former slaves who had been freed by their masters. "It is good before God if people free their slaves; that's why people do it," one woman explained to me. "It is like going on the pilgrimage to Mecca. You give the slave a cow or a camel [so he can support himself] and free him."

I put the terms "black" and "white" in quotation marks because, although they are another set of terms used to distinguish former slaves from former masters, they do not always describe the physical reality of actual skin color. Although Arabs are often lighter skinned than *haratin*, there are numerous "white" Arabs who are quite dark skinned, and "black" Arabs who are lighter than most "white" Arabs (see Plate 6, page 110). Light skin color is a sign of status for former slaves, and many "white" Arabs bemoaned the fact that their skin was "becoming" dark – it is because of illness, they would explain, or bad food, or lack of milk. People would describe the color of darker skinned "whites" as "green," rather than black.[6]

Haratin are distinguishable from Arabs to some extent by skin color, but also by dress: female *haratin* tend to wear black *hawlis*, in contrast to the white, indigo, or tie-dyed ones worn by Arab women, although this is changing as *haratin* move ever further from their former slave status and the practices of dress and adornment that accompanied it. *Haratin*, especially those who have gone to school or traveled at all, also dress more and more frequently in the batik cloth of the sub-Saharan West Africans.

Although Azawagh Arabs did sell and buy slaves in the past, and in many ways treated them as property, Moor slavery was less commodified and arguably less cruel than slavery in the Americas; slaves constituted "quasi-relatives" and the sense of mutual obligation between masters and slaves was greater than in the new world (Miers and Kopytoff 1977). Slaves were more like serfs in medieval Europe, owing allegiance to a particular family who in turn took responsibility for their well-being. In this way, the practice of slavery among the Azawagh Arabs was much closer to that of sub-Saharan African societies than to that of the New World. Where slavery among Moors was distinct from that among their neighbors to the south, however, was in the racialized character of slave status.

All Arabs who could afford it (and it often seemed to me that Arab women would give up almost anything to afford it) paid a *harataniyya* to cook, clean, and bring water to the household. In many of the households in Tassara, the *harataniyya* who was hired had some past connection to the family; for example, she was the daughter of a slave the family had owned in the past. There was a very high turnover, however, and many *haratin* were resentful of the small pay they received from their erstwhile masters. Only the wealthier Arab families, therefore, had regular servants – usually one or two women who spent much of the day in their compound. The only other option for employment in Tassara was to work for Hausa civil servants (the teachers, nurse, or policemen) or at the army base, but these jobs could not accommodate all the *haratin* women who wanted work in the village. Some *haratin* women whose husbands made enough money through their own herding, trade, or labor did not have to work outside their homes, but the majority of them worked at least on and off for other households in the community.

Like their womenfolk, *haratin* men are in a state of transition. Some work as herders for Arabs, or work around Arab compounds on such tasks as milking, taking care of animals, fetching water, and masonry. Some ḥaraṭīn men, however, have their own herds, small trading businesses, and stores, and like Arab men are frequently away from town attending to their economic activities.

Although there was clearly resentment on the part of ḥaraṭīn toward their former masters, on the surface at least relations between the two groups were generally good – they joked together, held each other's children, and hung out and chatted with one another when work did not call. And, as I said above, ḥaraṭīn would begrudgingly perform random tasks for Arabs if asked, just as Arabs would continue, however reluctantly, to give periodic gifts to ḥaraṭīn, each group pulled by past habits, or perhaps guarding against a rainy day when old allegiances and obligations might come in handy.

Opinions in Tassara about the state of slavery were varied, and, not surprisingly, it was Arab women of the chiefly family who were most bereft at its decline, since this entailed a necessary decline in their own freedom from work as well. Arab women still spoke of ḥaraṭīn who had previously belonged to their family as "our slaves," and seemed to consider it a slight to their very persons that these ḥaraṭīn did not continue to work willingly for them. When I expressed surprise at how well a group of women from the chiefly family seemed to know both Minnou and her family, one of the women said, "Yes, of course, she is ours; they are our slaves; her father and his fathers belonged to Khamayed's father [the chief's brother and husband to the chief's daughter]." I asked whether they had not been freed, and some discussion ensued, after which the women concluded that perhaps Minnou herself had been freed (i.e. by the Arab master, not national law), but that none of the others in her family had been. When later I drove Minnou out to the bush to visit her family, the chief's daughter and her kinswomen laughed at me for actually "working," in some sense, for someone of the slave caste.

Those of the former slave caste generally looked back on the era of slavery with less nostalgia. It was not easy for me, a white woman, to know what the former slaves thought, for with my white skin I was closer in identity to the "white" Arabs, however much of an outsider I was to both communities, and however much I shunned the hierarchical distinctions Arabs made. Some "black" women I spoke with, however, clearly resented the continued Arab expectations of them. One former slave woman emphasized to me that even twenty years ago her family were ḥaraṭīn, freed slaves, and that the woman her daughter worked for *paid* her; her daughter was not a slave.

Just as colonization and Nigerien independence opened up new opportunities for members of the artisan caste, these eras have also vastly expanded the opportunities for former slaves. When the French came to the area in the 1950s, and demanded that the Arabs put their boys in school, the Arabs sent their children to the bush to hide and sent their slaves' children instead. This pattern repeated itself across the Sahara, and has led to a generation of educated former slaves, while the Arabs belatedly try to "catch up." Indeed, the most educated children of Tassara were former slaves: one woman at university and one man who teaches at the *lycée* (high school) in Tahoua, the nearest large town. Ann McDougall (1988) has pointed out that the introduction of wage labor and monetization by the French in Mauritania benefited *haraṭīn* more than slaves, because the *haraṭīn* had a developed wage-labor work ethic already; they were used to working for incentives. In Niger, where there was never a large class of *haraṭīn*, I would suggest that changes in the economy often worked to the benefit of both *haraṭīn* and slaves.

Arab men realized fairly quickly that government schooling was increasingly necessary for success, and have adapted themselves to the changing scene. Arab women, however, find the erosion of slavery to be a more serious affront to their status. For the life of fattened, immobile leisure that is the ideal of female existence is entirely dependent on the presence of a forced worker caste. The following excerpt from a poem written down by Harry Norris in the 1950s or 1960s in Mauritania expresses the angst that the disruption of the caste system caused many Arabs:

> While the meager tributary is fat and filled, and the *hartani*
> [*sic*] – have no doubt – is proud and groomed
> The slave is owner of two flowing shifts, while the slave girl
> keeps her weight through drinking milk
> He who is learned in the faith has since forsaken it. Thus it
> remains, confused and in tumult
> This world is topsy-turvy, but the world to come is sure.
> Norris 1968, quoted in McDougall 1988

In fact, *haraṭīn* women often protested to me that they could fatten if they wanted to, and they certainly shared the Arab aesthetic for fatness. There was, however, only one *haraṭaniyya* in Tassara who could be considered of respectable Arab proportions, the wife of a man who was the son of an Arab father and slave caste mother. (Although such marriages did occur, I only knew of two in Tassara, and they were both looked down upon by the Arab community.) Minnou, however, frequently complained to me of the wasting disease she had suffered for many years now (brought on by witchcraft), and told me of the days when she had had a large behind and even the Arab men found her very attractive.

As Thorstein Veblen (1994) noted of late nineteenth-century Western society, the existence of a servant class enables a life of "conspicuous leisure" by those at the top, and particularly by women at the top, who are generally the first to be exempted from labor. Thus the existence of slaves in the past, and a still largely "captive" *haraṭīn* caste today, enables both the focus on capital accumulation by Arab men, and on capital consumption, if you will, by Arab women.

A license to leisure: women's "work"

When I asked the old *qāḍi* what people did in the past, when he was growing up, he described it like this: "Men herded, watered their animals, and traveled – they traveled to villages to get millet, clothes, and tea. Slaves herded." Since he had conspicuously left Arab women unmentioned, I asked, "And Arab women?" "They sat and they drank," was his curt reply.

The major tasks of everyday life can be categorized according to a tri-partite division of labor: Arab men trade and oversee herding, former slaves carry out the everyday tasks of herding and tent life, and Arab women are the beneficiaries of these efforts. They did not need to be mentioned in the *qāḍi*'s account of what people did in the past because their role, in a sense, was not to do, not to work.[7] Or rather their "work" is a kind of consumption rather than production, and a "task" whose ultimate product is not material wherewithal but the enhancement and expression of value by the "investment" of material goods in their own bodies, where it becomes transformed into the stuff of proper Arab honor and potential increase.

While the practice of slavery allowed Arab men to avoid certain kinds of labor and to bolster their sense of themselves as elite and powerful, it was in some ways even more important for Arab women, as I have noted, for it was virtually a precondition for the role they occupied in Moor society. Thus when I asked women why they were fattening less today than in the past, they invariably gave one answer: "All our slaves have left; how can we fatten?" As this reasoning reveals, fattening is both a sign of and a justification for abstaining from labor – a license to leisure. Fattening is both women's "work," and the sign of their freedom from work. Relying completely on the labor of others, Azawagh Arab women were able to devote themselves wholly to "eating and sitting," as they put it. As the unknown poet above laments, a world turned "topsy-turvy" is one in which slaves not only own nice clothes, but in which slave girls are fattening – a complete usurpation of Arab women's place in society, a complete disrup-tion of the order on which their prestige depends.

Azawagh Arab women spoke nostalgically of the time when a slave brought over their bowl of milk, they drank it, and then lay down, raising themselves only to pray. There was only one exception to this life of ease, and that was the making of tents, a task that requires relatively little move-ment and little exertion. It is perhaps logical that this one contribution Arab women made to the work of the camp involved investing in their own protection and vaunted place at the center of society.

The one time I heard a reference made to women's work – the quotation at the opening of this chapter – the context was ironic and involved a play on words. An aunt of Boukia's tried to convince me that girls need not attend school, and finally, exasperated with my incomprehension, concluded: "Boys' work is head work; girls' work is stomach work." Since we had just been discussing the fact that students at the elementary school had been asked to help with a construction project by carrying loads of sand on their head from one place to another, the "head work" referred to seemed to mean this labor, not "brain" work. Although this was her own invented metaphor of the moment and not a phrase I ever heard again, it captures well the centrality of fattening in girls' and women's lives. Girls' "work" in life – in reality a kind of anti-work – was to get fat.

Fattening was implied to be in opposition to "work" in two other contexts as well. Ketti, the female Koranic teacher in Tchin Tabaraden, told me she had never fattened because she had studied the Koran instead. The slight mobility required for going to study the Koran was considered incompatible with the complete refusal of all movement and work necessary for fattening. Ketti's son Daha, a young teenager at the time of my fieldwork, noted an antithesis between working and fattening in another context as well. After puzzling for some time over my curious (and always doubted) assertion that women in the United States wanted to be thin, he came up with a possible interpretation: "In America women move around a lot so they can't get fat, always going to another city, like you," he suggested. "Here, Arab women have no work but to eat."

Arab women's roles were commonly contrasted with the labor that slaves and *haratīn* performed, but also with the work that men do. As one well-placed Arab woman explained to me:

> It is not good for a man to make a woman work; *men* are the ones who work to provide food, clothes, and so on for the *women*. This is why Hassan [an Arab man who had been married to several women in rather rapid succession] married a *Sūdaniyya* [a Black; a Hausa woman] – he can tell her to cook or do some task, and he can't say this to an Arab wife.

In this defiant statement one senses the pride of Arab women, but also perhaps hints of a rising fear that, with the disappearance of slavery, Arab women too will be forced into labor, or else lose their menfolk to more obliging brides.

Even as Arab women's freedom from work becomes less and less guaranteed, however, or perhaps because of this, fattening continues to be a desirable symbol of female status for women themselves. While as children girls perceive the practice as cumbersome and often express resistance to it, with time women come to see what was at first constraining as liberating and empowering. The burden of having to stuff oneself daily becomes freedom from even more burdensome work; while others pound, cook, and fetch water in the hot Saharan sun, Azawagh Arab women sit; while others produce and process, they consume. Given how little direct control Arab women exercise in their lives, the body also constitutes the one domain over which they do have limited control, and through which they can make their own sort of contribution to their families and society. Fattening is thus a sort of anti-work, but it is in a broader sense of the term women's main "work" in life: their active contribution to the production of value in the society by their own act of consumption. By controlling and literally embodying the flow of milk, the most valued food and product of the society, Azawagh Arab women express and safeguard their society's vision of itself, as well as its continuation and increase.

In order for women to fulfill their part in the cycle and transformation of value, however, they depend on their menfolk to "bring them what they will eat," as they say. Having discussed the contexts of the Moor caste system, slavery, and Arab women's role in the economy, it is to these male strategies of subsistence and capital accumulation that I now turn.

Subsisting in the Sahara: men's work

Nigerien Moor society depends heavily on livestock, but it hardly fits the image of an isolated, self-sufficient pastoralist society, as indeed few pastoralist societies do (Galaty and Bonte 1991; Khazanov 1994). Instead, the economic strategies of Azawagh Arabs are two-pronged: herding (as-serḥa) and trade (at-tijār). Furthermore, the nature of both of these activities has changed over the centuries, as migrations and environmental changes have altered herding patterns, and as the demands and opportunities of trade have constantly shifted.[8] What have remained constant, however, are two overriding logics: (1) the quick increase in value that "wealth in blood" – livestock – is capable of; and (2) the substantial increase in the value of all kinds of goods that can accrue when they are moved over long distances. While livestock have always been the dominant form of capital, a frequent item of trade, and a basis of subsistence, I suggest that raising livestock, while a *sine qua non* of Moor subsistence, can in many ways be subsumed under a more overarching strategy – the rapid accrual of value to objects, by animal reproduction and by the movement of goods, including animals, over long distances in order to create a profit.

Virtually all Azawagh Arab men own animals – goats, sheep, cows, and camels. Even the few local men who have left the Azawagh to settle in towns still own some animals in the desert. Especially since settling in towns, very few Azawagh Arab men actually look after their own animals, however; the actual work of herding and watering animals is left to younger brothers, poor cousins, hired Tuaregs, and *ḥaraṭīn*. Indeed, one of the nice things about camels, goats, and cattle is that they do not require constant watch – they can be left to wander on their own and will make their way to a well when they need water. Thus the work of herding consists mostly of herding sheep, and watering all animals, in addition to branding them, treating them for illnesses, castrating males, and other less frequent tasks.

Larger herds are divided up, so that different sorts of animals are herded in different places. Land is not owned but wells are, by tribe, so men tend to have their animals herded in areas where they have rights of priority at watering spots. (However, anyone, even a non-Arab, is allowed to water his animals at a "foreign" well; he simply does not have priority.) Just as people do not count children for fear of provoking the evil eye, people do not count animals, so it is difficult to estimate the average size of men's herds. The richest men in Tassara had scores of camels and cattle in addition to sheep and goats; the poorest had much smaller herds of sheep and goats only.

Livestock is the main type of wealth that is inherited, it used to be the sole means of paying bride-price, and it constitutes the most appropriate gift. Although the Koran dictates that women should inherit their parents' wealth as well as their brothers', even if only half a man's share, few women in Tassara owned much livestock beyond a few goats or sheep. In the past girls were sometimes given a milk cow to provide milk for their fattening. Livestock can also still take the place of cash in many business transactions. One young unmarried man I knew was able to purchase a Toyota pick-up truck because the man he bought it from, a fellow Arab, accepted half the payment in animals.

Although Azawagh Arab society has been a cash economy for decades, Azawagh Arabs are still partial to "wealth in blood" (*māl ad-demm*). As they pointed out to me, animals were like no other product in their profitability – by reproducing, they could double in value in a matter of one or two years.[9] No other commodity the Arabs trade – tea, sugar, dried milk, macaroni, cloth – has the capacity to accrue so much value so fast, no matter how far one transports it to sell. Cash was a convenient medium of exchange, but its value was paltry compared to its equivalent in animals.

While camels and cows are valued more highly than any other good in Azawagh Arab society, no hint of the famous "cattle complex" informs Moor culture. The Arabs of the Azawagh are in no way "put together as the bull is put together," as Godfrey Lienhardt noted of the cattle-herding Dinka (1961: 23). In fact, Azawagh Arabs look down upon those who invest too much sentiment in their animals. Driving with Moussaysa across the desert once, we passed some Wodaabe with their cattle. "Look at all those bulls," Moussaysa said with scorn. "Just one of them could probably get one hundred thousand francs [about 300 dollars], but the Fulani refuse to sell. They could sell a bull and do commerce, but they don't. They just keep all those cattle and follow them around."

When I suggested this was because they liked their cattle so much, he readily agreed. To Arabs, devotion to animals in this way was foolish. Cows, sheep, goats, and even camels are means to an end, not ends in themselves. A beautiful animal is appreciated as such, but the level of attachment the Wodaabe exhibited toward their cattle was considered almost tantamount to idolatry.[10]

Instead it was commerce that for Azawagh Arab men was as much a *modus vivendi* as a *modus operandi*.[11] When I asked a young man, Dahanna, about the difference between men who primarily herded and those who primarily traded, he said there was no difference really. Herders raise their animals to sell them; herding is merely a highly successful means of creating a marketable product, with the added benefit, of course, of creating meat and milk for local consumption.

French colonial accounts begin testifying to Azawagh Arab commercial acumen as early as 1907, only seven years after France laid claim to their territory. The following passage from the colonial archives also illustrates the ever-changing nature of trade in the Azawagh, despite its seeming remove from world market forces:

Rich and respected, [the Arabs are] among the most involved in commerce in the Azawagh. Their horses and their camels have a well-deserved reputation there. It is they who sell the ostrich feathers and the giraffe skins. They have relations with the Hoggar [in Algeria] and bring down into the Azawagh *gandoura*s [men's robes] and camel-hair blankets made in the Touat [also in Algeria].

(Peignol 1907)

As the passage notes, the Arabs had accommodated themselves to European market demands for exotic plumes and skins, until the ostriches retreated further north and the giraffes further south (and feather hats went out of style). The Touat region of central Algeria mentioned in the passage is an oasis region from which most Arabs in the Azawagh today emigrated between the sixteenth and eighteenth centuries. That Azawagh Arabs were still trading with the region, 750 miles across the Sahara, hundreds of years later, is a testimony to the perduring nature of the Azawagh Arab commitment to commerce. French officials continued to comment on Arab prosperity throughout the colonial era (Abadie 1927: 153; Untitled document 1933; Nicolas 1950: 69).

Since *haraṭīn* men, Tuareg clients, and less enterprising young sons do most of the actual work of herding and watering animals, adult Azawagh Arab men are able to devote their energies to the more "exalted" task of long-distance trade, managing their herds from a distance. At any given moment during my fieldwork, the majority of the men of Tassara were away – at the weekly market in Tchin Tabaraden selling or buying animals and goods; in Algeria on a black-market trade mission; in some Nigerien city trying to sell for a profit some commodity transported over long distances, or occasionally out in the bush checking on their herds. Only older or less successful men were more likely to be found in town, spending the long quiet days at the small shops many owned, as much to have a place to go when not trading as to engage in such "stationary" commerce. Since all the stores carried virtually the same items, there was little real profit to be made here.

The converse of this is that the more important the man, the less often he was seen in Tassara. Some heads of families in the town even had houses in Tchin Tabaraden or Tahoua, where they would stay for stretches of up to several months. Younger men who had not yet married or made their way in the world tended to flit in and out of town more irregularly, taking off quite suddenly when an opportunity arose, and showing up again with little sign of the purpose that had called them away. A few times a week pick-up trucks roared in and out of little Tassara carrying men to and from larger towns to the south and east. When men traveled to Algeria more planning seemed to be involved; the trip was long and potentially dangerous since it required "stealing" over the officially closed border. Every so often a man or a group of men would take livestock to sell in Algeria, trekking with the herds all the way, or trekking with them to a point further north from which a large rig would transport them the rest of the way.

Although men trade items from wheelbarrows to biscuits to gasoline to flashlights, the mainstay of the economy is selling cattle and other animals south to the Hausa and even to Nigeria and other West African nations, and north across the border to Algeria. The border to Algeria, especially now that trade across it has been banned, is one of the most lucrative sites of business. Niger welcomes the dried milk, sugar, tea, dates, macaroni, and other products obtainable across the border, and Algeria needs animals. Consequently, at least while I was in Tassara in the early 1990s, the most profit to be made in trade was from selling animals in the southern Algerian town of Tamanrasset.

Back in Tassara, *haratin* men and older Arab men oversaw the watering of animals every day at the large troughs on the southeast edge of town. Animals would wander in from the bush of their own accord, or be led by a hired herder, and their owners would make sure they drank, brand new animals with their family sign, and make decisions about castrating, breeding, and selling animals. This was a world, like that of the trading expedition, that was off limits to me, and it was only after many months in Tassara that I felt it appropriate to accompany one old man to the watering troughs one day to observe the branding of animals. So although all this activity went on only a stone's throw from where Tassara's women lived out their days, it was a world apart, and one whose rhythms I cannot describe with the same detail that I relate women's lives.

Men who are unable to turn a profit from their economic activities are gently ridiculed, often by being compared to women. One man, for example, complained to me about the worsening economy by saying that men have no work now, "they just sit around like women." When on my return to Niger in 1991 I asked my old neighbor Omar what Boukia's hapless husband's work was these days, he said with a laugh, "Leaving girls in the world"; that is, no work worth anything. Maidou's misfortune at producing no fewer than six girls and only one son with Boukia exposed him to such teasing, especially since he, uncharacteristically for an Azawagh Arab man, seemed unable to succeed at any business venture he attempted.

Women don't complain about their menfolk's endless absences because this is what is expected of men; they will bring goods from the outside world back to the "hearth," where women stand guard, and invest those goods in their womenfolk. When my American boyfriend was coming to visit me, women in Tassara asked me if he was *zeyn*, an all-purpose word meaning "good" and "attractive." I answered that his heart was *zeyn*. (Having a good heart has connotations of sense and intelligence in Galgaliyya.) The women nodded in approval: "Women don't care about whether a man's face is *zeyn*," they asserted. "They care only that the man has money and can work."

Over the past century camel herds have dwindled and goat herds have grown, and ostrich feathers and giraffe skins have given way to Italian tomato paste and Algerian dried milk, but what has remained constant is the overarching logic of Azawagh Arab subsistence: to extract value from the outside world by moving an object from one place to another. By being attuned to the world's wants and the world's wares, and by being willing to go where no one else will go, Azawagh Arab men have managed to support their hearth and home by a strategic interdependence with the "outside world" (Khazanov 1994). Part of what endures in this relationship is the separation Arabs maintain between the center of their world – tents, women, and children – and the non-Arab, non-family exterior. This outside world provides the markets and the commodities necessary for Arab men to support themselves by moving things from place to place, thereby accruing value to them. This allows Azawagh Arab men to continually funnel money from the exterior world into their own interior world. It is not surprising, perhaps, that when men accumulate surplus, what does not go towards feeding the family and fattening women they often spend on obtaining means of transport – camels and horses in the past, trucks today – before acquisition of stationary objects for the tent. Here again is the dichotomy between creating value via movement, and holding it stationary in women's bodies.

Investment of milk from cows in women

Although Moussaysa scoffed at the Fulani herder who could not bear to part with his cattle, the animals Azawagh Arabs herd are not in fact treated entirely as mere commodities. The processes of milking, mating, fattening, and slaughtering animals are in several ways a mirror image of the ideologies that govern human society. To illustrate this, I will relate a conversation I had with Moussaysa one day about herding and animals.

I had recently come to understand how camels, goats, and cows essentially herd themselves; that is, they are left on their own to wander off and seek pasture, without anyone to oversee them. When they need water, Moussaysa explained, they will need to come to a well, where their owner (or a kinsman or paid worker) will call them over. "The animals all have names, by a color or a defect," he explained. Intrigued, I pointed to a sheep that was tied up and asked what its name was. "Oh, that's a ram," Moussaysa responded. "He has no name. He has no milk."

In startling opposition to Arab human society, in the animal world it is the females who have names and the males who are nameless, merely useful for reproduction. The fact that female animals are more valuable in general for their capacity to reproduce also inverts the human order. Whereas in the human world there is ululating and joy at the birth of a boy, and resignation at the birth of a girl, Arabs welcome the birth of female animals over male, and slaughter the less valuable male animals more frequently than the female. The inversions go even further: male animals are fattened for slaughter, and often castrated in order to increase their ability to gain weight. On the one hand it is their emasculation that leads to their fatness, a feminine characteristic, but on the other hand they are nonetheless male animals undergoing a regime similar to that which Arab girls undergo. A Freudian analysis could make much of the trauma young men go through as they watch the testicles of male animals being beaten or cut in order to fatten them up, and then return home to the comforts of a society where men reign supreme, celebrate their hard, virile, sexual masculinity, and fatten their womenfolk to cement the alternative vision.

Whether one subscribes to such a reading of Azawagh Arab practices or not, there are other, more direct ways in which the reliance on pastoralism "feeds into" elements of social ideology. First, animals essentially spend all of their waking hours eating, and if they do not, they are not well enough nourished to produce offspring. This observable fact about the natural world that Azawagh Arabs depend upon can be said to condition their understanding of the necessity of frequent eating among girls and women.

Second, the centrality of milk to a pastoral economy also helps explain why fattening makes sense. In all its nourishing, tasty, white richness, milk is a prime symbol of social bonds, health, and prosperity among Azawagh Arabs, as well as a creator of kinship. Not only is it the foodstuff of highest value,[12] but visions of heaven, as I described, were often expressed using metaphors of milkiness. Women used to fatten almost solely on milk and still favor it above all other foods. Men's production through the herding, watering, and finally milking of their animals is thus recycled into women's bodies. This "investment" of milk is transformed into a woman's sexiness, desirability, and, eventually, reproductive power. Though men cannot reproduce themselves on their own, by the investment of their production into women's bodies they contribute more than simply their seed to the creation of the next generation.

It is no coincidence that women do not generally milk animals, though women insisted they could if necessary. People had difficulty articulating to me why this was, but one man explained that it was "because of respect between a man and a woman." This need for respect derives, I believe, from the fact that women are providers of milk themselves, and to take milk from animals as well would be to appropriate the domain in which men have power over this most precious substance; it would violate the division of labor in the production of value.

Women's power through milk does not end with their ability to nurture the next generation of Allah's chosen through the vicissitudes of babyhood. As I discussed in the last chapter, women can create kinship by breast-feeding children not their own – milk kinship. Milk knits people to the natural world they live in, and it to them, as well as knitting together the society itself. While it is in men's productive activities that the milk needed to keep the cycle going is produced, only women have the capacity to transform that earthly product into the stuff of Arab pride and proliferation.

Imbuing life with value

Having discussed the material realities and cultural patterns of making a living among Azawagh Arabs, I want to return to my initial question about the relationship between the economic base of society and aesthetic bodily ideals. What does it mean to say that female fatness, and much of the gender ideology that is embedded within it, is grounded in economic realities but not determined by them and not a direct sign of them; that the practice of female fattening must be understood in its material context but is not an epiphenomenon of it?

The fact that there is scarcity in the desert, that animals with protruding bones are associated with drought and famine, that there have been slaves to do back-breaking work in the hot sun – all of these create fertile preconditions for a bodily ideal of luscious, immobile female fatness to develop.

But these circumstances cannot explain why the practice of fattening has developed among Azawagh Arabs but not among other peoples in the world living in similar conditions; nor do they explain why Azawagh Arabs give it the meanings they do. The natural and the social environments create appropriate conditions in which an elaborated aesthetic of female fatness can flourish, but these circumstances cannot in themselves constitute the sole explanation for an aesthetic ideal.

Neither can an explanation that relies on a simple equation that fatness = wealth account for the bodily ideal in all its complexity. As with bodily ideals everywhere, women who achieve it tend to "catch" rich men, but this sociologically observable reality says little about the meanings that people themselves read into a bodily ideal. As I have argued above, fatness can be said to be a sign of wealth for Azawagh Arabs only to the extent that thinness can be said to be a sign of wealth in the West – that is, very little in people's conscious interpretations of the ideal.

Another possible materialist explanation for female fattening is that it is thought to enhance fertility, the probably erroneous explanation often given for why the famous Stone Age Venus figurines are so plump (Nelson 2001). Fattening has no explicit or implicit association with fertility for Azawagh Arabs, however, that I could discern. Female girth is no more associated with fertility than it is with wealth. That is, while rich men are likely to have fat wives and fat wives are, it is hoped, fertile, feminine corpulence is decidedly not read by Azawagh Arabs, explicitly or implicitly, as a direct indicator of either of these traits.

Instead of these reductionist constructions of the relationship between the material realities of life and the cultural elaboration of a bodily ideal, I want to suggest that we need to leave Western divisions between value in an economic sense and value in a cultural sense behind. The female body has such "weight" in Moor society precisely because it can merge these two types of value, by taking into it men's production out in the world and turning it into Arabness, and all that this is thought to encompass. The female body has the capacity to transform value of a physical kind – milk and grain – into value of another kind – aesthetic value, sexual value, cultural value. It is women's bodies that perform this transformation so fundamental to human social life everywhere, whereby we imbue the natural and physical world with specific cultural meanings. Furthermore, not only do female bodies turn the stuff of men's labor into something enduring, fertile, and infinitely appealing, but in doing so they enhance that value immeasurably.

Although I have suggested that women's bodies commute the real into the aesthetic, to suggest a plain translation or transposition of grain into honor, or milk into sexiness, through the alchemy of women's bodies would still be to draw too simplistic a picture of the cultural work that women's bodies do. Echoing the human body's properties as biological yet social, tangible in its forms but intangible in its expressiveness, what women's bodies in fact accomplish is nothing less than the merging of the material/aesthetic divide. In effect, the female body "makes commensurable different forms of value" (Comaroff and Comaroff 1992: 150), infusing the transformed milk and grain of men's labors with Arabness, beauty, and allure. Women's bodies have the power to actually collapse the divide between material value – the products of men's labor – and social value – the ultimate "good." Thus do food, bodies, men, children, and women become inextricably linked to a set of aesthetic values and sexual imaginings that are more real than food and bodies themselves. As nature (milk and grain as of the physical world) is turned to culture (the achieved aesthetic of fleshy immobility), so is culture (milk and grain as products of men's labor) turned to nature (the given forms of women's bodies). Herein, I submit, lies the relationship between the economic basis of Moor society and women's fattening: the material and the aesthetic are merged into one in the profoundly natural but simultaneously profoundly cultural forms of women's bodies.

It may be worth noting that the body's ability to contain different forms of value is not dissimilar to money's ability to equate disparate forms of value (Simmel 1978: 292). Through money, a car and college tuition become reduced to a similar impersonal value. Unlike money, however, which reduces the particular to one impersonal form, the body does the opposite; it ennobles, enhances, and particularizes the impersonal and general.[13] Taking value into its own living self, the body uplifts that value. Christopher Gregory (1982) has pointed out that while in the West our economic system is dominated by "productive consumption," whereby the producer of things objectifies himself – gets "consumed" – in their production, indigenous societies in Papua New Guinea are more likely to follow a logic of "consumptive production," whereby produced objects constantly become personified through their consumption. This latter economic logic is more akin to the one I am describing as central to the logic of fattening, where women through their consumption of milk and grain actually produce an intangible of far greater value than the original products.

My argument theorizes a system of value that flows through all dimensions, making any ultimate distinction between the material and the symbolic, infrastructure and superstructure, economics and culture, beside the point. For material value is only meaningful in its capacity to become culture, just as that cultural form is always undergirded by the constraints and possibilities of material subsistence.

Interestingly, this understanding of value corresponds to a Galgaliyya term, *fayde*, which refers to usefulness, worth, or capability, but not necessarily in a mechanistic sense of usefulness. A medicine that works well is said to have *fayde* (*fihe fayde*, literally "there is usefulness in it"), referring to its capacity to effect a cure. Yet the term *fayde* is also used when talking about people, not to refer to their capacity for literal productive work, but to refer more to a notion of their social usefulness, their social value. A thin woman, for example, is said to have no *fayde* – no ability to do anything, to be functional, or to fulfill her proper role. Although Azawagh Arabs might not fully recognize my argument here in terms of value transformation, they would, I think, agree that fat women have *fayde* in a sense that corresponds neatly with my outside observer's analysis.

According to Terence Turner's definition of the term, "value" can be considered the goal of all social action and productive activity (Turner 1979: 30),[14] whether it be the management of herds, the fattening of a woman's body, or the application of a medicine. Women's "work" in and on their own bodies and men's productive work out in the world, interdependent forms of "social action," thus each contribute to the ultimate production of what makes people experience life as valuable in Azawagh Arab society.

Part III

VEILED LOGICS

Plate 7 Munni with her two youngest children (Tassara)

6

THE INTERIOR SPACES OF SOCIAL LIFE

Bodies of men, bodies of women

She is beautiful to the eyes, oh my lord, and God gave her,
Gave her a breast new and green appearing like two
    balanced weights,
Gave her two teeth solid and spaced, able to be ringed,
Gave her a forearm strong like steel of which houses are
    built,
Gave her upper arms that would never be sold without a
    merchant's great profit,
Gave her a waist lined with stripes,
Gave her a thigh with stretchmarks reaching from her
    stomach to her knee,
Gave her calves beautiful and soft, you have never seen such
    creations,
Gave her a heel like none a son of Adam ever walked on.
                         -Poem recited by Boukia, 1990

That the above love poem segments and celebrates each distinct region of a woman's body, and equates them with objects and ideas seemingly unrelated to bodies, is in keeping with the way Azawagh Arabs talk about the body in everyday life. The surfaces and forms of the human body have a profound centrality in Azawagh Arab discourse, imagination, and social practice, and are often projected onto the world in metaphor or spontaneous illustration: a car has a big behind, a child's body can be compared to a goatskin sack. Even women's descriptions of heaven tend to focus heavily on what happens to the body: after death the body becomes clean and pure. Perhaps most significantly, during their earthly lives women's chief "work" is not manual labor they do with their bodies, or any kind of work they do in spite of their bodies, but work that could be said to be to, on, and in their bodies. To be an Azawagh Arab woman is, in effect, to have a certain type of body – a fattened one – and to engage in maintaining that body throughout life.

135

Even if Azawagh Arab women did not practice fattening, much in their culture would still point to the salience of the human body in women's daily concerns, to the perceived malleability of the body, and to the body as a basic tool with which not only to act on the world around one (cf. Mauss 1973) but also to think about it. While theorists have forcefully argued that culture, meaning, and imagination are deeply embodied everywhere (Bourdieu 1977, 1990; Jackson 1989; Johnson 1987; Lakoff and Johnson 1999), I was nonetheless surprised by the degree to which Azawagh Arabs use and value the human body in everyday expression.

Discussing how the body can be central to a society through the medium of language poses a certain conundrum. Even if both bodies and words symbolize and represent, communicate and make values plain, bodies work in a different way from words, and that is partly the point of this book. Bodies can symbolize silently and holistically; words are in a sense more clumsy and obvious, and less multivalent. Since bodies are our natural, biological forms even as we make them socially meaningful with adornment, say, or by fattening, they also have a way of making any meanings attached to them seem very natural and grounded. Language is also a "given," but words are more fleeting and less concrete than bodies. So to reduce bodily experience and bodily meanings to words as I will do here is to violate much that is particular to how bodies work. Yet in the absence of a forum in which to dance, gesture, or eat my way to a communicable understanding of Azawagh Arab embodiment, I must turn to the imperfect equivalents of language. In what follows I will attempt to translate what it means to have and to be a male and a female body in Azawagh Arab society into the terms and concepts of social science, implicitly contrasting it with the received understandings of embodiment in the West. I will begin by elucidating ways in which Azawagh Arabs talk about the body and are aware of their own bodies, and then move to the more implicit assumptions made about the body, the things that go without saying.

Male bodies and female bodies

The fact that male and female bodies are perceived by Azawagh Arabs to differ so fundamentally has implications for how we understand the relationship between culture and bodies in their society. In fact, few of the models available for understanding the relationship of body to society acknowledge the two types of bodies which almost all societies perceive (Grosz 1994). While Bourdieu's notion of the habitus – roughly that our bodies and our actions, rather than primarily cognitive models, encode cultural meanings – heavily informs my understanding of what female fattening is about for Moors, for example, his model neglects the different bodies and physical potentials that males and females are born with, and the different preexisting cultural constructions of maleness and femaleness,

136

and hence the different ways in which men and women are able to "body forth the world" (Jackson 1989: 136). For as Jackson's well-turned phrase implies, we bring forth worlds, or make our lives meaningful, not only with language, rituals, and works, but also in and on our very bodies.

I suggest that among Azawagh Arabs there is a division of labor with regard to the transmission and expression of culture, and that women do much of the work of "bodying forth the world" for both sexes, both in their unique and valued capacity as reproducers of men, and in their life-long devotion to embodying the principal structures and values that bring order and meaning to Azawagh Arab life. When girls at age six go from studying the Koran and the Islamic rules of life to begin their fattening, they switch from learning through language to learning through the body, ingesting the principles and values of their culture, to eventually represent and reproduce them for their society as a whole.

While many in the West are increasingly convinced that there is either little difference between male and female bodies, or that their differences are largely the result of socialization, the sexed nature of bodies for Azawagh Arabs is inherent, inescapable, and determinative of the self's relation to the world and others at all times. The differences are present from before birth. Since the male fetus is thought to take form in the womb twice as quickly as the female fetus, for example, when Seyet miscarried at about three months, her friends explained that they knew it was a boy because it was "differentiated" (*mutafāṣl, mutafāreg*) in its body parts. A female fetus at that stage would have been "just meat, flesh" (*al-ḥamm*): women put up a fist to illustrate what it would have looked like – just a lump. This general opposition – differentiation and articulation vs. fleshy wholeness – remains a characteristic of the way men and women are embodied throughout their lives, even as girls reverse the pace of fetal development as they mature twice as quickly as boys outside of the womb en route to puberty.

Awareness of how corporeal forms differ by sex is instilled in children early. One day two cousins, a girl and a boy each around age eleven or twelve, got in a spat when the boy, Mohamed, asked his cousin tauntingly why she did not engage in some boyish type of play. "I am not like you," Nuna yelled back at him. "I am cut down there," she said, indicating her genital area. Mohamed replied by holding out his left arm, grasping it upright at the elbow and making a fist, announcing proudly, "And I am like a tree."[1] He then drew a line in the sand to depict how Nuna was cut, and presented his erect forearm once again for all around to contemplate. None of the older women or even other children around paid much attention, either to approve or disapprove of this reference to the corporeal/sexual nature of males and females. In fact, older women sometimes referred to a group of women as "all those who are cut" (*al-mashgūgāt*) and men in playful talk not infrequently represented their sex organs with

137

a tightened, upright forearm. This fundamental difference between female and male bodies – one cut, open, and vulnerable; the other strong, upright, and whole – is the bedrock on which expected female and male comportment, spatial relations, eating, dress, and all interaction are founded.

More elaborate intimations of Azawagh Arab views on male and female difference emerged in a local version of the creation story, which exists in Islam in similar form to that in Christianity and Judaism. The woman who told me the story was Maya, whose death in 1991 brought men from far and wide to chant the Koran. She was a vibrant and respected personality in Tchin Tabaraden, and left me with some of my most vivid impressions of the world she so warmly welcomed me into.

It was on a day shortly after my return to the Azawagh for fieldwork that she began explaining to me, as people were wont to do, that Westerners are really descendants of the Quraysh tribe of the Prophet Muhammad, and therefore brothers of the Arabs, with a shared descent from even earlier ancestors, Adam and Eve.[2] The story raises several of the themes that structure notions of male and female, and male and female bodies, among Azawagh Arabs.[3]

"The first person was Adama," she began. "He was made alone. He ate clay and water. Hawa was made from his rib; it grew some sort of growth, and Hawa emerged out of it. ...." She pointed at a lower right rib on her own torso and gestured an illustration of Hawa's genesis.

> When there were just Adama and Hawa, the devil (*al-blīs*) came to Hawa and said, "Don't you see that Adama is going to other women?" He gave her a mirror and when Hawa saw the woman in the mirror, the devil told her it was the woman Adama was going to. Hawa picked up her goatskin water bag (*girba*) and left.
>
> When she got to a certain place, she put her *girba* under her and sat on it. Adama came looking for her; he followed her tracks and found her. Hawa said, "You left and looked for other women." Adama said, "There's only you and me; what women could I have gone to?" Then they fought. Adama told Hawa that her buttocks were cold. They were cold because of sitting on the water bag.
>
> Then to find out who was telling the truth, they went to the tree of fire/hell (*ṣadra tʿat an-nār*). Hawa told Adama to drink the leaves of the tree. He did and they stuck in his throat, and made the Adam's apple (*garjūma*). Hawa ate it and it went right through her, and she got her period.

Maya did not speak about the morals and meanings of this tale, except to reflect that since the leaves stuck in his throat, Adam had been telling the truth. (She did not state explicitly that Hawa had been lying, however.)

138

In this first significant consumption of food by human beings, their sexual and gendered natures were revealed and fixed: men hold things in their bodies, and women are in danger of losing them. Food sticks in men, but leaks out of women; men are closed, women are open. That women tend toward coldness, especially in a body part that Maya probably meant as a euphemism for the genitals and vagina, was also established early in this version of the human story. The special metaphorical relationship between women's bodies and goatskin water bags is also hinted at in this telling. As I will discuss at greater length below, the bag's seams resemble a woman's "seams"; its coldness echoes a woman's coldness; its ability to contain fluids imitates a woman's ability to produce liquid secretions. This particular Moor version of Genesis also lays out one of the primary concerns of everyday life for Moor men and women: sexual fidelity. It suggests a perception of women as vain, desirous, and more susceptible to the devil's work than men, but of men as potentially unfaithful, this latter the more apparent truth of male–female relations in the contemporary Azawagh Arab world.[4]

Azawagh Arab bodies

I suspect that Azawagh Arabs would be unimpressed by the early French anthropologist Marcel Mauss' insight that the ways people walk, eat, and sit are highly socially conditioned. Both men and women are aware that to be a proper Arab one must adopt a certain bodily habitus (in Mauss' sense), that one must, as Mauss puts it (1973: 75), classify "the miscellaneous" movements and gestures of the body to be a properly socialized adult. In fact, the Azawagh region makes an interesting laboratory for considering Mauss' insight, because to outsiders Azawagh Arabs are often indistinguishable in appearance from the neighboring Tuareg, especially the men, who tend to dress identically in a long, flowing *jellaba*, wide pants, turban and sandals.[5] Yet Azawagh Arabs (and Tuaregs as well) can tell them apart even at great distance through what are to the outsider minute subtleties in the way members of each society carry their bodies.

I learned about this most tellingly from Maya's middle-aged, divorced daughter, Shweytima. Sitting one day long after Maya's death with Shweytima in the doorway of her house on a back lane, I watched a man who was to me indistinguishable from a Tuareg saunter down the street. Shweytima quickly pulled up her veil, which she would not need to do for a Tuareg, and when I asked how she knew he was Arab she assured me he was although she had never seen him before. "You can tell by the way they look around. A Tuareg will look everywhere, all over. He would know every little thing on that table [behind me] after he walked past." An Arab, however, will only look straight ahead, she explained, but his eyes will dart furtively sideways as he goes by. A little later another unknown man appeared down the sandy lane. Shweytima veiled, but I watched closely as he performed exactly as expected, stealing an irresistible, quick, sidelong glance toward us as he strode by. We laughed at the accuracy of Shweytima's description and enactment; even she seemed surprised at her ability to so vividly articulate this bit of received, generally unspoken knowledge.

What Mauss called "techniques of the body" – socialized ways of using the body – were also made vividly apparent to me when after months in Tassara I went to visit a Tuareg family in a distant encampment. Though again they dressed and adorned themselves similarly to Azawagh Arabs and resembled them in most aspects of physical appearance, the way they sat, used their arms, looked at each other, adjusted their bodies to the presence of the opposite sex, and moved was strikingly different from what I had grown used to. Where Arab women sit tall and immobile, moving only their arms in animated gesture, these Tuareg women draped themselves daintily and used their delicate hands in less accentuated ways to illustrate a point. Where Arab men hover at the edge of the tent, asserting authority and energy with legs widespread when they sit, and in constant motion when in the presence of women, these Tuareg men sat solidly under the tent, still and modest, unconcerned about where their limbs rested. Furthermore, while a young Tuareg woman perched herself on a raised bed platform, a young man sat unconcernedly on the ground, a physical hierarchy that one would be unlikely to witness among Azawagh Arabs. The attitudes of indifference to the presence of the opposite sex which were so clearly apparent in the physical behavior of the Tuaregs contrasted strikingly with the bodily adjustments, energy level, and tensions in Azawagh Arab mixed-sex gatherings.

In addition to the way Azawagh Arab women position themselves vis-à-vis men, the very form of their bodies defines them as Arab. To be an Azawagh Arab woman *is* to have a certain type of body, a fattened one, usually seated, and lumbering and swaying if walking. In their concern to convert me into a proper Arab woman, friends would not only try to fatten me, but also instruct me on how to sit, lie, and walk. The characteristic woman's walk, in which she swings her hips from side to side while throwing her hands out from the elbow at each step as if to balance her hefty lower torso, is referred to as *tefowsis* or *tefaydeḥ*. A popular and genial young *ḥaraṭāni* would send women into peals of laughter with his imitations of female behavior, which consisted chiefly of a very exaggerated performance of this walk. Men also said they could recognize the veiled forms of particular women at a distance by the individual swayings of their walks.

Azawagh Arabs' recognition of how bodily habitus encodes identity goes deeper than gestures, stride, and sitting posture, however. In questions women asked me about my body and the bodies of "my people," they made it clear that the particular biological characteristics of Arab bodies could not be presumed to apply to the bodies of all peoples. Did I menstruate? women commonly asked me. Do white women go through labor when they give birth? The physical character of their own feminine embodiment seemed to be potentially a correlate of their Arabness, rather than of female human bodies generally. Social difference corresponded to bodily difference with respect to illness as well. They could only make sense of my assertion that Westerners did not know of the humoral qualities of hot and cold by assuming that our bodies merely did not react to these forces in the same way, so that we did not recognize them. They understood the very experience of pain, illness, and menstruation to differ with one's ethnic identity, a notion that accords with recent radical rethinkings of embodiment in anthropology (Csordas 1994).

The belief that bodies differ as cultures differ also accords with racialist models of difference that Azawagh Arabs subscribe to within the Moor world. Although there is a considerable range of skin color within all the castes of Moor society, including black "whites" and white "blacks," as I have explained, perceived bodily hue is considered a potent sign that blacks, blacksmiths, Western whites, Arabs, and even Indians and Chinese are all profoundly different from one another. Skin color is read as an outer sign of inner moral and ontological status, lighter skin inevitably correlating with higher character and worth. When I asked Azawagh Arabs directly, several asserted that there were of course good and intelligent ḥaraṭīn, and bad and stupid Arabs. Yet those "white" Arabs who were distinctly dark skinned often made spontaneous excuses to me for their skin color, attributing it to changes in weather or temporary illness. And one ḥaraṭīn family, so light-skinned I thought they were Arabs for most of my stay, lived outside of Tassara, by themselves, seemingly unwilling to settle among other ḥaraṭīn even if their light skin alone did not earn them the status of "white" Arabs.

Qualities associated by Azawagh Arabs with blacks include lack of willpower, lack of self-restraint, untrustworthiness, and, not least, uncontrollable sexuality. Sexuality is perceived as a prime arena of physical and moral difference. An Azawagh Arab woman explained to me that black women have big vaginas, but light-skinned people – Arabs, Europeans, and "red" Tuareg[6] – have small ones, this latter being preferable. The general association between black women and a wanton yet ultimately unsophisticated and unrefined sexuality was made commonly by Azawagh Arab women. Moral, physical, and social differences are conflated, each level of difference taken as the expression of difference at another level.

I want to emphasize that whiteness is not so much a sign of stature as its concomitant, its embodiment: whiteness, goodness, beauty, and prestige are embedded in one another. The same is true of fatness: the fattened female body is not so much an indication of prestige and moral stature as synonymous with these qualities. By long and diligent manipulation of their own bodies into fattened form, Azawagh Arab women also assert their own identity both as non-male and as non-slave. In a society with few material belongings, the body is a prime arena, then, for marking identity. In sum, while Azawagh Arabs define themselves by and take pride in their own language, heritage, and way of life, their own sense of themselves is largely expressed in the realm of the corporeal.

Metaphorical bodies

In fact, the perceived sophistication of the Arabic language is itself not entirely divorced from things corporeal. Whenever Azawagh Arabs set out to test my language skills, both women and men invariably began by asking me the names of body parts. I could easily prove my dedication to their community and their world, it seemed, by knowing the word for armpit, forearm, navel, or heel.[7] Women were proud of the elaborateness of Arabic's corporeal vocabulary, with its specialized terms for the space between the collar bones, the fat that hangs from the upper arm, the cleft in the upper lip, and the side of the torso.[8] They often asked whether my language had terms for all the body parts theirs did. The detail with which their exalted language expressed the shapes, crevices, and fine distinctions of the body seemed proof of its refinement. Their own bodies, in turn, were the yardstick of differentiation and significance against which a language's power to know the world was judged.

Accordingly, the human body is used frequently as a model for imagining the world. That is, Azawagh Arabs tend to imagine the world's constituent elements in the images and forms of the elaborately defined object that is their own person. For example, rather than describing an absent object by shaping their hands to designate the space it would occupy, Azawagh Arabs tend to let a body part stand in its place. In this way, for example, the lower arm and fisted hand image the male sex organ, as described earlier, or a fist alone may be held up to represent a ball of butter. A woman once "enacted" a goatskin bag to me in order to explain what it was by pretending her body was the bag, her neck the bag's neck, and her mouth the bag's opening. In order to describe a camel saddle to me a man contorted his arm into its shape. To illustrate the drumming that goes on at a feast day, a woman tapped her cheeks. To describe the strange, back-heavy shape of a car that had rolled into town, a woman pointed to her behind, her body becoming the car, and the car becoming her body.

These examples suggest that the body is a particularly apt emblem for understanding the shapes and forms of the external, non-human world for Azawagh Arabs. The body's forms engender conscious and concrete models of and for the world, as less conscious sets of embodied relations to our world generate the image schemata and guiding metaphors that Lakoff and Johnson (1980, 1999) and Johnson (1987) discuss as so central to the nature of human cognition and rationality. The way the human body so readily "stands for" objects in the environment also suggests that Azawagh Arabs inhabit their world in a particularly active way, going so far as to inhabit figuratively the objects that constitute its material expression. Their very embodied persons suffuse the world, and the world can in turn suffuse their very embodied persons. The practice suggests a profound centrality of the human form for Azawagh Arabs, both in their lived world in a desert landscape of few human constructions, and in the imagination this world conjures up.

There are also established metaphorical connections between the body and the environment in discourse – routinized expressions that read bodily parts onto non-bodily entities that share some aspect of their form or function. The term for breasts (*lebzazīl*), for example, can also refer to stones set in earrings or faucets. The most prominent and significant of these body-based metaphorical connections, however, involves the mouth. Orifices are especially continuous from the sentient to the insentient world in Azawagh Arab culture: mouths (sing. *al-femm*) are vaginas are doorways are holes in the ground are wells. The entry to a village by the main road is even referred to as a *femm*, and the nipple of a woman's breast is referred to as either the "head" of the breast (*rās al-bazūla*) or as the *femm* of the breast.

While the term *femm* may be a relatively "quiescent" or inactive metaphor (Jackson 1989: 143) when referring to a door, its connotations not brought to consciousness, they are frequently made explicit in practice. When a woman gives birth, for example, all passageways between the outer world and her inner body – all the "mouths" – are kept covered, from her own mouth to the walls of her enclosure to the tent sides. The connection may become even more "active," as in the example above when a woman used her own mouth to play the part of the opening of a goatskin water bag. Perhaps Michael Jackson's two poles of "quiescent" and "active" metaphors are better conceptualized as a continuum. In the case of orifices in Azawagh Arab culture, the term *femm* may be used as a quiescent metaphor, or the relations within the term's applications may be activated in practice, or the relations may generally be at the level of consciousness. In all cases, the metaphorical connections between different sorts of openings are not without practical consequences: the relations between the door to a compound and a vagina may not be consciously envisioned every time a doorway is mentioned, but in practice they are treated similarly, as potentially endangering openings into the self and body.

The most "active" and also significant mouth metaphor is that between the two most prominent openings on the female body, the mouth and the vagina. While the vagina is generally referred to by a separate term (*lurāk*), it is considered a *femm* to the body. The homologies of the mouth and the vagina were made particularly apparent to me one day early in my field-work when Fatima was giving me a lesson on sex and health. "What comes out of a man is cold (*bārid*)," she explained, a quality women do not want. "After sex, therefore, a woman should take a cloth and wipe herself off," she continued. She then proceeded to take an imaginary cloth in her hands, and, very graphically, to wipe delicately around her mouth, and then dab gingerly at her lips. Sitting on a sandy, torn mat under a low-ceilinged tent, watching this full-faced woman with *kohl*-ed eyes and a heavy blue veil covering most of her body, I could not help but imagine an aristocratic lady wiping her mouth at a dinner party, so vivid and careful were Fatima's gestures. In fact, though, she was demonstrating to me how a woman should wipe clean her genitalia after sex. To Fatima, the connection she created through gesture between the vagina and the mouth did not require explanation; that the mouth was readily synonymous with the vagina went without saying.

The relations between the mouth and the vagina are further elaborated in the perceived relationship between eating and sex. As mentioned previously, to eat or talk openly in an inappropriate situation is akin to confessing sexual appetite or interest. A common euphemism for engaging in sex or sexual play is "to talk" or "to chat" (*lwinsa*). The body's forms, then, are used not only to image the external world, but also to image other parts of the body itself: the mouth is to the vagina as speaking is to having sex.

Along with the anus, the mouth and vagina form a trilogy of passage-ways into the body whose openness must always be guarded. With one more passageway than men, and an important one, women need to be especially careful of when and how they open their bodies. A woman once explained to me that men could only easily get "cold" if they had diarrhea; that is, if their anus was unusually susceptible to humoral forces because of an illness that "opened" this entrance to the body. Otherwise, women are naturally much more prone to such invasions.

To Azawagh Arabs the fact that the vagina, the mouth, and the anus all open to the outside world and let in objects and forces from that world – food, semen, men's bodies, wind, cold, heat – makes them analogous, even homologous. Out of the dialectic of experience of the body's physical forms on the one hand, and cultural emphases on closedness, purity, and containedness on the other, emerges a particular understanding of embodiment as well as an embodied understanding of the world. In the body's power to inhabit and image the world, a coalescence of sensory, affective, social, and material fields is brought about in the body (Devisch 1993: 42). Through the reading of the body onto the world, and a recognition of homologies even within the body itself, Azawagh Arabs achieve a sense of wholeness wherein the body – the very form of their own being –

legitimates and gives order to the world, and reinforces its own meaning-fulness and order in turn.

The connectedness of bodies to the world around them

As I noted above, Azawagh Arabs usually use the term *jild*, literally "skin," to refer to the body. This is fitting, given that the body seems to consist of an extension inwards of that surface that confronts the social and natural environment, rather than consisting primarily of inner states that are bounded off or disjoined from their social context and environment. The skin itself, moreover, is not an absolute boundary to the environment around one. Rather, forces of the body and forces of the world are of a piece, and the body is always and deeply vulnerable to the hot sands, sneaking winds, and invisible spirits of the world that surrounds it.[9]

Women are particularly vulnerable to outside forces because of what should by now be familiar: women's bodies are "open" not only during urination, excretion, and eating, but also during menstruation, sexual activity, and giving birth. Consequently, women are constantly mindful of keeping themselves veiled and "closed," by not urinating at dusk, for example, when spirits are especially abundant. The forty-day postpartum seclusion period is not, as I at first erroneously and ethnocentrically assumed, a chance for the baby to bond with the mother or to be kept from infection. It is a chance for the mother to close herself off again from the dangerous forces childbirth has opened. This is why during these forty days she lies silently, with legs kept ever together, under blankets even in the hot season, within a mat-wall enclosure, within the tent.

After giving birth, accordingly, women try to regain the fatness that the nausea and food taboos of pregnancy have often diminished. Abundant flesh effectively swells the thighs so as to close off the sexual opening, the most dangerous port of entry to the female body. Fat women are also thought to have tight vaginas, desirable both for the sexual pleasure this affords men and for the security it offers against dangerous outside winds and spirits. So fatness does not so much extend a woman into the world as it encloses her openings and inner spaces, helping her achieve the closed, containing body that is thought necessary for health and well-being. Fatness not only establishes beauty, allure, and potency within the body itself, but encompasses the body in relation to the world around it. It establishes an appropriate and healthy boundedness with respect to the forces of the world, diminishing the female body's porousness and reinforcing its solidity against the forces that threaten its integrity.

The essential porousness of the body to the outside world is one reason that Azawagh Arabs see no sense in measuring the body's weight. A woman once described to me at length a machine she had been placed on at a health clinic, something similar to an X-ray machine but different, she said, that, according to her understanding, figured out what was wrong with the patient. It took me a very long time to realize that she was talking about a weighing scale. In part the confusion arose simply because the woman was unfamiliar with the machines and equipment used in health clinics, and nurses rarely explain what they are doing, not least of all because of language barriers. (None of the nurses in Tassara or Tchin Tabaraden spoke Arabic, and as I have said, few Azawagh Arab women speak Hausa, and none speak French.) Even when I explained what a scale does, the procedure seemed to make little sense to her. Although millet, tea, gold, and numerous other items are weighed and measured in the Azawagh, for Azawagh Arab women, at least, it does not make sense to measure and weigh the body. The body is not equivalent to a bounded object that has a definite and determinable weight; it is fluid both in its size and its character, going from thinner to fatter, colder to hotter, according to varying external and internal circumstances. Fatness is not a matter of weight, but of abundance, not of sheer size, but of the quality of full limbs and protruding buttocks.

Like the goatskin bag that is sewn together and holds milk or water in amorphous, ever changing shape, the human body has its "seams," its openings to the world, as well as the ability to hold different contents and take on different forms. It requires constant care, constant filling, and constant attention to leaks. In contrast to Western models, notably Marx's (Marx and Engels 1970: 21), in which bodies shape consciousness via their labor on the world, Azawagh Arab bodies, especially women's bodies, shape consciousness by their inherent, passive relation of openness to the world, one could say. The body's natural attitude to the world conditions what it means to be a woman and to be a man. Whereas for a man this relationship arises also in production and exchange, activities that take place around and through the body's efforts, for women the "self" is shaped and attended to largely through attention to the body itself. Through consumption and management of bodily orifices, women create their adult selves out of their corporeal relationship to the world's forces and products. In contrast to Marx's model as well as other Western formulations that posit discrete, bounded selves, bodies, and environments – and relations formed through active engagement – for Azawagh Arabs these relations or pathways are by nature open, even in the absence of concrete productive activity. The body is necessarily in constant interaction and negotiation with the world around it.

The connectedness of bodies to non-bodily domains

The relationship between corporeal states and consciousness is also more fluid and open for Azawagh Arabs than the dualisms of Western thought presuppose. The physical forces that run through the world and the body can affect "the mind" as well, though the term does not exist as such in Galgaliyya Arabic. But physical states can lead to a loss of "self," *roh*, to becoming taken by spirits – to a loss of sanity. The best example of this is how "heat," in the humoral system, is a positive quality associated with closedness, fecundity, and sexual desirability if possessed in reasonable measure, but too much heat can make a person become dizzy, and at higher levels go crazy. A bodily state thus becomes transformed into what we would consider a mental state, a state of a different order. The somatic realm is not bounded off from the realm of spirit, but one fades into the other at its edges.

In at least one situation, bodies are even interchangeable with non-bodily material objects. This is at birth, when bodies are least formed, least socialized. When I arrived at a tent in the desert where a friend had just given birth, I learned that the midwife had made the small razor incisions on the temples and upper arms of the infant that morning, as is done to all newborns. This is not so that bad blood may be let out, I discovered, a rationale for such treatments later in life. Instead, it is so spirits will not be tempted to take the child. As an old woman explained to me quietly, so the spirits would not hear, "If the spirits see the child with cuts, they won't want it. Otherwise, if they see the baby without cuts, they will think it is their goatskin water bag and take it." At that liminal stage of human-ness, the body can be mistaken for an inanimate object. It has not yet been encompassed by society and *made* human, and therefore it is still inter-changeable with the non-human world around it. The unsocialized body is, in effect, not fully a body.

Fattening not only socializes bodies into Azawagh Arab bodies and increases women's protection against dangerous forces in the world, but is also the chief way in which female bodies become female bodies in the first place. For it is through fattening that girls' relatively inchoate forms are socialized to appropriate Muslim adulthood. While Allah has created two sexes, it is up to humans to embrace and enhance his scheme, elaborating on sexual differences and actively adding to the distance between female-ness and maleness. Further, the lack of an absolute, natural boundary between the bodily and the non-bodily opens the way for the transforma-tions that take place in women's bodies, that is, of milk into flesh, of food into the stuff of men's desiring, and of men's production of goods out in the world into women's reproduction of people.

Willful bodies

Azawagh Arab bodies act on the world not only as instruments of a self or a mind, but also of their own immanence, force, and volition. Bodies emit powerful intentions, desires, and perceptions, sometimes willed, but often unwilled. As bodies project their intentions onto the world, so other bodies receive the imprint of the intentions, also in ways individuals may or may not be immediately aware of.

An obvious example of this lies in the reason behind women's veiling. Once a girl's first teeth have fallen out, she starts to have "fire" in her skin and therefore must be careful around men, whom she now has the power to "burn" (*ḥaraga*). She should stop lying next to her father on a mat or bed, for example. Similarly, a boy's body will gain the capacity to be burned once his first teeth fall out, and therefore his mother should not lie on the same bed as him. The power of a girl's skin or body becomes even stronger after she reaches puberty, so when she starts to develop breasts and pubic hair, she takes on the veil. A woman's hair is especially invested with the power to burn.[10] When I went to visit the elderly *qāḍi*, the Islamic leader of the Azawagh Arabs, his wife frequently whispered admonishments to me to cover my hair more completely before I entered his presence; the wisps straying out on my forehead would burn him.

"Burning" here has the metaphorical sense of sending a person to hell. By exposing her body to a man not her husband or close relative, a woman condemns both herself and him to hell. While in any given situation a girl may veil more out of habit than out of fear of actually going to hell, veiling is not only a symbolic social form. The very materiality of the body contains forces for ill that must be protected against by similarly physical means. But the capacity to burn is also the capacity to attract. As a girl's skin becomes imbued with the ability to "burn" men, she is simultaneously becoming imbued with the power to attract men, and imbuing herself further with this power by fattening. "If a man sees so much as a small part of a woman's flesh," Dahmou told me, "he will want her." Veiling both protects against this danger, and enhances the value of what it hides: "Covered dung is better than exposed gold,"[11] as the saying goes.

By hastening the onset of womanly curves, girls embellish the power their bodies attain naturally with cultural visions of appropriate desirability. At the same time, they make the potentially troublesome sexual power of their bodies socially encompassed. By feminizing their bodies in socially appropriate ways, by grounding themselves, and by eventually taking on the *ḥawli*, they acknowledge their bodies' power, accede to it, and go about controlling it. In this way the fattening of a girl's body enables the "gut" male response to the female body to rise above a base urge, and to become a socially sanctioned yearning for something that holds material and ideal value.

That bodies emit forces is in keeping with the agentive powers of other types of inanimate objects. Most salient among these is Koranic writing which, when transcribed onto an amulet worn encased in a pouch around the neck (described in chapter 3), has the power to protect the wearer against spirits and various diseases and dangers. Almost all Azawagh Arabs wear one or more amulets. Passages from the Koran can also be written in ink on a Koranic board, and then washed off into water, to create another potent cure (al-mahia), evidence of the power of ink, when used to write down passages from the Koran and then turned to inky water, to transform and cure disease and other unfortunate circumstances. And from copper rings and bracelets emanates a power that deters witches. Thus the power of skin surfaces to burn or attract should be understood against this background of the potential power of things in general.[12]

Heavenly bodies

A final confounding of Western understandings of the body arises in Azawagh Arab notions of what happens to a person when he or she dies and, God willing (inshAllah), goes to heaven. Rather than a Christian paradise of disembodied souls, the final and eternal resting place of all good Muslims is a place of perfected embodiment. I would like to revisit Kia's vision of heaven that I first introduced in chapter 3, to consider it against the background of Azawagh Arab concepts of embodiment.

> Your body will become very good, with milk flowing through it, and you will be white. Men's bodies will be like glass, and you will be able to see yourself in their bodies. You will not defecate, or have mucous, or be sick.

Far from the mere soul (an-nefs) traveling upwards to receive the rewards of the afterlife, the body is the vehicle of the self that achieves and represents complete perfection and satisfaction after a life of suffering and unfulfilled desires. The troublesome passage of fluids and forces in and out of the body ceases, and contained embodiment is reached.

Another girl I knew once disagreed with her younger cousin's assertions that in heaven the tents would be very good, insisting there were no tents in heaven, but that milk would come out of faucets and food (l'aysh) would just appear; you wouldn't have to make it. When I asked what people did there, she said: "They sit, like in the world, but it's better than [the world]. They dress, and eat, and get married." As this description suggests, Azawagh Arab images of paradise tend to feature very concrete and embodied images of salvation as well. This is in keeping with Koranic visions of heaven, which emphasize material abundance and comfort – streams of water (4: 57), fruit and rivers of milk, wine, and honey (47: 15), luxurious carpets and cushions (55: 76), and rich adornment (76: 21, 44: 53).[13]

As in life, heavenly bodily states index moral, social, and emotional status as well as mere physical well-being. What is significant in life, what lends life its meaning and piety its power, resides in the material being of the self – the contoured, porous, given form through which and in which life and its struggles are negotiated. The promise of the afterlife includes not only surcease from the divisive and troubling differences between men and women but also surcease from the leaking, hungering, and discomforts this corporeal self is prone to on earth.

Plate 8 Tassara with approaching sandstorm

7

THE EXTERIOR SPACES
OF SOCIAL LIFE

Tent and desert

If an Arab woman stands up, you can blow her over, but if
she is seated, she can pull you to the ground.
                    -Words of a young man in Tassara

The ways in which men and women inhabit tents, villages, and desert
quietly but forcefully communicate and materialize Azawagh Arab values
and understandings of the world, including the logics that lie behind the
perceived beauty of fattened women. How space is organized and talked
about discloses a vision of the world in which women physically mark the
center of family and tribe, but in which men stand as the ideological pillars
around which society turns. People did not of course have a conscious
model of how space is conceived; what I describe here is a way of ordering
the world that exists tacitly in people's everyday practices, and as such
provides a powerful statement about what the world's natural state is
thought to be.

Orienting oneself in the world

When I first moved to Tassara, the woman I hired to help me cook and
clean, Minnou, casually turned my bed around 180 degrees each time she
swept the verandah on my house. After the third time, I decided it was not
mere chance or fancy that occasioned this rearrangement, and asked
Minnou why my bed always ended up facing in a different direction from
the one I had left it in. It turned out that it had indeed not been an accident. Realizing that I always switched the bed back, Minnou responded by
pleading, "You must not sleep with your head north!" She proceeded to
explain her worry that spirits would possess me in the night and turn me
into a donkey, the basest of animals. I was soon to realize that people
constantly attuned and positioned their bodies to this fact. A woman never
walks north to urinate in the night, for example, for fear that spirits who

dwell there will enter her, and while tent sides are often raised and lowered, the northern side of a tent is always kept closed.

Just as people are forever anchored in the social web they are born into, so are they forever and inescapably anchored in the directions of Allah's world. As fervent Moslems who pray to the east in a desert landscape where the sun rises and falls on unobstructed horizons, Azawagh Arabs are constantly aware of their orientation to the points of the compass. The dead are laid in their graves facing east, the direction of prayer and Mecca; people sleep with their heads to the south; and in a sweep of their arms from east to west people locate their history, an arc of travel out of Arabia and west to the Maghreb, with a final turn south to the land they now call their own. I was often asked in which direction we Christians prayed, as if this could define and situate for them our strange, floating, seemingly ungrounded religion. People also asked me frequently in which direction America was, as well as other countries they had heard of. "Is it this way or this way?" they would ask, pointing with their arms. I was never asked about what my country looked like or how far away it was; the direction in which it lay in reference to them was satisfying enough to define a place. When I traveled in the desert it was incomprehensible to the people I was with that I was not constantly aware of where north and south were, whether there were clear skies or not.

As all these examples suggest, the points of the compass impinged on people's very beings. Lines seemed to run from horizon through tent to body and outwards again, keeping the concerns of the most immediate bodily activity ever aligned with the forces and order of the wider world. In fact, coming from a world where space is largely imagined in terms of grids and graphs, it took me some time to realize that space was implicitly ordered very differently among Azawagh Arabs: more like a circle, with radii running out in all directions from the center. With time I came to have a recurring vision of this desert society: large, anchored women at the middle of a huge wheel whose spokes were elastic threads leading out from the center to men who bounded all over the world and from time to time back to the center, only to bound away again.

The gendered geography of everyday life

If the Azawagh Arab spatial world could be said to be imagined as lines radiating outwards from the center, women constantly gravitate to and occupy that center, while men gravitate constantly outwards toward the wider world. Put in other terms, men have a centrifugal orientation, and women a centripetal orientation.[1] These orientations are reflected in the way men make a living by extracting things from the periphery to invest, so to speak, in the center; in a social ideology that values centripetal in-marriage; as well as in the domains of daily movement, bodily management, and sexuality.

Related to this implicit model of space are two more explicit axes, already introduced, that take on expression in daily discourse as well as in how people treat their bodies and manage their movement: the contrast between closedness and openness, and between stasis and motion. Women strive for closedness and stillness, while men are less wary of openness, and strive always toward movement. The center of a tent, where women reign, for example, is equated with closedness and stasis; the outer world where men venture is open and full of movement.

As all of this suggests, space is, like everything else, profoundly gendered. Conceptions of space in fact constitute a key domain in which notions of maleness and femaleness are legitimized. Certain spaces, like tents, are "naturally" female, whereas others, such as the open desert, suit men much better. For men the tent resembles the Kabyle house as Bourdieu describes it: "not so much a place he enters as a place he comes out of" (1977: 91). When men stop by even their own tent during the day, they are often treated as, and act as, strangers to this female domain, hovering on its edges, passing quickly on to the house to get something, or settling down to rest quietly in one corner.

This contrast is the rule in the Muslim and Arab world; women are associated with interior, private spaces, and men with the public domain.[2] That women "belong" to interior spaces, and interior spaces to women, should not be read as necessarily correlating with inferior status. For the private interior space that women occupy is also the symbolic and affective center of the family and society, and thus a hallowed position in which to sit. Especially when women reach old age they rule the roost in their tents, and even sons and husbands must pass through during the day almost as visitors. Men are as "required" by culture as women to adhere to "their" spaces – a man who hangs around at home all day will be mocked. (In the dollhouses the little girls made, the female dolls occupied center stage, and the few male dolls – simple sticks lashed together and covered with pieces of folded cloth – lay strewn haphazardly at the back. Men were clearly as peripheral to their play worlds as real men often seemed to the daily lives of real women.)

The points I make here about the relationship between how space is inhabited and how the social world is experienced are not new.[3] Bourdieu has noted, in prose typical of him, that the spatial arrangements of a society enable "the appropriating by the world of a body thus enabled to appropriate the world" (1977: 89). In other words, by being socialized in spaces (houses, towns, schools) that are laid out in particular ways and given particular meanings, individuals absorb deep knowledge about the cultural categories and priorities of their society, which they then reproduce in their own actions. T.O. Beidelman has noted in less abstract prose that

[o]ur dwellings and our bodies are the primary models by which we try to imagine more complex and elusive aspects of our beliefs and society. Furthermore, it is in our homes and through our bodies that we are initially socialized, that we are related to other beings and things.

(Beidelman 1993: 46)

In the West, for example, merely by moving through the spatial layout of their own homes children learn about private/public distinctions and about the importance of individual autonomy. Western homes are as a rule divided into public spaces (living room, dining room) and private spaces (bedrooms, bathrooms), and ideally every child gets his or her own room which can be closed off and in which, presumably, his or her unique and autonomous individuality can develop. In the West, as in non-literate societies, moving in space becomes "so many structural exercises" (Bourdieu 1977: 91) that implicitly teach individuals key oppositions and values of their culture: that women should focus inwards and be still, for example, and that the back tent flaps should remain down at all times to guard against spirits.

Following on Bourdieu's insights, I want to emphasize that the relationship between space and social life is not one of mapping, metaphor, or model. Instead, both space and social life are conceived of according to similar mental models, neither the cause of the other but both structured according to a similar logic, each informing the other. As Henrietta Moore points out in her study of space and social life among the Kenyan Marakwet, "The organisation of space is not a direct reflection of cultural codes and meanings; it is, above all, a context developed through practice – that is, through the interaction of individuals" (1986: 116). In other words, when little Aichatou sees other girls eat their fattening food in a corner of the tent and sees growing boys shoo-ed out into the village; when Fatima yells at her not to "run around like a prostitute" and to keep her vagina covered, Aichatou absorbs the consonant messages of her spatial and social worlds at the same time. The centered, still, closed-off, fattened female body is consonant in its turn with this received vision of how the world is meant to be.

The tent: women's world

The Azawagh Arabs in towns live in adobe-walled compounds (ḥawsh) like other villagers in this part of the world, and like those other ethnic groups, build adobe houses within these compounds. Unlike other ethnic groups, however, they use these houses rarely, instead building their tents in the yard and continuing to reside in them as they did in the bush. Their tents consist of a square or rectangular arrangement of tentpoles with a roof frame of more sticks and poles lashed together, and over which is stretched a covering of many layers of burlap sacks, synthetic tenting material (that has trickled into the area from various aid projects), or, previously, goat skins. Whereas I was always nervous to be under a tent during a violent rainstorm, Azawagh Arabs were nervous to be in their houses at such a time – they consider houses fragile and fallible, and are especially reluctant to use them during storms, when they believe them most likely to fall. People occasionally sat in their houses on cold days, or if an influx of visitors necessitated that the women move indoors for privacy. In the more populous and cosmopolitan Tchin Tabaraden Azawagh Arabs used their houses more; they often had smaller yards, and were probably influenced by the non-nomadic, house-dwelling people around them.

Tents and their "furnishings" are always oriented to the points of the compass. The back of a tent is always its northern side, where the skin or burlap is tied close to the ground and belongings are stacked, a barrier of sorts to both wind and spirits. Milk stands (sing. *tajīkent*, from Tamajeq), the tallest objects in a tent, occupy the place of honor at the south side, elevating the most prized foodstuff and product in decorated splendor. Milk stands are made of wood, and consist of a long pole anchored in the sand, adorned with leather fringes, and ending in a funnel-shaped cage that holds the large wooden bowl (*gdāḥ*) where milk is kept to sour. Though today milk stands are not as common, in the past they were a standard element of dowries, and are still commissioned from artisans by those who can afford them. Also in an auspicious position in the tent are women's *garfas*, the decorated leather bags in which they have traditionally kept their special belongings. Note that milk stands and *garfas*, both associated with women's activities (since women are in charge of all milk distribution within the household), stand in opposition to the less valued and more "male" items – sacks of grain, trunks of clothing or other possessions – that help form the barrier at the north side of the tent.

Tents are built in such a way that any side but the north can be lifted to let in air or lowered to block out the sun. The danger of winds and spirits is always weighed against the simpler fury of the weather: storms, for example, always come from the east, so that tents must often be shut off from the direction of Islam. Doorways and openings are necessarily less flexible in adobe architecture. If at all possible, people build doorways to their walled compounds and to their houses facing east, west, or south.

The spatial arrangements of everyday tent life frequently appear more chaotic than the ordering of self and space that I have just described. Despite the standard arrangement of milk stands, beds, and goatskin bags with respect to north, south, east, and west, Azawagh Arab tents usually present an impression of considerable disarray: a lone torn sandal, a broken wooden spoon, goat droppings, a torn piece of cloth, and other scraps frequently litter their sandy floors, and worn blankets and mats are every-where. Nevertheless, women always know in what corner of the tent rafters a clean spoon is suspended, where a needle was stuck into the burlap roof for safe-keeping, or where the sandy ground of the tent is unclean from a child recently relieving himself.

Fittingly, women's arched hairstyles and the arched roofs of Arab tents are recognized to mimic one another, tents representing a projection of women's own veiled and protected forms.[4] Since tents are the female space *par excellence*, it is no surprise that tent making and repairing have been among the few work activities Arab women have engaged in, as discussed in chapter 5. In fact, both today and in the past much of the actual sewing and the erection of the tent are usually carried out by *ḥaraṭīn*. Nevertheless, the ideology persists that fabrication of the tent is an Arab woman's respon-sibility, and they noted this to me often. And I frequently came upon women repairing their tent, stitching up a tear or adding a piece of old *ḥawli* or a burlap sack to one "wall," most often to the side flaps.

The goatskin tents[5] that were the abode of all Azawagh Arabs until recent decades required scores of skins, and the ones of burlap that most live in today require almost as many used millet sacks.[6] Sewing these pieces together is no small task. It involves creating tight seams between the pieces of material so that as little sun, sand, and rain as possible can penetrate. It is in keeping with female nature, therefore, that this labor of closing off space, of ensuring unbroken cover for their bodies and persons, is one women readily engage in.[7] To assemble all these pieces into a good tent is to seal off, enclose, constrict entry, all acts that women also engage in toward their own bodies by fattening, veiling, and managing their bodily orifices. A song/poem (*gāf*) praising the features of a beautiful woman even compares her thighs to something sewed or tied together: "and her thighs tied together, belted with a knot" (see epigraph to chapter 9). Despite the little work of any kind that Azawagh Arab women do, and the few material objects or utensils they make use of, it is not uncommon for a woman to have a needle stuck into her top braid, handily placed for sewing up a torn *ḥawli* or repairing a corner of the tent.

Despite women's daily occupation of and responsibilities toward the tent, it is not women's property, as it is among the neighboring Tuareg. Among Azawagh Arabs the tent belongs decidedly to the man, and when a woman is divorced she must leave this conjugal shelter and return to her father's or brother's. *Khayme*, the term for "tent," also means "home" generally. Only through marriage can a woman come to "have" a tent; only through marriage can she gain a home, and the desirable protection, placehood, and prestige this confers. To get married is "to make a tent" *'adel al-khayme*, and if a woman is divorced she becomes "without a tent" (*bila khayme*). When I asked an old woman once where her daughter lived (liter-ally "where is her tent?"), she responded, "she has no tent [home]" ("ma 'andhe ḥate khayme"). A divorced woman, then, is not only without the shelter and support of a man, but also without the shelter of a tent. A divorced woman usually returns to live with her father, but like all un-married women, has no place to call her own in society, at least until she has grown sons who can support her as a husband would. I discuss the relationship between social placehood and maleness at greater length below.

The extent to which daily practice inverts the actuality of male owner-ship of tents, however, was brought home to me on one of my first days in Tassara, when I came across the girls playing with homemade dolls in miniature cardboard houses in a corner of a compound, described in chapter 1. The furnishings consisted largely of play pillows, mats, and scraps of blankets – the most prominent objects in any tent, for people to lean, sit, and lie on. Along the open side of the dollhouse sat the big, round female dolls. Only after a few minutes did I discover strewn haphazardly against the back wall two sticks lashed together with a simple covering – the male doll, in much smaller proportions than the female dolls, and with much less elaboration. The male doll was clearly not at the center of the tent in the girls' play, and indeed seemed an afterthought to the theater of daily life they were engaged in constructing, just as in daily life men are not part of the female-dominated tent scene.

Engendering space: center and periphery, stasis and movement

Women rarely raise themselves, and always move with slow, deliberate movements. The most characteristic "Arab" positions for a woman are to be sitting cross-legged, or to lie prone on one side, propped on an elbow. A large part of the fattening regimen for girls is learning to be still, not always flitting about, a type of activity women derogate by pointing one finger up in the air and moving it up and down as they wave their hand about. (Women are very expressive with their hands and arms, perhaps an especially well-developed arena of gesture in the absence of other physical movements permitted them.) The chief's daughter, one of the biggest women in Tassara, both figuratively and literally, often wore heavy anklets, a type of adornment that was more widespread in the past. Even when people lived out in the desert and shifted camp Arab women had little truck with movement, depending on servants to pack and unload the animals.

Men, by contrast, not only travel constantly, but on a day-to-day basis are in constant motion, and walk with a strong, quick, and deliberate stride. Even when young men pay visits to the tents of their sisters, mothers, and aunts, their behavior is in striking contrast to that of the women, who sit modestly and quietly and veil if the kin relationship demands it. Around women men seem to exaggerate the bodily postures and spatial mobility that are characteristic of maleness, by sitting with their legs sprawled wide apart, talking rapidly and moving from subject to subject, gesturing like live wires, and jumping up to leave abruptly as if important work suddenly called or the very subdued immobility of the women was starting to repel them.

If men and women must both be at home, as when both are elderly or the husband is sick, they sit as far apart as possible, usually with their backs to one another, or one sits in the house while the other occupies the tent. In the desert, families tend to have a small tent for visitors where men may spend the days at some remove from their main tent. Another solution is to erect a mat wall within the tent. Bakka used this solution in the tent with her husband, the *qāḍi*. A mat enclosed Bakka in the southeast corner of the tent, and the aging Sidi al-Mokhtar sat quietly on the other side. Once when I was visiting Bakka, a learned Islamic scholar (*'ālem*) arrived to visit Sidi al-Mokhtar. Bakka veiled even behind the mat (she was generally very modest), and to the *'ālem*'s quiet, invisible words of greeting she answered in a respectful, barely audible whisper. The *'ālem*, like all visitors to the *qāḍi*, sat partially outside the tent's covering, and as other men arrived to share the visit, Bakka's and my conversation came to an end. Our whispers ceased, and in this relatively unusual proximity of men who were both elderly and *'ulama*, their sex effectively took command of the space of the tent.

The way men and women occupy space varies throughout the life-cycle, a temporal axis which men and women also occupy differently. Recall that, according to Azawagh Arabs, female fetuses develop more slowly than male fetuses, but as children, girls mature twice as quickly as boys. Although they do not keep track of ages in years, a girl of twelve is essentially considered the equivalent in maturity of a man of twenty-four.[8] Childhood and old age are the times when men and women are closest to one another in spatial terms, for girls who have not begun to fatten run about as boys do, and old men often remain at home as women do. As men and women reach the point of maximal differentiation, as teenagers and young adults, they are most separated in space, and most separated in the way they occupy space. When women have fattened and are entering their roles as wives and mothers, and men are focused on supporting their families out in the larger world, women are most still and men most mobile.

Once married, husbands and wives rarely speak to each other at all in the presence of others, even when a husband departs for or returns from a long trip. The public silence of married couples does not indicate antagonism or a poor quality of marital relationship, however; rather, it indicates the respect/shame (*ḥeshme*) the two feel around the fact of their sexual relationship, as well as a cultural disinclination to show too much affection for a single person, especially one in as delicate a relationship to you as your spouse. Consequently, if couples do talk in public it may be in anger, or because they are older and beyond the peak of their sexual relationship. The extent to which many couples discuss their experiences in private, however, was brought home to me once when I joined several important men from Tassara for a meal when we were all in Tchin Tabaraden. As we sat around the bowl, Sherayef, a generally upstanding but shy young man, informed the others, "She doesn't eat meat,"[9] and "She eats with her hands; she doesn't need a spoon." I was very amused by his seeming expertise in my habits, since I barely knew him. Laughing a little, I asked, "But how do you know all this?" He looked a bit embarrassed, and his older brother a bit teasingly answered for him: "Fettam [his wife] told him." Clearly they had ample time to discuss the minutiae of daily life with one another, however little they even acknowledged each other's presence during daylight hours.

The social distance between men and women in public is inversely related to how close they are in private. At the time of highest sexual attraction, women are most shy not only of acknowledging their husband's existence, as when he walks into a compound, but even of uttering his name in his absence. Men also were embarrassed if I asked after their wives by name, rather than simply asking the standard greeting, "How is your family?" It is as if daytime behavior must compensate for nighttime closeness, when husbands and wives open themselves to one another not only through sex but also by sharing daily happenings and concerns.

In summary, men and women relate to space most differently and are most segregated from one another at the times when they are sexually closest and most attracted to one another: when they are married or seeking marriage. Women are least mobile when they are at the height of their desirability; fattening pubescent or pre-pubescent girls rarely leave their tents or compounds. Their husbands-to-be, by contrast, are the most mobile members of the community, men of late adolescence and early adulthood who are making their way in the world by seemingly incessant travel and movement.

While husbands and wives do share in each other's lives more as equals when they lie together at night, the qualities of male mobility and female immobility pertain to their love making that also goes on then. I was told by both women and men that women are always underneath during sexual activity, and should not move but receive men's caresses and squeezes passively. (These are presumably the same caresses and squeezes that some men described gesturally by doing something like kneading dough in the air.) Indeed, immobile, veiled, entirely contained women incited the most desire in men. One young male friend confessed to me his new love for a girl in the nearby camp of Amassara by explaining that what really impressed him was that if anyone else was around, she would not even talk, but just sit there, veiled, before him. The expectations of women to be immobile, closed, and distant from men are, like the appeal of fatness, ultimately cloaked in a sexual aesthetic.

The geography of daily social life recapitulates the geography of the society as a whole. People play out the opposition of center and periphery in the female–male dichotomy, and each sex is most fulfilled and most potent when best complying with expected bodily comportment. A young man once said to me, "If an Arab woman stands up you can blow her over, but if she is sitting she can pull you to the ground." Women frequently joked with me and with each other by trying to pull someone standing to the ground when shaking hands in greeting. Sometimes I read in this an envy of mobility (which a few women confessed to me in words at other times), sometimes I took it as a wish to make the person standing, especially when it was me, more appropriately grounded, as they were. In any case, women's metaphorical as well as physical strength resides in their being seated. Standing, a woman's balance is unsteady, her worth in question, her embodiment of social values compromised. Seated, a woman fulfills her part of the male–female opposition and exemplifies the core of her family and her family's morality. By fattening women anchor not only themselves, but by extension their families, encampments, and the whole society and its cultural identity. In a sense it is because women so ground their families and their society that men are free to travel as widely as they do, bringing that which is outside their world into it, strengthening their society at its core by their manipulation of that which is outside it.

Azawagh Arabs possess what one early French official described as "a very marked spirit of independence"(Abadie 1927: 153). They are willing to settle on lands few others care to inhabit and make them the center of their society. In these far reaches not only can they cherish their freedom, but Azawagh Arab men can have the best of both worlds: a protected sphere of tent and home, and a wider world of excitement, adventure, and economic possibility where no actions can ever endanger the core of their families and tribes. Azawagh Arab men may travel constantly, but despite this or perhaps because of it, they had a strong sense of ownership and attachment to the land they called home.[10] In summary, Azawagh Arabs resolve what I see as conflicting sentiments about mobility and stasis, involvement in the outside world and inner purity and containedness, in a sexual division of labor and living that allows for both. Men and women occupy space in opposing yet complementary ways: while men are constantly pulled toward movement, they are dependent on and drawn to the stability immobile women provide, just as women's immobility is dependent on the constant mobility of men.

Engendering space: placehood

While women are clearly markers and embodiers of physical space, it is men who mark and signify space in the social imagination by their ability to actually constitute a sort of space in their own persons. Let me explain.

In contrast to the daily physical fact of women's immobility, their lives consist of being moved about like pieces in a chess game, in which men provide the stable reference points. A girl moves first from her father's home to her husband's, then perhaps later to another husband's, and eventually perhaps to a son's or, in a few cases, to her own tent. When a man first marries, however, he becomes one of the lodestars around which people then orient themselves. He becomes, in effect, a "place." A woman can only be a "place" when she is old and widowed.

These relationships of people to placehood are expressed through the Arabic word 'and, which means something in between the English "at" and "with," or "at the home of," like the French *chez*. When asked to tell the story of their lives, women generally related a brief set of events located by their relationship to a man: "I was 'and so and so when I fasted, then 'and so and so until I was 'taken' [in marriage] by so and so," and so forth. Despite the careful labeling of each and every swell and tree clustering in their vast landscape, Azawagh Arabs generally describe a woman's place at any particular time by reference not to a geographical space but to a man. "She died 'and Muhammad," one might say, referring to her second husband. "Where were you at the time you got this sickness?" I might ask. "I was 'and these children's father" (never pronouncing a husband's real name, since that would be disrespectful).

Once when I ran into a young man I knew on the street in Tassara, he asked the inevitable question of where I was coming from (if not where I was going). I replied that I had been "at the place of the divorcées," or young unmarried women ('and al-hajajīl), a home where two such young women lived, and a third frequently visited. I commonly thought of it as the unmarried women's home, though I knew it was "really" the household of Nefou, the father of one of the women whom I only met after many months in Tassara because he was often away. In any case, the young man laughed and patiently explained to me that you cannot be "at" the unmarried women's. They have no house. If I said I was 'and them, people would think perhaps I had just seen them in the street. I could only say that I was " 'and Bukaha" (Nefou's wife) or "at Nefou's people" ('and hal-Nefou) – meaning those he has married, engendered, or in some way is responsible for – or, better yet, simply 'and Nefou. To acquire placehood status, then, is to marry and start a family. One can even be 'and (at the place of) a woman once she is married, though she herself will always be 'and her husband and this would be the more correct way to refer to her household.

The way in which Azawagh Arabs speak of kinship distance in terms of the number of men separating them also accords with this view of men as place markers. Again, men are the units of measurement that create the calculus of kinship, just as they are the markers of social place. In keeping with their social fixedness, and as discussed in chapter 4, men "take" or "bring" in marriage (*huwa jābhe*, "he took/brought her"), and "let go," to divorce (*huwa khellāhe*); a woman can only be the passive recipient of these actions. The verb "to marry" can only be conjugated with a male subject, "he married her" (*huwa sheddhe*).

How people occupy space at a concrete, corporeal level, then, seems to be the inverse of how space is talked about and mentally conceptualized. On a physical plane, and in one manifestation of personhood, it is women who (re)produce, provide, and anchor the society; but on an ideological plane, and in another guise of personhood, it is men who produce, provide, and are the still points in a sea of circulating women, birth, life, and death. This analysis, if correct, contrasts somewhat with conceptions of the relationship between physical space and cultural patterns espoused by Beidelman (1993), Bourdieu (1977), and others wherein schemas of spatial practice index or reflect more elusive aspects of cultural meaning. My analysis suggests that modes of occupying physical space and constructions of social space may at times be inversions of each other, even in dialogue with each other. For Azawagh Arabs, women's practical dominance of the physical center of society counterbalances men's dominance of social place and permanence in the society. Through fattening, lack of movement, and playfully pulling people to the ground, women assert their rights to the center of social spaces, just as men assert their rights by laughing when I suggest that I was "at" the divorcées, and by refusing to make long visits to the female spaces of the tent, rushing off instead to the market, bush, or well that constitute the public centers of their world.

Town and desert: women's changing worlds

After two years in Tchin Tabaraden, fifteen months in Tassara and numerous excursions into the surrounding desert,[11] I came to realize that while most of the Arabs I knew resided in villages, their imaginations still lived in the bush. Not only did women constantly wax nostalgic about bush life, but when I spent time at bush encampments I saw that the slow, meandering daily routine I observed in town was very well suited to the endless hours of bush life where "drinking and sitting" constituted the bulk of all female activity. Despite the fact that water was free and readily available in town, for example, people never kept extra on hand, only sending someone to get it long after it had run out.[12] They did not dig latrines,[13] and many did not have permanent wash areas in their yards; indeed, they washed seldom. The continuing dependency on bush plants for medicine

164

and the attachment of Azawagh Arabs to tents rather than houses also testified to the nearness of their lives to the bush life many had so recently left behind. Nonetheless, I also noticed how welcome the company of female kinswomen was after life among only a handful of other women in desert camps, and, as I will discuss below, when the opportunity arose, few women in fact wanted to return to desert life.

Amidst busy ethnographic analysis, the peace and silence of desert life is difficult to convey in words. Several times I arrived at desert camps to find a woman in a tent sitting alone, or alone but for a child, in my terms doing nothing, and yet exuding an aura of utter purpose and completeness and peace. In their terms, I came to realize, to sit or lie wonderfully still was to fulfill a purpose: simply to be fat and beautiful and closed off from the world's chaos and dangers, embodying the conditions of life's honor and increase.

Women spoke with considerable nostalgia of bush life, telling me again and again how milk was abundant in the desert, their "hearts were calm," and their bodies white, fat, and healthy. They also spoke with pride of the way they moved, or more accurately, were moved, from camp to camp. As Maya explained to me on my first visit with the women of Tassara, her voice wistful,

A camel was brought, it would lie down, and the woman would get on. Then they would move to where the next camp would be, the woman would get off, and lie in the shade of a tree, a slave would bring her a bowl of milk, she would drink, she would lie down.

One day Maya got so involved in the description of how women were hoisted up and placed on camels that she decided to act it out. She sent to a neighbor for a particular type of blanket (*leqtīfa*) that was positioned around women on their high saddles. She proceeded to wrap it around her on the ground as she sat cross-legged and straight-backed, and then grabbed three babies present and placed one on each side and one on her lap. There, her seated body made even wider by the cumbersome blanket, Maya basked in the image of her weighty and maternal glory, and I could easily picture her perched high on a camel, dominating the landscape in her luscious but hidden allure, being led to the next desert plain she would adorn. Women decorated themselves with jewelry when they moved camp, and the camels wore decorations of dyed, fringed leather as well. With the fading of this way of life, women no longer move as often, no longer traverse the same desert spaces that men do, and no longer have the opportunity for this moment of glory. It is part of a deepening chasm between male and female experience that is beginning to define a new generation of Azawagh Arabs.

Despite the decreasing numbers who live in small bush encampments, there is still considerable interaction between town dwellers and desert dwellers. It is common for one branch of a family to be in the desert looking after animals, and another to be settled in a town. Sometimes the more retiring men of a family may choose to settle in a desert encampment where life is simpler and less expensive, while the more adventurous brothers may go off to a bigger town for some years to make their fortunes. The desert also holds an attraction for the very religious: several of the most esteemed *ulama* remain permanently in the desert. Some women go out to the desert for weeks or months after the rainy season in order to fatten and/or recover from illness. Despite their constant romantic allusions to it, however, women tend to find the desert lonely and envy their sisters in towns. It was not unusual for sisters and daughters to come into town for extended stays with their natal families, and then be reluctant to return to the bush.

Although I thought most families in Tassara showed no signs of ever intending to move to the bush again, toward the end of my stay one quite established extended family moved 10 kilometers south to Amassara following the rains. After hearing such nostalgia for bush life over the year, I was now surprised to learn that the women quietly but adamantly opposed the move. Their husbands decreed it, however, apparently to be near their animals and avoid the higher expenses of town life. Once there, the women's lives did not seem appreciably changed, though they missed relatives who stayed behind. Without walls to bound the nuclear family units, the tents were further from each other than their houses had been in town.

In town women spend less time alone and visit or receive visits more often, though they venture into the lanes only after ascertaining that no men or only insignificant men will be able to observe their passage. Generally younger women spend the days at their mother's, grandmother's, or aunt's. They leave in the morning, and return at the end of the day, and their fattening food may be brought to them from their own home. Though younger women move back and forth between certain houses, none has ever seen the market, and older women almost never leave their compounds.

Once, forgetting myself, I turned to my female friend, Asseghiyera, in Tchin Tabaraden to ask whose store was next to Alhoussein's in the market. Asseghiyera, whose wedding I described in chapter 4, was one of my more worldly female acquaintances, fluent in Hausa and Tamajeq, with a husband who had spent many years in Libya, and a house on a main "thoroughfare," conveniently located for optimum observation of town happenings. When I asked her about the market stall, however, she laughed. "Reqia [my Arabic name], you *know* I have never seen the market! The closest I ever got to it was the day I went in your car to visit Shweytima on the other side of town." Women did not even see the comparatively bustling epicenter of their own towns, a mere 100 yards from where they were born, raised, married, became mothers, and died.

That women strive for closedness and immobility is understood as natural, a logical aspect of being female because these characteristics are embedded in the way women are socialized to set up their tent, position themselves within it, relate to men, treat visitors, relieve themselves, converse, eat, give birth, and make love. That women and men should lead their lives apart, ever controlling the strong passions liable to arise between them, is made an unassailable truth because the ideas and practices under-pinning it pervade every moment and every behavior, in body, heart, and mind.

Henrietta Moore has noted that in order to understand how the orga-nization of space comes to have meaning, one must relate it to the problems and challenges people perceive in their world. Of course the relationship is dialectical; the perception of those problems and challenges is itself shaped by daily life ordered within space in a particular way (Moore 1986: 107). For Azawagh Arabs, the tensions and forces they negotiate on a daily basis have to do with the potency of the sexual urge, the necessity of bodily closedness for well-being, the acquisition of food and wealth, and the protection and enhancement of family and tribe. Just as all of these are deeply embedded in the corporeal geography of the Azawagh Arab world, as I explored in the last chapter, they are also clearly played out in how space is occupied.

Part IV

NEGOTIATING LIFE'S CHALLENGES

Plate 9 The author with Faissa mint Moussaysa (Amassara)

8

WELL-BEING
AND ILLNESS

Don't you see the Arab women here, always dizzy? They take
medicine until they get very hot, and fall. They seek it out.
They want men not to dislike them.

-Words of a *ḥaraṭāni*

From my first days working at the health clinic in Tchin Tabaraden to my
last days in Tassara, a constantly recurring topic of conversation was
whether someone suffered from too much "heat" or too much "cold."
Although disease is also believed to be caused by spirits, the evil eye, and
witchcraft, all of which are treated by Islamic medicine, the first diagnosis
people make for most illnesses, from indigestion to weight loss to severe
fever, is almost always an excess of hot or cold. This near-universal way
of analyzing the state of the body, ancestor to the Western concept of
"having a cold," constitutes the major way in which Azawagh Arabs think
about health and disease. Despite the terminology, the categories have little
to do with temperature, but rather represent two overarching categories
that each encompass many different qualities, not least those to do with
sexual desire and desirability. To understand the mechanics of fattening,
and to understand the ultimate bodily state women seek to achieve, requires
understanding the complex way in which a balance between hot and cold
is a condition not just of personal health, but of the general well-being of
the world.

Understanding disease: "hot" and "cold"

Classification of diseases and foods into hot and cold qualities exists from
Latin America to the Far East, through the Middle East, much of Africa,
and south and central Asia.[1] Remnants of the system exist still in Western
cultures, where we talk of having "a cold" and where many still believe
that a draft can bring on a cold or muscle aches. Although there are some
fundamental similarities in the different humoral systems in the world, such

171

as their holism and the association of heat with flowing, procreation, and sex, there are many differences as well. Often the same condition is associated with heat in one place and cold in another. As near to Niger as Morocco, for example, spirits are associated with cold (Greenwood 1992: 298) whereas in the Azawagh they are associated with heat.

The anthropologist George Foster (1994) identifies three major humoral systems in the world: the ancient Greek, the Indian Ayurvedic, and the Chinese. They are not identical, and it is unclear whether one system preceded and developed into the others. It is generally accepted, however, that since their possibly disparate origins several millennia ago they have had contact with and influenced one another, as well as evolved indigenously. All also diffused outwards, with the ancient Greek system ultimately influencing Europe and later European colonies, from Latin America to the Philippines, as well as the Arab and the Muslim world. The original Greek four-category system of hot, cold, wet, and dry has been reworked and simplified in many of these places to focus on heat and coldness, a fundamental dualism that then embraces other dualistic qualities.

For Azawagh Arabs, because hot and cold (ḥamān and barūd) are considered part of the empirically perceptible natural world, it made no sense to people when I said that where I came from we did not have hot and cold. It seemed to be equivalent to saying that we cannot distinguish between saltiness and sweetness, or that we do not get stomach aches. If we did not have hot and cold where I came from, this could only mean that our natural world was of an entirely different order from theirs, and that our physical human bodies were of a different nature from theirs. Given that these states seemed to them to be as much aspects of the natural world as air and water, that is, utterly obvious and open to sensory perception, it is perhaps not surprising that no one I asked could explain in fact what "hot" and "cold" meant in a way that clarified the overall logic of the system. The meanings of hot and cold were also unreflected upon because they are taken so much for granted by all ethnic groups in this part of the world, even if there are differences in how each group applies the system.

It was only after a concentrated month of analyzing my fieldnotes and making lists and categories out of myriad ethnographic details that I began to see that how people used the terms "hot" and "cold" was neither arbitrary nor illogical, but rather belonged to a consistent system. One key to the system has to do precisely with the qualities of openness and closedness so central to life for Azawagh Arabs: heat is generally a quality of energy enclosed in the body, and cold a quality of the body being too open.

Pregnancy provides an excellent example of heat. When a woman is pregnant she becomes very hot, given that huge amounts of energy are surging inside her to create a new human being, all in the completely closed space of her womb. In many ways the same acts that increase the energy of a substance according to Western chemistry – movement in an enclosed space

– are what are associated with heat in the Azawagh. The image of food cooking in pots also conveys what heat is about: heat is contained in the closed pot, building up energy in a confined space. Thus heat is the quality of things moving, being processed, and gestating; of heightened emotion, and of sexual allure.

Cold, by contrast, is what women need to watch out for the minute after they have given birth: the energy and heat have escaped, and the body is bleeding and wide open for outside winds to enter. Cold, then, is the quality of things running out of the body, but also of things blocked and still in the body. Thus a runny nose, diarrhea, and various kinds of stomach complaints are all cold. Cold is associated with raw foods, with foods cooked in such a way that the heat can escape, for example in the ground (a common way of cooking bread, buried in the sand), and with foods sifted, because air enters. Cold is generally the quality of wind and air and inappropriate flow. Although semen, the product of free-moving males, is cold, too much cold is synonymous not with sexuality but with dreaded sexually transmitted disease, which is characterized by unnatural discharge. It comes on when what should be inner and what should be outer pollute one another, as when winds enter the body.

Put another way, heat is also a quality of energy concentrated, whereas cold is a quality of energy dissipated. It may be useful to offer a general summary of the two qualities:

1   Heat is the quality of things that are *enclosed* and *full of energy*, like a churning stomach ache without diarrhea.
2   Cold is the quality of things that are *wet*, *runny*, and *open*, like a cold that brings a runny nose, or sexually transmitted diseases that cause vaginal or penile secretions.

Neither heat nor cold is negative in and of itself; the key is to retain the correct balance in the body, and to be hot or cold at the right time and in the right way. A woman wants to be a little hot, for example, to be sexy. Boddy notes that among Arabs in the northern Sudan as well, heat and associated fluids are "markers of fertility and femininity," and that enclosure is crucial to creating the necessary moist environment for gestation (Boddy 1989: 69, 65). In the Azawagh, because heat in the body mounts when there are no openings for the escape of gestating and transformative processes, outward closedness and dryness of the body are also associated with heat. Within the emotional and moral domains, desire, appetite, and sexuality are both heat-laden and stimulated by heat. Foreign foods like tomatoes, peppers, and beans also bring on heat; perhaps because with origins far from the balancing powers of the desert, they come from a world of comparatively frenetic activity and immorality.

Heat is also associated with things flowing in appropriate ways, such as food dispersing quickly from the stomach into the body. Women who are fattening thus increase the heat of their bodies by drinking large amounts of water with their grain, or by subsisting entirely on milk. In this way, even as their bodies turn colder from cold-generating immobility and stuffing themselves with food, the proper dispersal of this substance into the body will create heat.

For women, cold is always the quality of desire and sexuality forestalled. Since they are generally trying to cultivate heat in their bodies, women avoid washing as much as possible because cold is brought on by putting water on the porous body, especially when it is at all windy. Women are in the greatest danger of cold when the body is "open" to the wind during the postpartum period, menstruation, or after having sex.

As the above description shows, the qualities of heat and cold are closely bound up with those of wetness and dryness, but not necessarily in straightforward ways. The best way to understand it seems to be that heat involves wetness in appropriate places, for example in women's body "meat" – here "wet" has the sense of fresh, new, and luscious; and heat involves fluids flowing in appropriate channels, though possibly in excess, such as frequent urination and large loss of blood. There can also be a dryness associated with heat; the outside of the body is dry, and too much heat can make the whole body dried up, pushing the wetness out of even the appropriate places. Cold, again, involves wetness in inappropriate places, such as the vagina, or in sores on the body, as well as fluids not flowing. Certain stomach problems are thought to result from cold, when food gets stopped up in the body, and body pains can be caused by cold when blood gathers and clots in one particular body area.

Because the etymology and symptoms of any given illness can be complicated, in practice the hot–cold "system" is open to negotiation and debate. For example, one day a man who had ridden in from the bush on a donkey showed up at a house where I was visiting, with a painfully swollen foot and aching back. The women present were cousins who were non-veiling (*meḥerima*) to him, and they immediately launched into a discussion of his ailments and general ill-health. "Is it from hot or cold?" one of the women asked him. "I don't know," he answered gruffly. The woman was surprised: "What? Don't you know what you have?" But her daughter chimed in that if he hadn't treated it yet, how could he know, with which the old man concurred. From there they went on to discuss the types of plants they could use, and what the likelihood was that ailments with such symptoms were hot or cold, comparing it to other similar ailments people had had. As this vignette suggests, many diseases can come from a surplus of either hot or cold, and only by symptoms' reaction to a known hot or cold medicine can one know the nature of a disease, hot treating cold, and cold, hot.

Although diagnosis can be ambiguous and complicated, no disease or medicine, including Western medicine available in the local health clinic, lies outside of the system of hot–cold classification. Many Western drugs, consequently, come to be used in ways not foreseen by the state medical establishment. When I found a packet of tetracycline pills stuffed in the tent rafters of a pregnant young woman who had been suffering from a urinary tract infection for weeks, I asked her why she did not take this medicine given her by the nurse. "Because we know that medicine is hot, we've seen it work. What I need is cold," she replied.

The qualities of hot and cold inhere not only in diseases and in medicines, but in all plants, all bodily conditions, sexuality, the weather, and even, to some extent, history. The forces of hot and cold are ubiquitous, linking bodies to their surrounding environment, so that a storm, inattention to diet, a walk on hot sand, or unsensed fluctuations in the air all inevitably affect the inner condition of bodies. Unifying the human body, the environment, the spirit world, and social life in a cohesive universe, the qualities of hot and cold entail that all of God's creations are mutually dependent and interacting.

Hot and cold vs. Western biomedicine

To further clarify the workings of the hot–cold system, it is worth comparing it more directly to its Western counterpart to illuminate how the two ways of understanding health and illness differ. Byron Good (1994: 101–115) has argued that humoral medical thinking is to a large extent incommensurable with Western medical thinking; in any case, the fundamental premises of the hot–cold paradigm run counter to biomedical wisdom in several ways. First, the logic of disease according to hot and cold is one of forces or energy interacting, rather than material entities invading, as in germ theory. The concept of health is thus one of balance: the forces of hot and cold must be kept in balance in the body, and though this often entails keeping one or the other at bay, it does not involve a notion of the body that must be kept bounded completely from outside antigens. Each force treats its opposite, so too much heat is treated by a cold medicine, and vice versa. All foods, medicines, and most bodily conditions lie somewhere on a continuum from very cold to very hot, with many degrees of variation in between, but nothing is neutral. Thus there are numerous ways to seek and achieve balance, but also endless opportunities for the balance to be thrown off.

Second, the system's logic assumes bi-directional influence: swelling in the body causes heat, for example, and heat is also a cause of swelling. This is very important; one cannot think about hot and cold in terms of cause and effect in the way that Western medicine separates what brings on a disease from its symptoms, because hot and cold run through everything, confusing any attempts to assert priority or causation. Even if people always seek to find a cause of illness, the symptoms are in themselves also creators of the disease, one might say.

Third, although hot and cold lie at opposite ends of a continuum, there is considerable ambiguity in their characters. Each can create confusingly similar conditions, such as swelling and wetness, but they are associated with different kinds of swelling and different kinds of wetness. Neither is wholly bad or wholly good, though it seemed that for women at least a tendency toward heat was better than one toward cold. Still, the goal, again, is balance. This too contrasts with the paradigm of Western medicine, where being wholly well is at one end of the continuum and very sick at the other; the goal of Western medicines is to drive out all traces of illness, not to reach a middle point on a range of qualities.

Fourth, the explanatory field of the hot–cold system acknowledges constant interaction between the environment and the inner human body, in a more profound way than Western medicine does, where air and wind are not considered threats unless they are thought to contain specific microbes. Fifth and lastly, this thermodynamic understanding of disease and the world integrally links sexuality and sexual health to the same forces that bring on stomach aches, blisters, and toothaches. Although in the West we associate sexuality with sexually transmitted diseases, we do not consider what happens with and to our sexual organs to be inherently connected to ill-being in other bodily organs. It is this groundedness of hot and cold in a sexual economy of allure, desire, and release that gives this understanding of disease its power and pervasiveness.

The social consequences of hot and cold

Although more implicit than the qualities of wet and dry, which are often discussed specifically in disease analysis and treatment, the qualities of closedness and openness constitute the most expressive link between the hot–cold system and the social structures in which they are embedded. It is through heat's essential quality of closedness, and cold's quality of openness, that the material, corporeal dualism of heat and cold responds to and orders the most salient aspects of Azawagh Arabs' social existence.

As discussed in previous chapters, being "closed off" and containing flow are as crucial to women's bodily health as they are to their social health. The closed spaces of their bodies create the protected space necessary for gestation; the closedness of their person insures that both they and their children will have intact honor and identities. Men, however, produce in the unbounded spaces of their world, and their honor and identity are tied to their ability to convert that production to sons and large families, and to this end to maintain a wife who embodies and upholds their integrity and ability to be productive. Cloaking these activities of production and reproduction are the flames of sexual desire and fulfillment, also expressed and modulated in the vocabulary of hot and cold, demanding that women maintain heat, and men cold. While both men and women seek a balance between hot and cold, cold is seen to strengthen men, who go out into the open world, and whose semen is cold. Women, on the other hand, are ever desirous of leaning toward the hot end of the continuum, as long as they can avoid its deleterious side-effects.

In general, cold is seen as the worse pole because of its association with sexually transmitted diseases, one of people's greatest fears, but the preeminent female healer in Tassara pointed out that, in the extreme case, cold is the lesser evil.

> Heat kills. If a woman comes to be really "gotten" by heat, she will no longer be a woman, she will no longer thrive [be *fālḥa*, literally "generous"]. If a woman has cold, and is treated, she will thrive again. Too much heat cannot be treated. Its medicine is very difficult.

Heat, as I have said, is associated with gestation and the creation of life, with sexuality and female allure, but too much of it may not only cause sickness and a swollen fetus, but may cause a woman to "become no longer a woman," going overboard as it were, losing her very femininity and humanity. This quality of heat speaks to the contradictory and ever conflicting impulses in Azawagh Arab society to heighten desire to its utmost point and celebrate it, and yet to control it and deny it at the same time. Desire leads to pleasure and offspring, yet also potentially to chaos and disorder. While women want to increase their heat to maintain their sexual attractiveness to husbands or potential husbands, too much heat can also draw the attention of ever lustful spirits, with disastrous consequences. They also must not be seen to be seeking such heat too actively, for there must be a contradictory passive but enticing sexuality.

Discussing the three different types of medicine found in most Arab-Islamic societies – popular or humoral (including hot and cold), sacred (i.e. Islamic), and "cosmopolitan" (i.e. Western biomedicine) – Byron Good suggests that, of these, it is popular medicine that responds in particularly appropriate, expressive ways to local cultures. "From the products of diverse historical periods and high theoretical traditions, popular medicine constructs illness configurations which articulate conflicts and stresses peculiar to that community, and often provides therapies which reinforce integration and conservative values of the community" (Good 1977: 30). Among Arabs of the Azawagh, hot and cold conform to Good's observation: that is, they speak about bodies and disease in the image of Azawagh Arab society. Through the two forces or states of hot and cold, the social is writ onto the body and its disorders, and the bodily logic they convey

177

in turn gives a material alibi to the Azawagh Arab social world of divergent sexes, openings and boundaries, and contained value discussed in this work so far.

Open women, closed men

In keeping with the other perceived differences between male and female bodies, women's and men's bodies also work differently when it comes to hot and cold. An Azawagh Arab woman's path through life, replete as it is with substances entering and leaving the body – getting fat, retaining fatness, menstruating, pleasing men sexually, giving birth, breastfeeding – requires her to be more vigilant about the forces of hot and cold than a man must be. When I asked Aichata, a woman renowned for her knowledge of healing plants, if wind, one of the main causes of cold, hurt men, she said, "Only ones with wounds, open cuts. It can't enter him from below, only women" (i.e. through the vagina). Only women have an opening "below" that is wide to the world during menstruation, sexual intercourse, and childbirth, leaving the body extra vulnerable to sneaking winds that cause cold and heat, that rise up from the ground and seep into the body. The perceived porousness of female bodies means that managing and closing off the body, in part by fattening, is a full-time occupation for women, and gives an anatomical alibi to the social injunctions that women veil, sit still, and remain tent-bound. The natural closedness of men, by contrast, is a condition for their ability to range far and wide over windy plains and to sleep without a covering at night.

Aichata's sister Fatima, another respected older woman in town, did not contradict me when I suggested that men seemed able to eat a greater range of foods than women without worrying about hot and cold. "Some men," she explained, however, "have cold in them, and others have heat in them." That is, their bodies *do* conform to and are affected by the same forces as women's. Their bodies do not necessarily react in the same way, though. "What makes a woman sick, does not make a man sick." As to cold, women's greatest bodily fear, she explained how men could get it despite the absence of the bodily openings her sister had mentioned: "Men get cold from women." Men need not worry so much about winds that could bring cold and the sexual dysfunction it causes, as about women who have been careless and allowed their own sexual organs to become affected. And women's own sexual organs can easily be harmed by cold if they do not pay careful attention to keeping the openings to their bodies closed, and watch the heat of the foods that make up their daily diet. As this conversation illustrates, women's concern about hot and cold is largely a concern about sexuality and the physical act of intercourse itself, when bodily states are most volatile, and when things merge which are otherwise kept radically apart – men and women. In a social world in which men and women go through life maximally differentiating themselves from one another, sexual intercourse is both the supreme articulation of this opposition as well as the supreme resolution of it.

Whereas cold, then, is deleterious to women's health, men are strengthened by it in small measure. Cold is a state of stillness within the body but volatile forces without, a bodily version of men's social and economic strategy in which goods flow around them because of their own agency. Men's social and economic health, one might say, depends not on what happens within their bodies, but on what happens outside their bodies – what they do with their arms and legs, their capacity to think, speak, and act. Their bodies are stable elements, points of agency able to effect transactions without being affected themselves. For women, what is important is that there should be activity – flow, if you will – within their bodies, where future generations take form. Their work is not on the world, converting value on the outside, but within themselves, transforming value on the inside. Cold and openness both endanger this generative capacity and compromise the value-laden, secure condition that attracts men to their necessary opposite, women, whose heat provides the conditions of sexual tension that fuel society. Cold swells women's bodies with the wrong kind of value, empty winds that could be spirit-laced; its swelling is false and without worth. Heat contains in the proper way, with energy enclosed, allure intact, and the independence and "closedness" of Arab society as a whole embodied.[2]

Pregnancy, childbirth, and postpartum

Pregnancy and its surrounding stages are the moments when the character of hot and cold, and women's vulnerability to them, come most to the fore. As soon as a woman knows she is pregnant, she must stop eating hot foods. She is "stoppered" (*meghelga*) by the child, her blood no longer flows, and if she is not careful the heat will build up and harm the child. "She drinks only milk that is not cooked; [otherwise] it heats up the infant." She eats only the most raw forms of the millet and milk porridges that are women's food; couscous that has been sifted in the wind to "cool" it, or millet that has been cooked in dough balls in the ground and is then repounded. She stays away from salt, oil, pepper, and porridge and other foods that have been cooked for a long time in a pot.

During the birth itself, especially at the moment the infant emerges, the tent sides are put down. As many women as possible attend and surround the struggling woman, and while one or more hold the woman in labor in a squatting or kneeling position, the midwife reaches up under the garments of the woman to catch the baby. No clothes are removed, and the genital area is never exposed. In one birth I witnessed, there was great concern when the afterbirth did not emerge immediately – a potential problem in itself, but also leaving the woman open longer and therefore in great danger. She was given a peppery powder to sniff that made her vomit, expelling the placenta with the convulsions.

As soon as she has given birth, a woman is at the greatest danger of cold of any time in her life. Torn open and bloody, she keeps her legs together under a thick blanket even in the hot season, either on the ground or on a low bed with layers of mats preventing any wind from getting through, and this within a mat enclosure built within the tent. In the past a woman did not wash for the entire forty days of her confinement, and today some do not wash for a week. During her confinement a woman does not open her body in other ways either – she speaks little, keeps her eyes cast down, and eats with her back to others, not letting her open mouth turn to society and the outside world of dangerous forces.

To avoid disease in her sexual parts, a woman not only keeps covered and enclosed, but eats the hottest foods possible. Hot tea and milk fresh from the cow, considered hotter, are given to her immediately after birthing, and later she eats pounded dates and a dish of pounded meat, oil, and pounded rice, one of the hottest foods the Azawagh Arabs have. "What is pounded, that is what treats/medicates (*yudāwi*) the stomach of a woman who has just given birth." Some women are even given butter to drink, another supremely hot food. Some drink almost no water, which brings on cold. In addition to special foods, plant medicines are also taken to heal the open, torn, wet vagina and womb.

Aichata explained why wind was so bad for women after they give birth: "It makes a woman swell [as with air], and she gets cold, and her husband cannot go to her [i.e. sexually]. If he goes to her he too will be sick." As Aichata's statement reflects, the forty days of confinement are not only a healing time for the woman but her preparation to return to her husband. Her proximate concern is for her tears to heal, but the ramifications of potential cold are not simply the woman's own discomfort. Ultimately her worry is about her sexual parts being damaged, and in turn not pleasing her husband. By seeking heat, she seeks to heal her vagina and make it tight again so as to please her husband when, on the fortieth day, the baby is taken around to see relatives and she dons a new *ḥawli* sent by her husband, has her hair braided, her face decorated, and returns to the marital bed.

The daily diet

Outside the time of pregnancy, the negotiation of heat and cold in the body is still a pervasive, everyday concern, and one that requires constant adjustment of foods. Women's chief consideration in what they eat each day is how much heat or cold their bodies need. Once I walked in to find a young woman eating a steamed form of *deghnu*, the millet porridge women fatten on. This particular steamed type is called *mufowwer*. "Why are you eating *mufowwer*?" I asked. "I need neither heat nor cold right now," she answered by way of explanation. In fact, women sometimes use the word for medicine, *duwe'*, when referring to food, because it is used to maintain the balance of their bodies and treat their conditions as much as plants or Western medicines are. "She needs [a particular type of porridge] today; that is what will treat/medicate her," women might say. Although *deghnu* is on the whole a colder food than *l'aysh* that men and non-fattening women eat, the many varieties of *deghnu* are themselves on a continuum of hot to cold, based on how finely the millet is pounded, how it is cooked (boiled, steamed, in the ground, not cooked), and whether or not it is sifted.

'Aichettu explained to me why girls and women fatten on *deghnu* and not *l'aysh*. "*L'aysh*, in the evening, if a woman eats it, it will touch the fat of her kidney, and eat it." Why? "Because it is hot. *L'aysh* in the evening melts fat. A woman wants only something cold, like flour, so that if she eats it and drinks water, her stomach will swell. What is good for a woman is something that will swell her." As a group of foods generally on the cold end of the continuum, *deghnu* does not flow through the body, but stays in the stomach, creating the desired swelling and expansion. When taken in huge mouthfuls with water to gulp it down, without chewing, the highly expansive, unprocessed food goes directly to the center of the body, where the water serves to disseminate it adequately into the rest of the body.

This type of imagery, of food dispersing (*yetefarreg*) evenly into the body, was often invoked when I asked women about *deghnu*. Once explaining this concept to me, Fatima put some sand in her palm and said, "See, this is now grouped together. If I put water on it will be spread out, dispersed." The cold *deghnu* taken with cold water goes in an orderly fashion to its resting place in the body's limbs, "flowing" just enough without generating too much heat. Women want food to stick in their bodies and to amass weight, but it must disperse evenly and not cause stomach ailments by staying in the stomach. What they ingest must flow, but to the appropriate resting places, not through and out of them. In order to get fat a woman must eat things that because of their sticking power are cold, and that could therefore lead her down the path to sexual disease and unattractiveness at the same time as they launch her body into the desired state of corpulent sexual allure. Hence the oft-cited prescription that "fat women want heat," or "fat women want hot medicines." Only by eating plant medicines that create heat in the body can the fattened woman turn her body to its appointed use, attracting, pleasing, and holding onto a husband. Often when discussing hot and cold, women would point out to me that a person could be cold in one part of her body and hot in another. "A woman could be cold in her stomach and hot in her head."

181

Furthermore, this seemed to be something more likely to befall women than men. This mixing of hot and cold in one body allows, I would suggest, for the tendency toward cold of a body fattening on milk and coldish foods, but also for the necessary heat of a woman's vagina.

Sex

The public discourse about hot and cold is one of foods, illnesses, plants, and cooking methods, but, as has by now become apparent, the underlying text is one of sexuality. Guided conversations that I had with women about hot and cold invariably followed a set pattern: first, disbelief and incomprehension that we did not "have" hot and cold; second, a listing of what foods and plants fall into each category; and third, a discussion, usually in a lowered voice,[3] about what hot and cold do to the vagina of a woman, and its consequent effects on her marriage.

Such a conversation was one I had with Fatima, the respected, honorable, and shrewd woman who is mother to several of the men who are rising leaders of the Nigerien Arab community today. After she was forced to accept that we in America are sadly blind to the qualities of hot and cold inherent in the living world, she went on to name for me foods that are hot and cold: "Things that contain salt, dried onions, hot pepper, and oil are hot, and ones without these things are cold." "And how would a person know if she had hot or cold?" I asked. "If one has cold, the stomach becomes distended/swollen (yentfekh). If one has heat, food won't stay in the stomach." She explained heat with a gesture, blowing imaginary dust off the upturned palm of her hand. It gave the impression of something dry and airily light, like ashes in the wind, able to disappear in an instant.

I asked then whether a woman should eat hot or cold to get fat. "Some women, because they have cold, will only get fat if they eat hot medicine." Then, Fatima continued, but on a different topic: "There are women, who are married by a man, and then they get cold, and their husband doesn't like them anymore." As she said the word "cold," she made a gesture with her hand indicative of water flowing out from down below (i.e. her vagina). "If a woman gets cold, she is wet. Also a woman's vagina will get large if she has cold." She made a large hole using the forefingers and thumbs of both hands. "With heat her vagina will become small," and she made a tight fist and pointed to the small hole within her curved forefinger.

Directly she explained to me what the medicine for this husband-alienating condition is: a medicinal powder sprinkled over coals, which a woman then sits over making a tent of her sari-like garment, so that the steam dries her out. "Your body will spill sweat and down below [pointing] you will become good." Going on to discuss the symptoms of cold, she explained that a woman could have cold and not know it.

There is a cold [i.e. a type of cold], where a woman becomes dry and it gets her. It becomes so that the woman is with her husband, and if he enters her, he takes a long time at her, he doesn't leave her; that is cold. When a man comes quickly, that is heat. That is good. Have you seen chickens? Like that is good – right away.

Although men are always physically the initiators of sex, clearly much of the responsibility for both its onset and its outcome rests with women. Sexual pleasure for the man is entirely a function of whether the woman is hot enough, as well as whether she has *shaytān* – literally, a devil, but figuratively something more like pheromones. Satisfying male desire is more than one of a series of conjugal obligations for a woman; in many ways, it is her ticket to a continuing marriage, or at least it is perceived as such. Since Azawagh Arabs divorce and remarry with great frequency, women have a strong incentive to be very concerned about holding onto a husband, especially as they get older. Not only women's present status, but their path to future status through sons, as well as their claims on goods to which they themselves have no access, come predominantly through their husbands. Since divorce is so common, men travel so often, and extra-marital affairs are the norm, women feel considerable pressure to continue to please their husbands in order to keep them. And during the periods of late adolescence when first marriages have often ended and many girls enter the freer but precarious status of divorcées, it is also imperative that they keep a certain level of heat in their bodies for the courting and late-night trysts that can lead to second, more chosen, and more successful marriages.

I once asked a *haratāni* to tell me about hot and cold in men. He broke into a wide grin, and, freer in his speech than a "noble" Arab man might be, immediately began telling me in graphic terms about the sexual strength of men. There was no mistaking what hot and cold were about in his mind. If I could bring medicine for cold, he said, seeming to immediately conflate any quality of cold with cold as a sexual problem, all the men would take it from me. When I asked him about heat in men, he said, "Women get that. Don't you see the Arab women (*'arabiyāt*) here, always dizzy? They take medicine until they get very hot, and fall," he added, somewhat disparagingly. "They seek it out. They want men not to dislike them." Such levels of sexual attractiveness as these women seek seem to become dizzying in the force of the desires they provoke, affecting the women's very reason and sanity.

The *haratāni's* last sentence, "They want men not to dislike them," expresses well the position from which women attempt to regulate the heat of their bodies. Amidst the vicissitudes of nature, women try to attune their bodies to the heat that will bind men to them, sexually and thereby socially.

Azawagh Arabs certainly recognize that marriages end for reasons of personality conflict, but they consistently frame male–female interaction in a vocabulary of sexuality. The dualism of hot and cold by which Allah has ordered his creations, be they plant, animal, or mineral, necessarily serves the preeminent dualism by which he ordered humanity, male and female. Hot and cold are nature's expression of the sexuality that pulls male and female together to satisfy the most base human passions as well as the most noble human aims, to be fruitful and multiply in one's own and in Allah's name.

Mind and body, women and men

Elaine Combs-Schilling has written that, "[w]e still do not have a vantage point that lets us see mind and body as part and parcel of the same process of cultural construction so that they cannot be severed without losing the understanding of what they in combination build" (1989: 37). Yet in order to understand hot and cold, al-ḥamān and le-barūd, as the Azawagh Arabs understand these qualities, we must see not only mind and body but also lived social life as part and parcel of one thematic process of making sense out of a chaotic universe. "Hot" and "cold" are ultimately meta-categories by which realms of experience are linked into a comprehensive universe. Much more than simply a system for dealing with disease, hot and cold both classify and unify all aspects of a vast, windswept world: day and night, hot sands and swirling breezes, cooking, pounding, and sifting, eating and sex, and all the many diseases that afflict people.

While I am not arguing for some sort of corporeal reductionism[4] in which all mental categories for thinking about social life are founded on a perception of bodily experience, Azawagh Arabs do inhabit a world where the body, the self, and the social are mutually constituting, indeed a piece, each affecting the others in an uninterrupted flow of force and causation. This is in stark contrast to Western philosophy and epistemology that have traditionally divided the mental from the physical, treating them as fundamentally separate forms of reality rather than mutually interacting.

Hot and cold both stand for and are the central forces that create the see-saw, vitalizing movement that urges social life forward. These forces or qualities are a naturalized form of the instability and asymmetry, but also the attraction and complementarity, that exist between men and women and motivate life's passage. Encompassing the guiding categories of Azawagh Arab culture – closedness and openness, sexual attraction, male and female, outer and inner – hot and cold encapsulate and express much that is central to Azawagh Arab lives. Hot and cold give physical expression to cultural values and social principles by representing them in the perceived empirical reality of natural forces.

Exercising agency

Most women can easily name forty or more plants and rocks and their healing qualities, and women with special knowledge of healing know many more. Men may know the plants' and rocks' basic qualities, but are less likely to have detailed knowledge about how to use them. When both men and women fall ill, they turn first to this female-dominated form of therapy, and only if several attempts at treatment have failed does an ill person turn to the more expensive, male-controlled Islamic therapies. Not only are women holders of the knowledge about these fundamental forces of hot and cold, but in the daily management of their own bodily states of hot and cold, in large part through the process of fattening, women maintain the necessary equilibrium for society as a whole. It is they, after all, who bring cold on men, and who by their care for their own bodies insure functioning, procreative, pleasurable sexuality; health; and the transformation of transient into lasting value for the society as a whole. Women's responsibilities and vulnerabilities to hot and cold are also their power.

The outsider does not immediately see that women are engaged in exercising this form of agency over their own lives, but it is in fact a constant preoccupation for them. In their endless debates over the heat or coldness responsible for a neighbor's stomach aches, and in their daily decisions about how hot or cold to make their own fattening porridge at each meal, Azawagh Arab women construct, control, and imagine their own bodies, writing macro-patterns of social life onto the micro-screen of these bodies. They are acting upon their world in otherwise highly confined circumstances. While they leave the world's endless expanses to men, through management of hot and cold women concentrate on the closer, more controllable arena of their own bodies and the encasings – fatness, skin, garments, tent – that insure their enduring protection and value. Women's bodies become the active seat of their being-in-the-world.

Plate 10 Young women enjoying themselves at a naming ceremony for a
newborn baby (Tchin Tabaraden)

9

BEAUTY, SEX, AND DESIRE

A *gowfa* [hairstyle][1] with six small braids:
With a scale I weighed it,
And eyebrows sewn in a line,
And eyes like pools beneath,
And a cheek yellow, without defect.
Pimples never marred it.
And a mouth generous to kiss
Cleaned by its possessor,
And a neck long as a cubit,
And a chest smooth below it,
And breasts to be sold
That just now emerged,
And a stomach with three folds.
Her pubis I measured with a hand-span,
And her thighs yoked together,
Sewn and belted with thread.
                    -Poem recorded in the Azawagh, 1991

In this visually powerful love poem, the eyes of the man travel down from the beauty of a young woman's face, to her voluptuous stomach, her alluring pubic area, and her swelling thighs which guard the treasure he seeks. With this expression of male admiration for the perfected female form, we come full circle, back to the "singular idea of feminine perfection" that Mungo Park described among the Moors, a notion of female beauty and allure quite at odds with Western aesthetic and sexual conceptions. By placing the aesthetic of female corpulence and the practice of childhood fattening in their social, cultural, and economic contexts, I have tried to demonstrate how an aesthetic ideal is predicated on and motivated by a wide set of understandings of the world. I have suggested that, while a "prevalent taste for unwieldiness of bulk" is grounded in a Moor view of faith, kinship, and livelihood that undergirds the meanings of fatness, the aesthetic is ultimately read as just that – an aesthetic – and in particular a sexually laden aesthetic. Female fattening makes women sexy at the same time as it anchors and tames women's own potential lusts. By inspiring desire in men at the same time as it curbs desire in women, female fattening socializes female sexuality, channeling it into acceptable forms. By managing the sexualization of their own bodies, women could be said to exercise a crucial kind of agency, controlling and harnessing the powerful forces of sex and desire not just for themselves, but for society as a whole.

A review of the argument

Although we may be aware that other ideals of beauty have held sway in different places and in different times, it is as hard for a Westerner to look at a fattened Arab woman and view her as attractive as it was for Azawagh Arab women to behold a willowy, fast-moving Western woman and see any redeeming features in her appearance. Even if by the end of my research I felt I could begin to see with Azawagh Arab eyes when it came to appreciating female appearance, it would be untruthful to say that I ever became free of my conditioned negative associations with rolls of fat and stretchmarks. When Azawagh Arab women I knew encountered Western women, they could recognize a warm smile, pleasant features, and a person at ease in her own body, but they could only pity women even with these assets if they were accompanied by what to them were haggard, bony bodies, and mannish movements. A Western model in a photo, if they could make out that she was a person at all (unused to pictures, some Arab women had trouble making sense of them), only looked either ill or like a man to them. The positive messages of agility, power, and self-discipline that a lean body represents in the West were as unreadable to them as were the less qualifiable aspects that constitute Western beauty. Similarly for Westerners, it verges on the impossible to train the eye to see in heavy folds of fat and massive thighs a sensual groundedness, an essence of womanliness, and a sexy closedness or containedness, all made more attractive for its immobility and unattainability.

What I have tried to do in this book, however, is to lead the reader into the world that defines beauty in quite opposite terms to those of the West, and to analyze the logic behind this aesthetic. As I have pointed out, the aesthetic of fattened women is not particularly a matter of conscious analysis for Azawagh Arabs themselves – it is obvious to them that fat women are good, beautiful, and desirable. My argument is that the obviousness of this "fact" is grounded in a wider cultural context. I review that context here, concluding with the way in which sex and desire are understood for Azawagh Arabs, and how these inform the meanings that make the fattened female body so pleasing to the eye.

A society's beauty ideals seem to float above concrete worldly concerns, in a realm of their own where another logic reigns. And to some extent they do – no environmental condition, economic pattern, or political structure can fully explain what people find beautiful. I have argued, however, that although social context does not determine beauty ideals, it predisposes people in favour of certain aesthetic tendencies and sets the framework within which a beauty ideal is elaborated.[2] For Azawagh Arabs these contexts include Islamic notions of men and women as profoundly different types of beings, Arab kinship expectations that one will desire and marry close relatives, and an economic pattern in which men make wealth out in the world and then bring it to and invest it in the center of their families and lives via their womenfolk. Beauty ideals also partake, I have argued, of cultural values that operate in several domains: in the case of Azawagh Arabs, closedness, stillness, and contained wetness which also feature in kin ideals (marrying in), how space is used (stillness vs. mobility), and ideas about health (where closed, still, contained moisture is considered characteristic of a healthy body).

How do these diverse aspects of Azawagh Arab society connect in a female beauty ideal? A large part of the ideal's power and tenacity lies precisely in its capacity to give expressive form to Islamic doctrine, economic logics, and notions of status simultaneously, while grounding them in the weight of palpable flesh and sexual allure. Their crystallization in the female body makes these logics in different arenas of experience not only natural and necessary, but mutually entailing, each providing the moorings and metaphors for the other.[3] Because a body heavy with wet, meaty flesh is the paragon of sexual attractiveness, women seek to achieve it, at the same time limiting their ability to work and requiring the presence of a servant caste, which in turn supports their own status and that of their families. In order to best achieve the cultural ideal, women must ingest large quantities of milk that only cows – male property – produce, making women dependent on men, men who are dependent in turn on women for transforming their production into the stuff of sexiness, female virtue, and, eventually, sons. Far from being a "pure" or "mere" aesthetic, and far from relying on a functional logic of economic production or reproduction, therefore, the material and ideal motivations of fattening are embedded in one another, and embodied in a figure whose aesthetic and material values constitute one another.

To put it another way, I have tried to demonstrate that women mediate a translation of material value into social value through their bodies in a way that enhances that value immeasurably. In crudest terms, the practice of fattening turns the products of men's labor – foodstuffs – first into aesthetic and sexual allure, and second, via women's reproductive capabilities, into what is even more valuable and lasting – sons. According to this analysis, women's bodies constitute far more than mere icons of wealth, instead holding the significance they do within Nigerien Moor society because of their capacity to make different forms of value – material and social – commensurable.

Socializing sexuality

Whatever the contextual underpinnings of the fat beauty ideal, to the Azawagh Arab beholder a fat woman is not a repository of male wealth or a conscious symbol of closedness; a fat woman is attractive in large part because a fat woman is sexy. The overdetermined logics of desired female corpulence are transposed with a singular unifying force to the idiom of sexuality. That is, the many threads of meaning embodied in women's expansive, weighty bodies seem to unite their forces in a powerful sexual aesthetic, an aesthetic informed by and enhanced by the many positive qualities a fattened girl explicitly and implicitly represents. The relative silence around fattening and fat women is due to this: to discuss someone's beauty is to risk casting the evil eye, but it is also to stray into areas of male attraction and sexuality that require circumspection. Discussing women's bodies is tantamount to discussing sex in a way that honor dictates must always be kept hidden.

Although attractiveness is looked for in a woman's face (as the above poem suggests), and though her innate forces of attraction, her *shaytān*, ultimately determine her "pull" on men, fatness is certainly the first trait noticed in a woman. Although a woman may be thin but have *shaytān*, this state of affairs is less promising than its opposite. My friend Boukia once said to me that a woman could have "no nose, mouth, or eyes" (i.e. be homely of face) but if she had folds of fat around the stomach (*lʿaqūn*) men would go to her. When discussions at the celebration of the ʿId-al-Kabir, the biggest Muslim holiday, turned to which of the women in their finery and high hairstyles were pretty, the conversation quickly turned to who was fat. One girl of a highly placed family, for example, despite all her gold, her finely henna-ed hands, and her new *ḥawli*, could not be judged attractive by the other women because she lacked the crucial plumpness.

The aesthetic of the fattened female body, then, is a sexualized aesthetic, pleasing to the eye because of its promise to be pleasing to the body. Fatness is seen very tangibly to improve the quality of the sexual pleasure a woman affords. Sidi once explained, "A fat woman is hot. A thin woman is like a man. You don't want to be able to touch a woman's ribs. A fat woman is seductive to a man." As I related earlier, Boukia also described the appeal of fatness in graphic terms, once when she was in a particularly expressive mood: "Oh, yes, they say 'oh what a girl!' They squeeze her breasts and stomach, and her pubis becomes big, like that of a woman, like that teapot." Two spirited young women also once teased me that I should get fat, "to make my vagina good, like sugar." Since unmarried adolescent girls are courted by young men who "steal" to them in the night, sneaking up beside them where they sleep to caress them and, perhaps, engage in sexual play, the attractiveness of a fattened young girl is not, as Boukia's comment suggests, a mere abstraction. As far as I could determine, unmarried young girls never engage in sexual intercourse – I never heard of a single Arab child born out of wedlock – but a man might please himself between a women's thighs. This practice may make fat thighs especially appealing, in addition to a fleshy, squeezable torso, and a large pubis.

How does fat equate with sexiness? For Azawagh Arabs, the spark of sexual attraction is understood to arise precisely out of otherness, a physics of opposites in which those bodies most different from one another possess the greatest magnetic attraction to each other. Veiling, seclusion, and the immobility of women also serve to enhance the perception of distance, difference, and unattainability that fan the flames of sexual desire. When young men remarked that if a woman had no fat it would be like touching a man, as in Sidi's comment above, it was as if to say: "What would be the point if a woman felt like a man?" Given this understanding of sex, it is perfectly logical that women and men should enhance their differences in order to enhance sexual attraction. Or that at least one sex, in this case women, should take on the task of exaggerating the difference, to the best of their abilities. Fattening accomplishes this, by altering both the appearance and the feel of the female body, lessening qualities associated with maleness – hardness, uprightness, mobility – and enhancing the quintessential qualities of femaleness – softness, pliability, stillness, seatedness. Fatness also exaggerates the sexual parts of the female body – the behind, the genital area, the stomach, and the breasts (although breasts play a much lesser role in the sexual imagination than in the West, since Azawagh Arab women are normally engaged in breastfeeding throughout the majority of their fertile years).

The sexual desirability of the female body is not an insignificant concern in a society where sex and the possibility of sex between any given man and any given woman is a paramount ordering principle of life. In the face of what are understood to be ever present and irrepressible sexual forces, Azawagh Arabs seek ways to socialize, control, and organize that sexuality. Fattening is one way. Janice Boddy (1982) wrote of female circumcision in northern Sudan that it ultimately serves to socialize female fertility. In a similar way, fattening among Azawagh Arabs could be said to socialize female sexuality. But this socialization is not only something done *to* girls and women. It is also something that women do to and for themselves. As Aline Tauzin (1981) has pointed out of Moor women in

Mauritania, the same sexuality that can be seen to bind women is also the seat of their power, for it is in large part by controlling and manipulating their sexuality that women control their own lives. For Azawagh Arab women their embodiedness is a prime mode of their engagement with, and influence upon, the world. Indeed, it constitutes their "work," as the woman who commented that "girls' work is stomach work" playfully but forcefully expressed (see chapter 5). Female fatness among Azawagh Arabs is thus not only expressive and symbolic of fundamental cultural tenets, but also provides women with a powerful way of exercising agency over their own lives.

To argue that sex is so central a pivot on which Azawagh Arab culture and social life turn runs the risk of exoticizing and orientalizing Azawagh Arabs, turning them into some sort of oversexed "other" in contrast to supposedly more rational, less instinct-driven, Western individuals. This risk may lie behind what has been a relative neglect of the subject of sex in anthropology (Herdt 1994: 12), especially before the age of AIDS. The problem could be said to lie, however, in the tradition of Western intellectual endeavor which has asserted the place of rationality, mind, thought, and ideas, above the equally human, and equally cultural, qualities of sexual desire and sexual pleasure. Even the Western term "sexuality" is misleading in discussing Azawagh Arab society, for it implies a theorized, abstract version of sex, more connected to individual identity, a particularly Western preoccupation, than to the sexual act and sexual desire. To understand the way in which the fattened female beauty ideal is a sexualized aesthetic requires understanding sex as drive, sex as act, and, perhaps most of all, sex as desire.

Feeding desire

Desire seemed in some sense a more significant emotion in Azawagh Arab culture than it is in the West. Perhaps it struck me this way because while desire in the West is encouraged, both by the capitalist economic system and by identity politics in which what you desire (people of the same sex, French wines, a particular type of music, a jewelry style) is largely defining of who you are, desire in the Azawagh is more problematic. "Desiring," which is my English summary translation of a number of different words and concepts used frequently by Azawagh Arabs,[4] is not so much a specific intention or emotion directed toward a specific object as a general state of being that can take many objects, each implying the other. This is especially true of food, money, and sex. To eat with too apparent pleasure and eagerness, for example, readily raises the specter of rapacious sexual lusts. This explains why as girls and women fatten, they must and do evince distaste for their food, eating "just to fill their stomachs," as they often

192

emphasized. (It is also, of course, unappetizing to have to eat so much bland food.) To evince intense interest in their fattening foods, which perform the function of sexualizing their bodies, would be tantamount to evincing interest in sex.

But why is evincing interest in sex so threatening a prospect? Sex may be the most profound of social acts but it is at the same time highly anti-social. In the private, dizzying desiring of two people for one another, everyone else is effectively excluded. In the rapture of the sex act, less passionate bonds to family, kin, and friends reduce their hold on the soul and the pleasure they afford pales. And of course, if desire runs rampant, children can result who do not fit neatly into the established social order, violating what are seen as natural and right distinctions of ethnic group, caste, and family. Desire, sexual and otherwise, is dangerous because of this. Even if society is dependent on the sex act for its continuation, sexual desire also has the power to pull society apart. The distinction between the two antagonistic forms of relationship, sexual and otherwise, is captured in the distinction discussed in chapter 4 between the two types of love, "love according to Allah" (ḥubb 'ala Allah) and "love according to Satan" (ḥubb 'ala Shayṭān) – love for kin and sexual love.

The concept of the prostitute in the Azawagh Arab world is telling of how desire and its destructive consequences are imagined. People explained to me that girls did not go to school because if they did they would become prostitutes. They would see men and see money, went the reasoning, and perceiving these things would lead them automatically to desire them. Being young and immature, girls would necessarily give in to these desires. A prostitute is one who lets her desires, for money and for men, get the better of her, bringing shame on herself and her family. (Women who were pros-titutes were said to want money too much.) Small girls who ran around rather than sitting still were also accused of being prostitutes; they were unable to tame their unruly longings, to avert their interest and their gaze from the temptations of the world. And if someone drank a lot of tea, it was said he "prostituted himself" to tea; again, his desires got the better of him.

Desire is also dangerous because, like perception, it leaves its imprint on the world. The lusts and longings of the heart are not merely an inner, subjective state, as in the West. When Boukia bore a daughter with a blue birthmark on her torso, for example, she explained to me quite matter-of-factly that Miriam had the mark on her body because while she was pregnant I had come to visit her wearing an indigo skirt that she coveted. Her desiring had left its mark on the child in her womb. Other kinds of intentions and emotions can also have visible, palpable effects on the world, as happens with the evil eye. When a young woman who did my hair for one of the holidays got a swollen eye the following day, for example, people said that others were jealous of how well she had done the hairstyle, and

193

their jealousy had led to her eye infection. Like the Azande whose witch-craft beliefs Evans-Pritchard (1937) described, people recognized that there was a more proximal cause of ills that befell people, such as an insect bite, but the question was: why was *I* bitten by an insect, and why was I bitten right *now*? This could only be explained by people's thoughts, perceptions, intentions, and desires.

Just as it could be said that one "emits" desire, one also "emits" attrac-tiveness. As I have mentioned, all people, men and women, have varying degrees of *shaytān*, something like pheromones that they emit and that attract others to them, largely but not only sexually. If a woman has *shaytān*, a man cannot resist her, and women will be drawn to her (asexually) as well. A woman can be unattractive but still have *shaytān*. Although it falls outside the purview of standard anthropological analysis, it is interesting to note that when my friend Asseghiyera and I once fell into discussing the degree to which various young men in the community possessed *shaytān*, we were in total accord. "X has so much *shaytān* that if you go near him you feel weak," Asseghiyera said of one local Don Juan, and I could only assent. Of another she noted that, "Y is the type of guy that would be good to marry, but he doesn't really have *shaytān*," an assess-ment that again matched perfectly my own. We went through the entire list of Tchin Tabaraden's eligible bachelors, and our *shaytān*-meters were in perfect agreement.

To withstand the pull of powerful *shaytān*, and indeed the pull of wanting altogether, whether things, people, or qualities, poses a constant challenge. The fact of wanting enables marrying, making a living, and creating kin, but it also constantly threatens these pivotal social activities. Having desire and intentions toward the world may be necessary for sur-vival, but to show desire of anything is a weakness. In particular, to show too great an appetite for pleasures of the mouth and stomach, so close to the pleasures of sex, is to evince lack of maturity and honor.

The ability to control desire is thus the central hallmark of mature, proper adulthood. This contrasts markedly with the modern West, where even if we are socialized to curb and channel our wants, part of becoming an adult is realizing, developing, and fulfilling our true inner passions. For Azawagh Arabs the route to maturity is not through recognizing and acting on one's desires, but through reining them in. This ability is called "having heart," where the heart represents the seat of maturity, or "having sense," *'aqal*, an Arabic term with a cluster of meanings in English relating to "sense" and "intelligence." As Bakka explained to me,

> If a person has no *'aqal*, whatever he sees he wants, from lack of heart. He will go and say "give me" about anything he sees, from lack of *'aqal*. If a person has *'aqal*, however, he will not want every-thing he sees. His heart is calm (*mesekken galbu*).

Thus rationality and emotion, intelligence and desire, are combined for Azawagh Arabs, both in their language and in the metaphorical seat of both, in the heart. When I asked Bakka if a girl who was beginning to fatten had heart yet, she said no, "there is no heart" at this age. To mature is to acquire heart. An expression describing someone with low intelligence is "decreased" or "lacking" in heart (*makhsūs min galbu*). But unlike the Western paradigm that separates the seat of emotions – the heart – from the seat of reason – the mind – for Azawagh Arabs both of these constituent elements of humanness, emotions and reason, are conceived of as located in the heart.

To want uncontrollably, then, is the opposite of intelligence and sense. A person "with heart" is able to control him or herself at all times, and to give away rather than want. Accordingly, the highest compliment paid to someone is that he or she is *falāḥ*, a term women defined for me as having a tendency to give things away. It is used, however, as often as we might use the term "nice" in English, to reflect general positive character. This positive trait consisted not primarily of friendliness, however, but of generosity and openness – the opposite of wanting, and a detachment from things and desiring. Khadijatou, describing to me the ways in which men were superior to women, included their generosity: "They give to the poor." When I asked whether women did not also give, she answered that they had less to give. Men have greater *'aqal* (sense, intelligence) and courage, and are also able to achieve a higher state of having heart because, with more to want and more to give away, they can both exemplify greater control over their desires and greater generosity.

All individuals learn to manage their desiring as they mature. But while women are thought more susceptible to desire's pull than men, both in Azawagh Arab society and throughout most of the Muslim world, their careful management of desire serves not only themselves but society as a whole. Men must go out in the world and make a living, people told me many times, and therefore have no choice but to be confronted with temptation. It thus becomes women's lot to control the desiring that exists in the world, a force almost like gravity, by veiling and by restricting their own movement. Women's expected comportment, often read in the West as a sign of their oppression by men, can instead be understood as women's contribution to the complementary efforts of both sexes to maintain propriety and well-being in their families and communities.

In another twist on Western conceptions of desire, for Azawagh Arabs individual struggles over impulse, desire, and jealousy are played out not so much between a person's higher, rational self and his or her bodily or irrational half, as between individuals and the social world around them. It is less important, for example, that a woman struggle to suppress her own inner sexual desiring to achieve a higher personal moral status, than that she suppress any expression of that desire, and, even more importantly, that she suppress the outer world's desiring of her, by veiling and keeping her body out of sight. For a man as well, it is not a sin to desire, only to act on inappropriate desires. And if a man does act, as long as no one finds out, little harm will have been done; the orderliness and bonds of family, tribe, and community will not have been disrupted. (When a man flirted with me and I demurred, saying I had a boyfriend, his response was, "But no one will find out." Therefore it should not matter, either to me or to my boyfriend, went the logic.)

Desire must be managed, but never obliterated, for in the end, desire is the pivot on which society turns. This is borne out both by the logic of fattening and by the way women talk about change in their society. Women spoke of the "changing" or "turning over" of the world (*teqlīb ad-dunye*), sometimes in terms of realignments in the balance of the ever present forces of hot and cold. The bush of nostalgic memory was cold, overflowing with milk and devoid of the suspect hot foreign foods with which they must now contend. By its coldness women also imply that the bush was free of the moral problems and surfeit of temptation that exist in the villages and towns that they are forced to become accustomed to. Women complain that men no longer marry, and that they no longer want/like Arab women. Shweytima bemoaned: "The world has turned over, become confused (*tegellebet, tekhelltet*). . . . Women's hearts used to be desirous of (*mshenneqīn*) men, because men were desirous of them. Now what do we want with them?"

In Shweytima's wistful and poetic words, desire, of men for women and women for men, becomes something positive rather than destructive. Yet the conditions of this desire – desire as a driving force of society – are fading. She lives in a larger town, where there are too many temptations:

> too many sweet things: tea, the sound of the radio, the noise of cars, prostitutes. The men are full. If a man's stomach is empty, he has desire for all things, whether it be work, women, or intelligence [learning]. If a person is full, where is he? Is not his heart dead? A man is not like a woman; if he is full, his intentions/desire (*niyye*) are dead. If a woman is full, her desire seeks/searches (*tlawwad*).

Men are going to prostitutes and there they slake their desire, becoming hotter in a sense from letting their desires go. Women, on the other hand, now washing more often, neglecting to fatten and take the hot medicines now less obtainable in towns than in the bush, seem to be becoming colder. The central, driving division of Azawagh Arab society is being compromised, that of maleness and femaleness, with the tension of sexuality, its primary expression, being reconfigured. Furthermore, the tension of desire between men and women is being thrown out of kilter. When one uses up all one's desire, as men can do too easily now, the source of the individual's and society's vitality is depleted.

As Shweytima's comments reflect, desire may be troublesome and threatening, but it is also absolutely necessary. Desire and the conditions for its continual inspiration must exist, for having sex and eating and acquiring beautiful things make up the very essence of life, even while channeling and properly controlling those desires remain one of life's enduring challenges. Fattening speaks directly to this existential challenge. The beauty of fattening is that it feeds desire – creating it, inducing it, inviting it – while simultaneously creating the conditions of desire's control – its anchoring, its closing off, its grounding.[5]

In effect, then, fattening justifies desire. To desire just any woman is tinged with the threat of sin and chaos, but to desire a woman who has devoted her life to embodying an honorable way of being is acceptable. For fattening does not make a woman desirable – all women are by definition desirable. What fattening does is make a woman an appropriate object of desire, culturally sanctioned: immobile, most different from men, her milk-producing father's daughter, her successful husband's wife, one who has in the most concrete way possible demonstrated her adherence to the highest social virtues: interiority, closedness, a body fit for sex and child-bearing but not physical labor. In this way it is like an extended initiation, bringing a girl into acceptable adult personhood in society.

As men reach out into the spaces of the vast world, women go about their days deliberately and meticulously focusing their energies on the economy and well-being of their own interior spaces. While men go about transporting objects across the desert, increasing their value in the process, women go about transporting foodstuffs into their own bodies and beings, actually transforming their value in the process. Out of milk and millet they create sensual beauty, well-being, and reproducibility, turning men's production into something uniquely Arab, while concretizing and encapsulating in forceful idiom that which is of paramount value and meaning. In this work that is not work, women manage the all-powerful forces of sex and desiring, eloquently contributing to the vitality of their world.

NOTES

PROLOGUE: THERE IS MORE TO BEAUTY THAN MEETS THE EYE

1 Agbasiere (2000: 99) suggests that the fattening of Igbo girls that occurred while they were in seclusion before marriage was merely a by-product of the fact that they were immobile for a period, and not a distinct aim of the seclusion practice.

1 COMING INTO THE AZAWAGH

1 Between 1987 and 1991 when proper rainfall records were kept in Tassara, the yearly rainfall was 113.2 mm (4.5 inches) at its lowest and 198.9 mm (almost 8 inches) at its highest. According to one report, rainfall regularly varies by 40 percent from year to year in the northern Azawagh (Swift 1984).
2 For history of the Azawagh Arab tribes and related Kunta, see Whitcomb (1975a, b), Marty (1921), Martin (1908), and Nicolas (1950).
3 Based on calculations from figures in the Nigerien *Recensement général de la population* (1990).
4 The term *neṣrāni* (pl. *anaṣāra*) is derived from "Nazarene," and is the term used not only in Arabic but also in Hausa in Niger to refer not just to Christians but to Westerners in general.
5 As of the early 1990s there was some electricity and a few television sets in the largest Azawagh town of Tchin Tabaraden.

2 GETTING FAT

1 The term Berber refers to a number of non-Arab North African groups including the Tuareg of the Sahara and the Kabyle of Algeria.
2 Traveling down the Niger river from Timbuktu to Gao, Ibn Battuta stopped at the village of the "excellent governor" Farba Sulayman, where "[w]e were served with a drink of theirs called *deqnu*, which is water containing some pounded millet mixed with a little honey or milk" (Ibn Battuta 1985: 300).

   Levtzion and Hopkins indicate that *deqnu* is not a term of Arabic derivation (1980: 473), and the people who served it to Ibn Battuta sound more like sub-Saharan Africans than Berbers, though this region bordered on the area of the Bardama. The recipe seems to have altered little over the centuries, although the *deghnu* that Azawagh Arab women eat is appropriate specifically to fattening and is not eaten by men. Honey is also relatively unknown in the northern Azawagh, though sugar is often added to another drink known by the similar name *zeghru*, rarely taken by women because of its "coldness." Interestingly, the term *deghnu* does not exist in Hassaniyya Arabic to the west, suggesting that while the notion of fattening women itself may have been adopted generally by Arab/Moors and Tuareg from the Bardama who lived across Sahelian West Africa, different, isolated groups of Arab/Moors and Tuareg may have adopted different terms for the new foods they ate.

3 In the original *magot*, which refers to grotesque Chinese porcelain figurines.

4 In the Azawagh such hairdos are common on young children, and are to ward off spirits by making the child look unattractive.

5 People in this region clean their teeth with sticks which they often chew on as people in the West might chew gum or smoke a cigarette.

6 The Tuareg comprise numerous loosely related groups across much of the central Sahara. There is less indication that the more northern Ahaggar Tuareg (mostly in Algeria) practiced the fattening of girls (Duveyrier 1973). In the Azawagh and northern Mali, however, Moor and Tuareg cultures seem to have shared the custom (Hildebrand *et al.* 1985) along with other features (dress, certain terminology for the natural environment, material culture).

7 The second paragraph refers to the custom of the wives of marabouts, or Muslim scholars, who only walk with a mat wrapped round them in a large, protective cylinder.

8 I do not know how he knew that more had been written about these other Nigerien ethnic groups, but he was right. What he probably had noticed was that of the Westerners in Niger, a number had learned Hausa or Tamajeq (the Tuareg language) and generally seemed interested in these peoples, while none other than I had spent time with the Arabs and learned their language.

9 The related term *blah* is listed in Hans Wehr's dictionary of standard Arabic (1976) as a botanical term for dates, and in Taine-Cheikh's dictionary of Hassaniyya (1988) as referring in particular to the "first dates, not yet arrived at first maturity, very juicy and appreciated."

10 Unfortunately, Taine-Cheikh's many-volume Hassaniyya–French dictionary has not yet reached the letter "gh," and so I do not know what her glosses for the term are. Hans Wehr translates the standard Arabic term as "deception," however, and Taine-Cheikh's much smaller French–Hassaniyya dictionary (1990) translates the French "déception" by the same term, *gharr*.

11 The term for simply "fat," *semīna* (feminine form), is common throughout the Arabic world. In the Azawagh it is also commonly used in the verb form *tesmin*, "she fattens," to describe a girl, woman, man, or animal gaining weight.

12 I actually collected the names of no fewer than eleven such preparations from women, but only seven seemed to be clearly distinct (others had more than one name): *fūra*, *maghsu'ub*, *zāmite*, *al-migli*, *mugayyem*, *akeynef*, and *kusuksu*. All *deghānu* (pl. of *deghnu*) are distinct from the thicker grain-based firm porridge that is always cooked in quantities of water, *ʿaysh*, which women eat when they aren't actively fattening, and which men always eat. Women do not want such a wet food, because it could bring on cold; thus they eat the drier *deghānu* and merely use water as a "chaser" to make it flow into their bodies.

13 *Tezwīz* means "to accompany," and is also used when referring to animals being accompanied to the desert to graze.

14 A slightly different interpretation of the relationship between sexual desire and fattening is offered by Aline Tauzin (1986: 153), who examined the practice among Moors in Mauritania. She suggests that fattening accomplishes a sort of displacement whereby female sexual desire is satisfied by oral indulgence.

The fact that women channel their desire orally (or it is channeled for them) further contributes, she argues, to the separation of the sexes, and the continual delaying or avoidance of sexual desire's satisfaction that she finds marks Moor culture.

15 What I have translated as "Oh my, what a girl!" is literally, "Oh my liver oh that girl" (*"ya kebdi ya thi-l-'azba"*). The liver is an organ used metaphorically in somewhat the way the heart is in English. Teapots are common objects lying around tents: plastic ones used to carry water for washing after relieving themselves, and metal ones used to make tea on small braziers.

16 *"Okli, bash t'ūdi eragāsh!"*

3 IN THE NAME OF ALLAH, MOST BENEVOLENT, EVER MERCIFUL

1 Transcriptions here are of how these phrases were uttered in spoken Galgaliyya Arabic, and are not the same as modern standard Arabic or Koranic Arabic.

2 Some interpreters of the Koran claim that it actually stipulates equality between men and women, but the passages used to support this view only speak of men and women together; they do not actually state that they are equal. (See Ali 1984, verses cited under "Women, equality," in index.) Leila Ahmed (1992: 63 ff.) also suggests that a close reading of many passages shows that the Koran fundamentally curtails men's rights over women. She also points out, however, that in practice Islam cemented a growing trend toward a more patrilineal and patriarchal society in Arabia, even if it originally put a stop to some of the more egregious practices curtailing women's dignity in seventh- and eighth-century Arabia (Ahmed 1982).

3 Numerous passages in the Koran describing heaven mention the presence of desirable women to attend on those to whom the Koran is addressed, men. For example: "And they shall have fair spouses then, and live there abidingly" (92: 25); "But those who believe and do good deeds, We shall admit into gardens ... with fairest of companions and coolest of shades" (4: 57); "We shall pair them with companions with large black eyes" (44: 54); "They would recline on couches set in rows, paired with fair companions (clean of thought and) bright of eye" (47: 15); "In them [gardens] maidens with averted glances, unde-flowered by man or by jinn before them" (55: 56).

4 TIES OF BLOOD, TIES OF MILK, TIES OF MARRIAGE

1 One could say that in the West we have the reverse situation: instead of assuming that men and women are at loggerheads by nature and that marriages are stressful affairs, we have an expectation, or at least hope, that men and women can readily achieve a meeting of souls. But then we have a large popular psychology industry from John Gray to Deborah Tannen explaining why conflicts of interest in fact arise so often.

2 In modern standard Arabic, the term is *maḥram*, defined as "unmarriageable, being in a degree of consanguinity precluding marriage" (Wehr 1976: 172). The triliteral root of this word, *ḥ-r-m*, is also the basis of the word "harem," where women who are forbidden to other men reside.

3 When Hildred Geertz asked Moroccans who their relatives were, she noticed that no one mentioned any women (1979: 350).

4 Carol Delaney (1991) has described at length Muslim understandings of conception and gestation in Turkey, demonstrating parallels between the agricultural imagery of Turkish village livelihood and folk models of conception.

5 The terms used for semen are *bo'l*, literally "urine"; *al-me*, literally "water"; and, here at least, *goṭr*, "drops."

6 "*Ileyn teṭhmer gīs akhwālek, wa ileyn tenḥān gīs 'amāmek.*"

7 *Ahel* also has other uses: the *ahel* of animals is the one who owns them, and *ahel* of money are people who have a lot of it.

8 Hans Wehr lists the *fusḥa* term *shaqīq(a)* as referring to a full brother or sister (1976: 480).

9 The line of male ancestors cited is identical to that in published accounts of Kunta history, for example in Batran (1979: 113).

10 Hildred Geertz (1979) has suggested that family relationships in Arab societies are the model for other relationships, such as those among unrelated peers or even among patrons and clients. I would add tribal relationships to this list.

11 Fredrik Barth notes that matrilateral relations are characterized as warm and supportive in many Middle Eastern societies (1973: 14).

12 When I say Azawagh Arab women "never" marry outside their community I am not exaggerating. Over the seven years that I traveled back and forth to the Azawagh, I never heard of an Arab woman who married an outsider. Once I was told of a "white" Arab woman I didn't know who married a "black-smith" Arab (of the artisan caste), but apparently she had had to be bewitched for this to happen.

13 Milk siblings are referred to in Galgaliyya Arabic by one of two terms, *khūt fi-lben*, literally "brothers (or siblings) in milk," or *khūt fi-l-ratha'a*, literally "brothers in nursing."

14 See Altorki (1980) for a detailed description of the rules surrounding milk kinship.

15 Colostrum is the nutrient-rich, watery liquid that a woman's breasts produce soon after she has given birth, before the milk proper comes in a few days later.

16 Altorki tells the story of a couple who married even though they were milk siblings, and had three children who were born with handicaps. People considered this to be divine retribution for the couple's violation of the milk-kin marriage taboo (1980: 243).

17 See Abu-Lughod (1986) and Trawick (1990) for a similar take on kinship.

18 There were no local Arabs I ever met or heard of who had married Westerners, so this was more a manner of speaking than an observation people had made. Some Arabs had, however, seen the children of Tuareg–white Westerner matches, and may have made their determination on this basis.

19 Pierre Bonte has noted that letting women marry "up" is one of the central ways in which Moors are able to preserve social hierarchies while still allowing some degree of social mobility (1987).

20 My statistics on marriage undoubtedly underestimate the amount of divorce among Azawagh Arabs because people usually don't mention early marriages that did not last. That said, my calculations suggest that at least half of both women and men had been divorced at least once: 31 of 63 women over age 14, and 26 of 54 men over age 20. Of men over age 35, I estimate that two-thirds had been married more than once. The chief, his recently deceased brother, and the *qāḍi* had each been married at least three times, and several of the most senior women in town had also been married three times. There were several prominent men in the community who had been married eight times, though this was always noted with a bit of a snicker by others,

especially women. (The ages I give are approximate since Azawagh Arabs do not keep track of ages.)

21 Thus, as in much of sub-Saharan Africa, marriage is a process (Radcliffe-Brown and Forde 1950: 49; Comaroff and Roberts 1981: 134), but unlike marriages in many African societies, there is a definite line between when a woman is married and when she is not. After the contract has been made, a woman (and a man) is considered married, though the marriage is more easily (and more readily) broken at this stage than after the wedding proper.

22 Emrys Peters, whose analysis of Cyrenaican Bedouin marriage focuses more on the attenuation of father–son ties that occurs than on sexuality, notes that marriage is the one time in men's lives when they can "sing their defiance of an older [generation]," which they do by joining in lewd songs and shouting obscenities during the wedding ceremony (Peters 1965: 131).

5 "THE MEN BRING US WHAT WE WILL EAT": HERDING, TRADE, AND SLAVERY

1 This view has been espoused not infrequently by observers of Moor culture. Odette du Puigaudeau, for example, the intrepid French traveler who visited Mauritania in the 1930s, suggested after describing a particularly voluptuous young girl, that "a woman's obesity is the sign of her husband's fortune" (1992: 138).

2 The term *ḥurra*, "free" or "noble," was also used in other contexts to connote something of good quality, such as *koḥl*, the antimony used as eyeliner. "Free people," *nās ḥurra*, referred to superior people, people whom the Arabs respected.

3 Clare Oxby (1978: 35) discusses the distinction between castes in India and castes among the Tuareg, which are similar to those among Moors.

4 Caste division is somewhat less pronounced among Moors in Niger than among Moors in Mauritania (Bonte *et al.* 1991). In particular, there is not as strict a division between priestly (Zwaya) and noble (Hassan) families in Niger. While some families and tribes or tribal subsections in the Azawagh, such as the Haj Hamma branch of the Deremsheka, are considered by tradition to be learned religious men (*'ulama*), they are not so large and they regularly marry with other "noble," non-priestly castes. In the Azawagh, all "white" (*beythān*), "noble," or "free" (*ḥurra*) Moors call themselves simply "Arab" (*'Arab*), a usage I have retained here. Even though a Tuareg or Hausa in the region might refer to a Moor artisan as an "Arab," within Moor society an artisan would only be referred to by the caste title, and never by the term "Arab."

5 The term *haraṭīn* does not exist in standard Arabic, though it is thought to be derived from Arabic. It may be derived from the Arabic term for "free," *ḥurra*, or it may be derived from the Arabic term for "to cultivate," *haratha*, since the people the Arabs enslaved when they came into West and North Africa were originally cultivators. See Ilahiane (2001) for a discussion of the term's etymology in reference to a *haraṭīn* population in Morocco.

6 Light skin, as this suggests, is an important feature of the aesthetic ideal of Azawagh Arabs. When I returned from a trip to the encampment of Egawan, the first questions a woman asked me about her daughter whom I had seen there were, "Is she a little fat? Is she 'yellow'?" – another term used to refer to a gradation of light skin. Women of all skin colors applied several herbal treatments to their faces to bring out light skin, and might explain to me that they had been lighter before some misfortune had befallen them.

7 The term for "work" in Galgaliyya Arabic is *khedma*, hence the term for a female slave, *khādem*. The term *isheghel*, from Tamajeq (the Tuareg language), was also used occasionally. Another word for work from standard Arabic, *'āmel*, was also used, but had slightly different connotations: it could mean to make or to work an object, such as leather, and it was also used to refer to the "work" of witchcraft.

8 Edmond Bernus (1990) discusses the transformations and diversity within the pastoral systems of the neighboring Tuareg over the last century.

9 Fredrik Barth notes these features of capital in the form of livestock in his analysis of economic strategies among the pastoral Basseri of Iran. There were potential capital gains of 40 percent a year, he notes, although there is also the risk of sudden heavy losses from epidemic or warfare (Barth 1968: 416).

10 Note the similarities between the Wodaabe and other Bantu peoples, such as the Tswana, for whom cattle were also much more than a medium of exchange (Comaroff and Comaroff 1992).

11 The renowned scholar, Sidi al-Mukhtar (d. 1811), a leader of the neighboring Kunta Moors, was recorded to have said that trade is "not only legitimate but honourable. It was the profession of the Prophet and an obligatory injunction prescribed by law for all Muslims" (quoted in McDougall 1986: 54).

12 In his study of ethnomedicine in Rwanda, Christopher Taylor has noted a similar "hierarchy of consumption," in which the higher caste Tutsi drank milk and the lower caste Hutu ate solids; liquid food was considered the more prestigious (1992: 130).

13 See Comaroff and Comaroff (1997: 175) for a similar argument about the nature of cattle for the Tswana in the nineteenth century.

14 David Graeber has developed this type of notion of value even further, following in large part on Terence Turner (1979) and Nancy Munn (1986), suggesting that a universally valid definition of value might be "the way in which actions become meaningful to the actor by being incorporated in some larger, social totality" (Graeber 2001: xii).

6 THE INTERIOR SPACES OF SOCIAL LIFE: BODIES OF MEN, BODIES OF WOMEN

1 Nuna: "*Ana māni kīfek; ana shegg mashgūga.*" Mohamed: "*Wa ana kīf al-'ūd.*"

2 In fact, I explained to Maya that Eve is known as Hawa in Arabic; she only knew Adama's name. The Koran only refers to her as Adama's wife or the first woman.

3 I did not tape record her words, so the following passage is not verbatim.

4 A creation story similar to that told in Genesis in the Old Testament is recited at several points in the Koran (2: 30–39, 7: 19–25, 20: 120–121) but does not contain the details of female jealousy, the goatskin bag, and swallowing leaves mentioned in Maya's tale. There are other details in the Koranic version, however, that are significant to Azawagh Arab conceptions of maleness and femaleness: the tree of good and evil is *al-shajarah*, a term whose basic meanings include disagreement and opposition as well as tree or bush. God's warning to Adam against eating of the tree is thus also a warning "against differences and opposition (through growing needs and jealousies)" (Ali 1984: 16). In all three mentions of the tale in the Koran, it is also emphasized that God's reaction to Adam and Eve's transgression is to make them enemies of one another

(2: 36, 7: 24, 20: 123). This vision of human sexual difference is very much in keeping with Azawagh Arab visions of men's and women's intertwined yet troubled fates vis-à-vis each other on earth.

5 Since the outbreak of the Tuareg "rebellion" around 1990, Azawagh Arabs are making a greater effort to differentiate their own appearance from that of Tuaregs, largely by tying their turbans in ways more characteristic of Arabs to the north, or by abandoning the turban altogether.

6 Tuaregs, though often as or more light skinned than Azawagh Arabs, are defined as "red."

7 Al-bāṭ, al-zind, al-ṣerra, al-gidm.

8 Al-menhar, al-ṭābig, al-remmeh, al-jinb.

9 The perception that forces of the environment, the body, and the person are interconnected is common in non-industrial societies; see for merely a few examples Hanks (1990: 86) on the Maya; Knauft (1989: 254) on Papua New Guinean societies; and Riesman (1986) on another African society.

10 See Hallpike (1969) for one theory of the sexual significance of hair.

11 Zibla maghattiya wa la thahāba meleggiya.

12 Note the similarities to the power of the sacred that Carolyn Bynum describes of the bodily secretions and the like of medieval saints: people bathed in their leftover bath water, and holy people spat or blew into the mouths of others to give grace or cure (Bynum 1989: 163).

13 In sharp contrast, hell is a place where people will "be given boiling water to drink which will cut their intestines to shreds" (47: 15).

7 THE EXTERIOR SPACES OF SOCIAL LIFE: TENT AND DESERT

1 Although some version of this is a common scenario in the Arab world, there is a nearly opposite construction among other African peoples, such as the Tswana, where the center is male space and there is a centripetal movement of men in toward it (Comaroff 1985: 55).

2 See, for example, Ahmed (1992: 117) on medieval Arab architecture, Altorki (1986: 30–31) on the Saudi elite; Boddy (1989: 70–75) on Sudan; Delaney (1991: 114) on Turkey; Fernea (1965) on Iraq; and Wikan (1982: 36) on Oman.

3 See, for example, Ardener (1992); Comaroff (1985); Devisch (1993); Griaule (1965); Hugh-Jones (1979); Jacobson-Widding (1991).

4 Urvoy (1942) claimed that the Moors in Niger had adopted the Tuareg ahakett, with a flat, square roof. He wrote of the 1930s. This may be, but it seems that he got most of his information from Tuaregs, and I have not seen evidence anywhere else, or heard from Azawagh Arabs, that they used to build their tents this way.

5 Some Azawagh Arabs told me that their tents were made of camels' hair in the past. Although I have found no recorded observation of this, the Moors to the west did build tents out of sheep's wool, at least in the 1930s, as described by Urvoy (1942: 33) and du Puigaudeau (1992: 85,162).

6 As animal skins became rarer and more expensive, and burlap more plentiful, Arabs began making higher and larger tents out of layers of these sacks (tefāla), similar to the shelters built by neighboring ethnic groups. In contrast to the flatter roofs of other groups' structures, however, the Arabs have maintained the higher, rounded roof, now building vaulted coverings to their modern burlap-based shelters.

7 Some younger women have taken up crocheting, something learned in Algeria and then passed along. Using very small hooks, they make brightly colored pillowcases of geometric patterns that are knit excruciatingly tightly.

8 This general relation mirrors Islamic laws that give to a woman half of what is given to a man, as in the case of inheritance.

9 For the record, I do eat meat, but since meat was often either tough and old, or consisted largely of stomach parts, I often deemed it best to leave it for others who needed the nutrition more than I did in any case.

10 The fact that wells rather than land belong to particular tribes offers another example of space organized according to key central points rather than to bounded-off expanses.

11 I made a number of overnight visits to Boukia's tent at the encampment of Egawan. I also visited smaller camps at Tassa Taqorat, Amassara, Armajegh, Neme, Tende, and Gharo.

12 Desert camps were not necessarily near water. At a camp I visited not far from Tassara a *ḥaraṭaniyya* spent most of day on a donkey going to a pond 13 kilometers away to fill up several goatskin bags and a few old plastic water jugs.

13 They urinate in the streets, women crouching down and letting their *ḥawlis* form a tent around them. They use the bush to defecate, women making slow excursions with one another every few days.

8 WELL-BEING AND ILLNESS

1 See, for example, Currier (1966) and Foster (1979, 1987, 1994) on Latin America; Weiss *et al.* (1988) on India; Tuschinsky (1995) on Malaysia; Wall (1988) on West Africa; Greenwood (1992) on Morocco; and Good (1980) on Iran. Many studies of humoral systems are largely ethnoscientific, but some examine hot and cold in wider social contexts, such as Daniel (1984: 184–194), who discusses how basic categories and qualities of Tamil personhood are mapped onto the hot–cold dichotomy in southern India.

2 Carol Delaney writes that in Turkish Muslim village society men are also seen as essentially bounded and women as essentially unbounded and needing closure (1991: 38).

3 When a woman speaks about anything having to do with sexuality, she exhibits *al-ḥeshme*, modesty, shame, embarrassment, respect. This term so central to the emotional and social life of Arab societies generally has no English equivalent, but in the context I cite here the lowered voice conveys a sense of *ḥeshme* that connotes respect, propriety, and seriousness, but not necessarily shame or embarrassment, particularly among older women. Younger women, however, would talk of sexuality, something so central to their lives and statuses at that age, amidst great giggling and blushing (not entirely dissimilar to how the subject is often discussed in the West by teenage girls). For a discussion of the complexities of *al-ḥeshme* that applies for the most part to the Azawagh Arab case as well as to the Egyptian Bedouin case it describes, see Abu-Lughod (1986: 103–117).

4 See, however, Johnson (1987) and Lakoff and Johnson (1999) for illuminating considerations of the ways in which our actual bodily presence in the world forms and shapes our mental categories.

9 BEAUTY, SEX, AND DESIRE

1 Hans Wehr's dictionary of Arabic lists the following definitions for terms related to the Galgaliyya *gowfa*: *qaffa*, to bristle, stand on end (hair); *quffa*, large basket. Either of these meanings may be related to the apparently elaborate *gowfa* hairdo, now no longer in fashion in the Azawagh (Wehr 1976: 781).

2 See Bordo (1993) for an exploration of how the demands of late consumer capitalism could be said to predispose if not determine the body ideals of the West.

3 I borrow the metaphor of crystallization from Bordo (1986), who has written of the way in which anorexia crystallizes a number of tendencies, some contradictory, of modern Western society.

4 *Al-beghi* (wanting, liking, desire), *al-izza* (liking), *al-niyye* (intention, desire), and *al-khelāga* (appetite).

5 Tauzin (1991: 48) offers a somewhat different but not entirely incompatible interpretation of the workings of desire in Moor society. She argues that the Moor man ultimately seeks to keep the woman always at arm's length, his desires potential but never satisfied; he "maintains the woman in her perfection and completion, making her the immobile and supreme object of his desire." Women are to be pleased by men, by being given things they want and by being fed (Tauzin 1986).

GLOSSARY

Al-, *le-*, and *l-* are forms of "the," and are not listed attached to the words below, even if the word almost always occurs with a definite article. A single quotatation mark before a vowel indicates the Arabic letter " 'ayn," a guttural sound made deep in the throat. Most of the spellings correspond with those used in Catherine Taine-Cheikh's dictionary of the Hassaniyya Arabic of Mauritania (1990).

'ālem, 'ulama (pl.) learned Islamic scholar
'am, 'amām (pl.) paternal uncle
'abid, 'abīd (pl.) slave in general; male slave in particular
anaṣāra see *neṣrāni*
'and at (the home of)
'aqal sense, intelligence
'aysh thick porridge, usually of millet, that constitutes the main food for people not fattening
barūd cold (noun)
blūḥ fattening
deghnu, deghānu (pl.) porridge-type foods that women fatten on
falāḥ, falḥa (fem.) generous, nice (of a person)
fayde usefulness, utility, worth, benefit
femm mouth or door
galb heart
garfa decorated leather bag in which women have traditionally kept their belongings
gharr forced fattening of girl
girba goatskin water bag
hajāle, hajajīl (pl.) divorcée or unmarried woman past adolescence
ḥamān heat
ḥaraṭāni (masc.), *ḥaraṭaniyya* (fem.), *ḥaraṭīn* (pl.) freed or former slave
ḥawli sari- or toga-like garment women wear
ḥeshme shame, modesty, respect
ḥubb love

209

ḥurra free, noble

jinn, janūn (pl.) spirit

khādem female slave or servant

khāl, akhwāl (pl.) relatives related by ties through women

khayme tent, household

kohl black eyeliner

labās literally "nothing bad"; the standard Arabic greeting in the Azawagh

m'ālem, m'ālemīn (pl.) artisan, blacksmith

marwa tent or house where bride and groom spend the wedding night

meherima (fem.) state of being able to greet or go unveiled before someone of the opposite sex because of close kin relationship, via blood or milk

neṣrāni, neṣraniyya (fem.), *anaṣāra* (pl.) Westerner

qāḍi Islamic judge, highest religious authority

qabila, qaba'il (pl.) tribe

ṣaḥra desert, the bush

semīn, semīna (fem.) fat (adjective)

shaytān, shayaṭīn (pl.) literally devil, figuratively power of attraction

ṣiniḥ tent or house where a newlywed couple spends the night in the early months or years of their marriage, usually somewhat apart from other tents or houses

sulṭān chief, leader

tefāla tent of burlap sacks, built in town compounds

tezwīz the act of swallowing down a mouthful of grain or porridge with water or soured milk (also refers to accompanying animals to pasture)

'ulama see *'ālem*

uld 'am, ulād 'am (pl.) relatives by ties through men; also relatives in general

zeyn, zeyna (fem.) good, beautiful

BIBLIOGRAPHY

Abadie, M. (1927) *La Colonie du Niger*, Paris: Société d'Editions Géographiques, Maritimes et Coloniales.

Abu-Lughod, L. (1986) *Veiled Sentiments: honor and poetry in a Bedouin society*, Berkeley: University of California Press.

—— (1997) "Is There a Muslim Sexuality? Changing constructions of sexuality in Egyptian Bedouin weddings," in Caroline B. Brettell and Carolyn F. Sargent (eds) *Gender in Cross-Cultural Perspective*, 2nd edn, Upper Saddle River, NJ: Prentice Hall.

Agbasiere, J.T. (2000) *Women in Igbo Life and Thought*, London: Routledge.

Ahmed, L. (1982) "Western Ethnocentrism and Perceptions of the Harem," *Feminist Studies* 8(3): 521–534.

—— (1992) *Women and Gender in Islam: historical roots of a modern debate*, New Haven, CT: Yale University Press.

Ali, A. (ed. and trans.) (1984) *The Qur'an: a contemporary translation*, Princeton, NJ: Princeton University Press.

Altorki, S. (1980) "Milk-Kinship in Arab Society: an unexplored problem in the ethnography of marriage," *Ethnology* 19(2): 233–244.

—— (1986) *Women in Saudi Arabia: ideology and behavior among the elite*, New York: Columbia University Press.

Amidié, F.B. (1985) "Engraissement de la femme dans la ville de Tomboctou," Mémoire fin d'études, l'Ecole Normale Supérieure, Bamako, Mali.

Ardener, S. (ed.) 1992 *Women and Space: ground rules and social maps*, rev. edn, Oxford: Berg Publishers.

Asad, T. (1986) "The Idea of an Anthropology of Islam," *Occasional Papers*, Georgetown University.

Barth, F. (1968; 1st edn 1964) "Capital, Investment, and the Social Structure of a Pastoral Nomad Group in South Persia," in E.E. LeClair, Jr. and H. Schneider (eds) *Economic Anthropology: readings in theory and analysis*, New York: Holt, Rinehart, and Winston.

—— (1973) "Descent and Marriage Reconsidered," in J. Goody (ed.) *The Character of Kinship*, Cambridge: Cambridge University Press.

Batran, A.A. (1979) "The Kunta, Sidi al-Mukhtar al-Kunti, and the Office of the Shaykh al-Tariq al-Qadiriyya," in John Ralph Willis (ed.) *Studies in West African History, vol. I: The Cultivators of Islam*, London: Frank Cass.

211

Becker, A.E. (1995) *Body, Self, and Society: the view from Fiji*, Philadelphia, PA: University of Pennsylvania Press.

Beidelman, T.O. (1993) *Moral Imagination in Kaguru Modes of Thought*, Washington, DC: Smithsonian Institution Press.

Bennett, W.C. and Zingg, R.M. (1935) *The Tarahumara: an Indian tribe of northern Mexico*, Chicago: University of Chicago Press.

Bernus, E. (1990) "Dates, Dromedaries, and Drought: diversification in Tuareg pastoral systems," in J.G. Galaty and D.L. Johnson (eds) *The World of Pastoralism: herding systems in comparative perspective*, New York: The Guilford Press.

—— (1991) *Touaregs: chroniques de l'Azawak*, Paris: Editions Plume.

Boddy, J. (1982) "Womb as Oasis: the symbolic context of pharaonic circumcision in rural northern Sudan," *American Ethnologist* 9(4): 682–698.

—— (1989) *Wombs and Alien Spirits: women, men, and the Zar cult in northern Sudan*, Madison: University of Wisconsin Press.

Bonte, P. (1987) "Donneurs de femmes ou preneurs d'hommes?: les Awlad Qaylan, tribu de l'Adrar Mauritanien," *L'Homme* 102(27:2): 54–79.

Bonte, P., Conte, E., Hamès, C., and Ould-Cheikh, A.W. (1991) *Al-Ansāb: la quête des origines: anthropologie historique de la société tribale Arabe*, Paris: Maisons des Sciences de l'Homme.

Bordo, S. (1986) "Anorexia Nervosa: psychopathology as the crystallization of culture," *The Philosophical Forum* 17(2): 73–104.

—— (1993) *Unbearable Weight: feminism, Western culture, and the body*, Berkeley, CA: University of California Press.

Borgerhoff Mulder, M. (1988) "Kipsigis Bridewealth Payments," in L. Betzig, M. Borgerhoff Mulder, and P. Turke (eds) *Human Reproductive Behavior*, Cambridge: Cambridge University Press.

Bouhdiba, A. (1985; orig. French 1975) *Sexuality in Islam*, trans. A. Sheridan, London: Routledge & Kegan Paul.

Bourdieu, P. (1977; 1st edn 1972) *Outline of a Theory of Practice*, trans. R. Nice, Cambridge: Cambridge University Press.

—— (1979; orig. French 1960) *Algeria 1960: the disenchantment of the world, the sense of honour, the Kabyle house or the world reversed*, trans. R. Nice, Cambridge: Cambridge University Press.

—— (1990; orig. French 1980) *The Logic of Practice*, trans. R. Nice, Stanford, CA: Stanford University Press.

Brachet (1938a) "Rapport de tournée effectuée par l'administrateur-adjoint Brachet: campagne vétérinaire et affaires politiques," Document 17.3.54, Niamey: Archives Nationales du Niger.

—— (1938b) "Rapport de tournée effectué par l'administrateur-adjoint Brachet, 13 octobre 1937–14 janvier 1938," Document 17.3.60, Niamey: Archives Nationales du Niger.

Brain, R. (1979) *The Decorated Body*, London: Hutchinson.

Brewster, S. (1992) "Women of the Sahara: force-fed for marriage," *Marie Claire*, UK edn, February: 32–34.

Brink, P.J. (1989) "The Fattening Room among the Annang of Nigeria," *Medical Anthropology* 12: 131–143.

Brown, P.J. (1991) "Culture and the Evolution of Obesity," *Human Nature* 2(1): 31–57.

Butler, J. (1993) *Bodies that Matter: on the discursive limits of "sex,"* New York: Routledge.

Bynum, C. (1989) "The Female Body and Religious Practice in the Later Middle Ages," in M. Feher, R. Tadoff, and N. Tazi (eds) *Fragments for a History of the Human Body*, New York: Zone Books.

Caillié, R. (1968; 1st edn 1830) *Travels Through Central Africa to Timbuctoo and Across the Great Desert to Morocco, Performed in the Years 1824–1828*, Travels and Narratives no. 36, J.R. Willis, Editorial Adviser, London: Frank Cass.

Cleaveland, T. "Introduction to 'Home in Walata: a history of marriage, reproduction, and kinship in a nineteenth century Saharan oasis'," paper presented at the African Studies Association Meetings, Boston, November 1993.

Comaroff, J. (1985) *Body of Power, Spirit of Resistance: the culture and history of a South African people*, Chicago, IL: University of Chicago Press.

Comaroff, J. and Comaroff, J.L. (1992) "Goodly Beasts and Beastly Goods: cattle and commodities in a southern African context," in J. Comaroff and J.L. Comaroff (eds) *Ethnography and the Historical Imagination*, Boulder, CO: Westview.

—— (1997) *Of Revelation and Revolution, vol. 2: The Dialectics of Modernity on a South African Frontier*, Chicago: University of Chicago Press.

Comaroff, J.L. and Roberts, S. (1981) *Rules and Processes: the cultural logic of dispute in an African context*, Chicago, IL: University of Chicago Press.

Combs-Schilling, E. (1985) "Family and Friend in a Moroccan Boom-Town: the segmentary debate reconsidered," *American Ethnologist* 12(4): 659–675.

—— (1989) *Sacred Performances: Islam, sexuality, and sacrifice*, New York: Columbia University Press.

Csordas, T.J. (ed.) (1994) *Embodiment and Experience: the existential ground of culture and self*, Cambridge: Cambridge University Press.

Currier, R.L. (1966) "The Hot–Cold Syndrome and Symbolic Balance in Mexican and Spanish-American Folk Medicine," *Ethnology* 5: 251–263.

Daniel, E.V. (1984) *Fluid Signs: being a person the Tamil way*, Berkeley, CA: University of California Press.

Delaney, C. (1991) *The Seed and the Soil: gender and cosmology in Turkish village society*, Berkeley, CA: University of California Press.

Denny, F.M. (1987) *Islam and the Muslim Community*, San Francisco, CA: Harper and Row.

Devisch, R. (1993) *Weaving the Threads of Life: the Khita gyn-eco-logical healing cult among the Yaka*, Chicago, IL: University of Chicago Press.

Douglas, M. (1982; 1st edn 1970) *Natural Symbols: explorations in cosmology*, New York: Pantheon Books.

du Puigaudeau, O. (1992; 1st edn 1936) *Pieds nus à travers la Mauritanie*, Paris: Phébus.

Duveyrier, H. (1973; 1st edn 1864) *Les Touareg du nord: exploration du Sahara*, Nendeln, Lichtenstein: Kraus Reprint.

Eickelman, D. (1989) *The Middle East: an anthropological approach*, 2nd edn, Englewood Cliffs, NJ: Prentice Hall.

Emecheta, B. (1976) *The Bride-Price*, New York: G. Braziller.

Esposito, J.L. (1988) *Islam: the straight path*, Oxford: Oxford University Press.

213

Etcoff, N. (1999) *Survival of the Prettiest: the science of beauty.* London: Little, Brown.

Evans-Pritchard, E.E. (1937) *Witchcraft, Oracles, and Magic among the Azande,* Oxford: Clarendon Press.

—— (1969; 1st edn 1940) *The Nuer: a description of the modes of livelihood and political institutions of a Nilotic people,* Oxford: Oxford University Press.

—— (1949) *The Sanusi of Cyrenaica,* Oxford: Clarendon Press.

Fernea, E. (1965) *Guests of the Sheik: an ethnography of an Iraqi village,* New York: Doubleday.

Foster, G.M. (1979) "Methodological Problems in the Study of Intracultural Variation: the hot/cold dichotomy in Tzintzuntzan," *Human Organization* 38(2): 179–183.

—— (1987) "On the Origin of Humoral Medicine in Latin America," *Medical Anthropology Quarterly* 1(4): 355–393.

—— (1994) *Hippocrates' Latin American Legacy: humoral medicine in the New World,* Amsterdam: Gordon and Breach.

Frisch, R.E., Fevelle, R., and Cook, S. (1973) "Components of Weight at Menarche and the Initiation of the Adolescent Growth Spurt in Girls: estimated total water, lean body weight, and fat," *Human Biology* 45: 469–483.

Galaty, J.G. and Bonte, P. (eds) (1991) *Herders, Warriors, and Traders: pastoralism in Africa,* Boulder, CO: Westview Press.

Galton, F. (1878) "Composite Portraits," *Nature* 18: 97–100.

Gampel, B. (1962) "The 'Hilltops' Community," in S.L. Kark and G.E. Stuart (eds) *Practice of Social Medicine,* London: E. and S. Livingstone.

Geertz, H. (1979) "The Meaning of Family Ties," in C. Geertz, H. Geertz, and L. Rosen (eds) *Meaning and Order in Moroccan Society: three essays in cultural analysis,* Cambridge: Cambridge University Press.

Gellner, E. (1969) *Saints of the Atlas,* Chicago, IL: University of Chicago Press.

—— (1981) *Muslim Society,* Cambridge: Cambridge University Press.

Ghannam, F. (1997) *Fertile, Plump, and Strong: the social construction of the female body in low-income Cairo,* Monographs in Reproductive Health, no. 3, Cairo: The Population Council.

Gilman, S. (1999) *Making the Body Beautiful: a cultural history of aesthetic surgery,* Princeton, NJ: Princeton University Press.

Good, B. (1977) "The Heart of What's the Matter: the semantics of illness in Iran," *Culture, Medicine and Psychiatry* 1: 25–58.

—— (1994) *Medicine, Rationality, and Experience: an anthropological perspective,* The Lewis Henry Morgan Lectures 1990, Cambridge: Cambridge University Press.

Good, M.J.D. (1980) "Of Blood and Babies: the relationship of popular Islamic physiology to fertility," *Social Science and Medicine* 14(B): 147–156.

Goody, J. (1976) *Production and Reproduction: a comparative study of the domestic domain,* Cambridge: Cambridge University Press.

Graeber, D. (2001) *Toward an Anthropological Theory of Value: the false coin of our own dreams,* New York: Palgrave.

Gray, J. (1993) *Men Are from Mars, Women Are from Venus: a practical guide for improving communication and getting what you want in your relationships,* New York: Harper Collins.

Greenwood, B. (1992) "Cold or Spirits? Ambiguity and syncretism in Moroccan therapeutics," in S. Feierman and J.M. Janzen (eds) *The Social Basis of Health and Healing in Africa*, Berkeley, CA: University of California Press.

Gregory, C.A. (1982) *Gifts and Commodities*, London: Academic Press.

Griaule, M. (1965; 1st edn 1948) *Conversations with Ogotemmêli: an introduction to Dogon religious ideas*, intro. G. Dieterlen, London: Oxford University Press.

Grosz, E. (1994) *Volatile Bodies: towards a corporeal feminism*, Bloomington, IN: Indiana University Press.

Hallpike, C.R. (1969) "Social Hair," *Man* 4: 256–264.

Hamet, I. (1911) *Chroniques de la Mauritanie Sénégalaise: Nacer Eddine*, Paris: Ernest Leroux.

Hanks, W.F. (1990) *Referential Practice: language and lived space among the Maya*, Chicago, IL: University of Chicago Press.

Herdt, G. (ed.) (1994) *Third Sex, Third Gender: beyond sexual dimorphism in culture and history*, New York: Zone Books.

Hildebrand, K., Hill, A.G., Randall, S., and van den Eerenbeemt, M.-L. (1985) "Child Mortality and Care of Children in Rural Mali," in A.G. Hill (ed.) *Population, Health, and Nutrition in the Sahel: issues in the welfare of selected West African communities*, London: Routledge and Kegan Paul.

Hirschon, Renée (1993) "Open Body/Closed Space: the transformation of female sexuality," in S. Ardener (ed.) *Defining Females: the nature of women in society*, Oxford: Berg.

Hubbard, R. (1996) "Gender and Genitals: constructs of sex and gender," *Social Text* 46/47 14(1&2): 157–165.

Hugh-Jones, C. (1979) *From the Milk-River*, Cambridge: Cambridge University Press.

Ibn Battuta (1985) in Joseph M. Cuoq (ed.) *Recueil des sources arabes concernant l'Afrique occidentale du VIIe au XVIe siècle (Bilad al-Sudan)*, Paris: Editions du Centre National de la Recherche Scientifique.

Ilahiane, H. (2001) "The Social Mobility of the Haratine and the Re-Working of Bourdieu's Habitus on the Saharan Frontier, Morocco," *American Anthropologist* 103(2): 380–394.

Jackson, M. (1989) *Paths Toward a Clearing: radical empiricism and ethnographic inquiry*, Bloomington, IN: Indiana University Press.

Jacobson-Widding, A. (ed.) (1991) *Body and Space: symbolic models of unity and division in African cosmological experience*, Stockholm: Almqvist and Wiksell.

Johnson, M. (1987) *The Body in the Mind: the bodily basis of meaning, imagination, and reason*, Chicago, IL: University of Chicago Press.

Khazanov, A.M. (1994; orig. Russian 1984) *Nomads and the Outside World*, trans. J. Crookenden, Madison, WI: University of Wisconsin Press.

Knauft, B. (1989) "Bodily Images in Melanesia: cultural substances and natural metaphors," in M. Feher, R. Tadoff, and N. Tazi (eds) *Fragments for a History of the Human Body*, vol. 3, New York: Zone Books.

Lakoff, G. and Johnson, M. (1980) *Metaphors We Live By*, Chicago, IL: University of Chicago Press.

—— (1999) *Philosophy in the Flesh: the embodied mind and its challenge to Western thought*, New York: Basic Books.

Lancaster, W. (1981) *The Rwala Bedouin Today*, Cambridge: Cambridge University Press.

Langewiesche, W. (1996) *Sahara Unveiled: a journey across a desert*, New York: Random House.

Langlois, J., Roggman, L.A., and Rieser-Danner, L.A. (1990) "Infants' Differential Social Response to Attractive and Unattractive Faces," *Developmental Psychology* 26: 153–159.

Levtzion, N. and Hopkins, J.F.P. (eds) (1980) *Corpus of Early Arabic Sources for West African History*, Cambridge: Cambridge University Press.

Lienhardt, G. (1961) *Divinity and Experience: the religion of the Dinka*, Oxford: Clarendon Press.

McDougall, E.A. (1986) "The Economics of Islam in the Southern Sahara: the rise of the Kunta clan," *Asian and African Studies* 20: 45–60.

—— (1988) "A Topsy-Turvy World: slaves and freed slaves in the Mauritanian Adrar, 1910–1950," in S. Miers and R. Roberts (eds) *The End of Slavery in Africa*, Madison, WI: University of Wisconsin Press.

McGarvey, S.T., Bindon, J.R., Crews, D.E., and Schendel, D.E. (1989) "Modernization and Adiposity: causes and consequences," in M.A. Little and J.D. Haas (eds) *Human Population Biology: a transdisciplinary science*, New York: Oxford University Press.

Malcom, L.W.G. (1925) "Note on the Seclusion of Girls Among the Efik at Old Calabar," *Man* 25: 113–114.

Martin, A.G.P. (1908) *Les Oasis Sahariennes*, Algiers: Editions de l'Imprimerie Algérienne.

Marty, P. (1921) *Etudes sur l'Islam et les tribus du Soudan, tome III: Les Tribus maures du Sahel et du Hodh*, Paris: Editions Ernest Leroux.

Marx, K. and Engels, F. (1970) *The German Ideology*, Part I, New York: International Publishers.

Masquelier, A. (2001) *Prayer Has Spoiled Everything: possession, power, and identity in an Islamic town of Niger*, Durham, NC: Duke University Press.

Massara, E. (1989) *Que Gordita! A study of weight among women in a Puerto Rican community*, New York: AMS Press.

Mauss, M. (1973; 1st edn 1935) "Techniques of the Body," *Economy and Society* 2(1): 70–88.

Meillassoux, C. (1972) "From Reproduction to Production: a Marxist approach to economic anthropology," *Economy and Society* 1(1): 93–105.

Mernissi, F. (1975) *Beyond the Veil: male–female dynamics in modern Muslim society*, Cambridge, MA: Schenkman.

Miers, S. and Kopytoff, I. (eds) (1977) *Slavery in Africa: historical and anthropological perspectives*, Madison, WI: University of Wisconsin Press.

Moore, H.L. (1986) *Space, Text, and Gender: an anthropological study of the Marakwet of Kenya*, Cambridge: Cambridge University Press.

Mosko, M. (1985) *Quadripartite Structures: categories, relations, and homologies in bush Mekeo culture*, Cambridge: Cambridge University Press.

Munn, N.D. (1986) *The Fame of Gawa: a symbolic study of value transformation in a Muslim (Papua New Guinea) society*, The Lewis Henry Morgan Lectures 1976, Cambridge: Cambridge University Press.

Nelson, S.M. (2001 [1990]) "Diversity of the Upper Paleolithic 'Venus' Figurines and Archeological Mythology," in C.B. Brettell and C.F. Sargent (eds) *Gender in Cross-Cultural Perspective*, 3rd edn, Upper Saddle River, NJ: Prentice Hall.

Nichter, M. (1994) "Fat Talk: body image among adolescent girls," in N. Sault (ed.) *Many Mirrors: body image and social relations*, New Brunswick, NJ: Rutgers University Press.

Nicolas, F. (1950) *Tamesna: les Ioullemmeden de l'est ou Touareg "Kel Dinnik,"* Paris: Imprimerie Nationale.

Norris, H.T. (1968) *The Arab Conquest of the Western Sahara*, Beirut: Longman, Librairie du Liban.

Oxby, C. (1978) "Sexual Division and Slavery in a Twareg Community: a study of dependence," unpublished Ph.D. thesis, School of Oriental and African Studies.

Park, M. (1954; 1st edn 1799) *Travels into the Interior of Africa*, London: Eland Books.

Peignol (1907) *Monographie du Cercle de Tahoua*, Document 17.1.4, Niamey: Archives Nationales du Niger.

Peters, E.L. (1965) "Aspects of the Family Among the Bedouin of Cyrenaica," in M.F. Nimkoff (ed.) *Comparative Family Systems*, Boston, MA: Houghton Mifflin.

—— (1990) *The Bedouin of Cyrenaica: studies in personal and corporate power*, ed. J. Goody and E. Marx, Cambridge: Cambridge University Press.

Piot, C. (1999) *Remotely Global: village modernity in West Africa*, Chicago: University of Chicago Press.

Popenoe, R. (1997) "Barbie and Ken in the Sahara: dolls, sex, and gender among Moors in Niger," *Antropologiska Studier* 58–59: 27–37.

Powdermaker, H. (1997) "An Anthropological Approach to the Problem of Obesity," in C. Counihan and P. Van Esterik (eds) *Food and Culture: a reader*, London: Routledge.

Radcliffe-Brown, A.R. and Forde, D. (eds) (1950) *African Systems of Kinship and Marriage*, London: Oxford University Press.

Recensement général de la population du Niger 1988 (1990) Niamey, Niger: Bureau Central du Recensement.

Riesman, P. (1986) *Freedom in Fulani Social Life*, Chicago, IL: University of Chicago Press.

Roscoe, J. (1915) *The Northern Bantu*, Cambridge: Cambridge University Press.

—— (1923) *The Banyankole*, Cambridge: Cambridge University Press.

Rosen, L. (1984) *Bargaining for Reality: the construction of social relations in a Muslim community*, Chicago, IL: University of Chicago Press.

Ross, C.E. and Mirowsky, J. (1983) "The Social Epidemiology of Overweight: a substantive and methodological investigation," *Journal of Health and Social Behavior* 24: 288–298.

Simmel, G. (1978; orig. German 1907) *The Philosophy of Money*, ed. D. Frisby, trans. T. Bottomore and D. Frisby, London: Routledge and Kegan Paul.

Sims, J.H. (1979) "A Study to Identify and Evaluate the Attitudes toward Obesity among Three Ethnic Groups of Women in Oklahoma," unpublished Ph.D. thesis, University of Oklahoma.

Singh, D. (1993) "Body Shape and Women's Attractiveness: the critical role of waist-to-hip ratio," *Human Nature* 4(3): 297–321.

Smithson, C.L. (1959) *The Havasupai Woman*, Salt Lake City, UT: University of Utah Press.

Sobo, E.J. (1993) *One Blood: the Jamaican body*, Albany, NY: State University of New York Press.

Stearns, P. (1997) *Fat History: bodies and beauty in the modern West*, New York: New York University Press.

Stewart, C.C. (1973) *Islam and the Social Order in Mauritania: a case study from the nineteenth century*, Oxford: Oxford University Press.

Strathern, A.J. (1971) *The Rope of Moka*, New York: Cambridge University Press.

—— (1994) *Body Thoughts*, Ann Arbor, MI: University of Michigan Press.

Styles, M.H. (1980) "Soul, Black Women, and Food," in J.R. Kaplan (ed.) *A Woman's Conflict: the special relationship between women and food*, Englewood Cliffs, NJ: Prentice Hall.

Swift, J. (ed.) (1984) *Pastoral Development in Central Niger: report of the Niger Range and Livestock Project*, USAID, Niamey, Niger.

Taine-Cheikh, C. (1988) *Dictionnaire ḥassāniyya–français: dialecte arabe de Mauritanie*, Paris: Geuthner.

—— (1990) *Lexique français–hassaniyya: dialecte arabe de Mauritanie*, Nouakchott: Centre Culturel Français Antoine de Saint Exupéry.

Tannen, D. (1990) *You Just Don't Understand: men and women in conversation*, New York: Morrow.

Tauzin, A. (1981) "Sexualité, mariages, et stratification sociale dans le Hodh mauritanien," thèse IIIème cycle, Ecole des Hautes Etudes en Sciences Sociales, Paris.

—— (1986) "La Femme partagée: contrôle et déplacement de la sexualité féminine en Mauritanie," *Côté Femmes: approches ethnologiques*, Paris: Editions L'Harmattan.

—— (1987) "Massages corporels des fillettes en Mauritanie," *Quel Corps?*: 45–57.

—— (1988) "Excision et identité féminine: l'exemple mauritanien," *Anthropologie et Sociétés* 12(1): 29–37.

—— (1991) "Souffrance du désir: figures poétiques de la femme au Yémen et en Mauritanie," *Intersignes: Paradoxes du Féminin en Islam 2.*

Taylor, C.C. (1992) "The Harp that Plays by Itself," in M. Nichter (ed.) *Anthropological Approaches to the Study of Ethnomedicine*, Langhorne, PA: Gordon and Breach.

Thiellement, A. (1935) "Rapport de tournée du 1 novembre au 12 décembre," Document 17.3.23, Niamey: Archives Nationales du Niger.

—— (1949) *Azawar*, Rennes: L'Amitié par le Livre.

Trawick, M. (1990) *Notes on Love in a Tamil Family*, Berkeley, CA: University of California Press.

Turner, T. (1979) "Anthropology and the Politics of Indigenous Peoples' Struggles," *Cambridge Anthropology* 5(1): 1–43.

Tuschinsky, C. (1995) "Balancing Hot and Cold – Balancing Power and Weakness: social and cultural aspects of Malay *jamu* in Singapore," *Social Science and Medicine* 41(11): 1587–1595.

Untitled document (1933) Document 17.3.16, Niamey: Archives Nationales du Niger.

Untitled document (1944) Document 17.3.113, Niamey: Archives Nationales du Niger.

Urvoy, Y. (1942) *Petit atlas ethno-démographique du Soudan (entre Sénégal et Tchad)*, Mémoires de l'IFAN No. 5, Paris: Librairie Larose.

van Damme, W. (1996) *Beauty in Context: towards an anthropological approach to aesthetics*, Leiden: E.J. Brill.

van Gennep, A. (1960; orig. Dutch 1908) *The Rites of Passage*, trans. M.B. Vizedom and G.L. Caffee, Chicago, IL: University of Chicago Press.

218

Veblen, T. (1994; 1st edn 1899) *The Theory of the Leisure Class*, New York: Dover Publications.

Wall, L. (1988) *Hausa Medicine: illness and well-being in a West African culture*, Durham, NC: Duke University Press.

Webb, J. (1995) *Desert Frontier: ecological and economic change along the Western Sahel, 1600–1800*, Madison, WI: Wisconsin University Press.

Wehr, H. (1976) *A Dictionary of Modern Written Arabic*, 3rd edn, Ithaca, NY: Spoken Language Services.

Weiss, B. (1992) "Plastic Teeth Extraction: the iconography of Haya gastro-sexual affliction," *American Ethnologist* 19(3): 538–552.

Weiss, M., Desai, A., and Jadhav, S. (1988) "Humoral Concepts of Mental Illness in India," *Social Science and Medicine* 27(5): 471–477.

Whitcomb, T. (1975a) "New Evidence on the Origin of the Kunta I," *Bulletin of the School of Oriental and African Studies* 38(1): 103–123.

—— (1975b) "New Evidence on the Origin of the Kunta I," *Bulletin of the School of Oriental and African Studies* 38(2): 403–413.

Wikan, U. (1982) *Behind the Veil in Arabia: women in Oman*, Chicago: University of Chicago Press.

Wilde, O. (1994; 1st edn 1891) *The Picture of Dorian Gray*, London: Penguin Books.

Zainaba (1990) "Lecture on Clitoridectomy to the Midwives of Touil (1987)," in M. Badran and M. Cooke (eds) *Opening the Gates: a century of Arab feminist writing*, Bloomington, IN: Indiana University Press.

INDEX

Comaroff, J. 205n1, 205n3
Comaroff, J. and Comaroff, J.L. 131, 204n10
Comaroff, J.L. and Roberts, S. 89, 98, 203n21
Combs-Schilling, E. 59, 69, 90–1, 184
conception 61, 84
confinement *see* childbirth
corporeality *see* body
courting 80, 97, 101, 106, 183, 191
creation story 138–9
Csordas, T.J. 141
Currier, R.L. 206n1
cutting of infants 147

Daniel, E.V. 171n1
daughters: birth of 88; relationship to fathers 88, 197; relationship to mothers 76, 87–8, 92–3, 106; *see also* affection; children; fattening; mothers; sons
death: chanting of Koran at 66; of children 30
deghnu (porridge) 34, 47–8, 180–1, 200n12
Delaney, C. 59–60, 84, 205n2, 206n2
Denny, F.M. 59
Deremsheka 90–1
desert 9, 13–15, 23, 24; as locus of imagination 164
desert camps 54, 64, 66, 88, 159, 164–6; relations with towns 166
desire 8–9, 188, 190–7; dangers posed by 193; and fattening 8, 40, 196–7; in heaven 58, 69–70; and humoral system 171, 173–4; link between sex and eating 48; and marriage 76; nature of 26, 29, 48, 148; as sparked by male/female difference 107; of spirits for women 68, 177; terms for 207n4; in West 192–5; *see also* sex; sexuality; sexual attraction
Devisch, R. 144, 205n3
divorce 100–1, 164, 183–4; and children 84, 86; examples of 63, 75, 80, 106; in Islam 61–5; and loss of household for women 158; reasons for 82, 184; young age at 79; *see also* marriage; divorcées

divorcées 42, 80, 106, 159, 163, 183; *see also* divorce
dolls 24, 43, 155, 159
dollhouses *see* dolls
Douglas, M. 8
dowry 157
dreams 56, 58, 65
dress *see* clothing
drought 16, 17, 21, 22, 55, 130
dryness: as central trope 8, 50; and fat 5; in humoral system 172–4, 176, 183; *see also* wetness
du Puigaudeau, O. 36–7, 203n1, 205n5
Duveyrier, H. 36, 200n6

eating *see* fattening; food; mouths
eating disorders 1
economic strategies 111–32, 162, 189
Efik: and fattening 6
Egypt: and fatness 5
Eickelman, D. 89
Emecheta, B. 6
emotion: Azawagh Arab concepts of 195; and kinship 92, 96–7; *see also* affection; kinship; love; marriage
endogamy *see* marriage
Esposito, J.L. 59
Etcoff, N. 3, 4
ethnic relations 15, 50, 56–7, 113
Evans-Pritchard, E.E. 20, 89, 194
evil eye 44, 124, 171, 190, 193

falaah, falha 195
family: importance of 76; *see also* kinship
fashion 2
fasting 57, 60, 73, 163; first fast 41, 45; women and 57, 60; *see also* Ramadan
fat: qualities of 5, 8, 181; *see also* fatness; fattening; women's bodies
fathers *see* children; kinship
fatness: as anchoring of society 162; as body ideal in Moor world 18, 44, 188; cross-culturally 4–7; and fertility 6, 107, 130; and Islam 70; meanings of for Azawagh Arabs 48–50, 111–13, 129–32, 187, 197; as sign of wealth 111–13, 130; and weight 145–6; *see also* fattening; immobility; sexual attraction; women's bodies